WHITENESS AND POSTCOLONIALISM IN THE NORDIC REGION

Studies in Migration and Diaspora

Series Editor:
Anne J. Kershen, Queen Mary, University of London, UK

Studies in Migration and Diaspora is a series designed to showcase the interdisciplinary and multidisciplinary nature of research in this important field. Volumes in the series cover local, national and global issues and engage with both historical and contemporary events. The books will appeal to scholars, students and all those engaged in the study of migration and diaspora. Amongst the topics covered are minority ethnic relations, transnational movements and the cultural, social and political implications of moving from 'over there', to 'over here'.

Also in the series:

European Identity and Culture
Narratives of Transnational Belonging
Edited by Rebecca Friedman and Markus Thiel
ISBN 978-1-4094-3714-7

Migration, Citizenship and Intercultural Relations
Looking through the Lens of Social Inclusion
Edited by Fethi Mansouri and Michele Lobo
ISBN 978-1-4094-2880-0

Ethnicity and Education in England and Europe
Gangstas, Geeks and Gorjas
Ian Law and Sarah Swann
ISBN 978-1-4094-1087-4

Masculinity, Sexuality and Illegal Migration
Human Smuggling from Pakistan to Europe
Ali Nobil Ahmad
ISBN 978-1-4094-0975-5

Globalization, Migration and Social Transformation
Ireland in Europe and the World
Edited by Bryan Fanning and Ronaldo Munck
ISBN 978-1-4094-1127-7

Whiteness and Postcolonialism in the Nordic Region
Exceptionalism, Migrant Others and National Identities

Edited by

KRISTÍN LOFTSDÓTTIR
University of Iceland, Iceland

LARS JENSEN
Roskilde University, Denmark

LONDON AND NEW YORK

First published 2012 by Ashgate Publishing

2 Park Square, Milton Park, Abingdon, Oxon OX14 4RN
711 Third Avenue, New York, NY 10017, USA

Routledge is an imprint of the Taylor & Francis Group, an informa business

First issued in paperback 2016

Copyright © Kristín Loftsóttir, Lars Jensen and the contributors 2012

Kristín Loftsóttir and Lars Jensen have asserted their right under the Copyright, Designs and Patents Act, 1988, to be identified as the editors of this work.

All rights reserved. No part of this book may be reprinted or reproduced or utilised in any form or by any electronic, mechanical, or other means, now known or hereafter invented, including photocopying and recording, or in any information storage or retrieval system, without permission in writing from the publishers.

Notice:
Product or corporate names may be trademarks or registered trademarks, and are used only for identification and explanation without intent to infringe.

British Library Cataloguing in Publication Data
Whiteness and postcolonialism in the Nordic region : exceptionalism, migrant others and national identities. – (Studies in migration and diaspora)
   1. Nationalism – Scandinavia. 2. Exceptionalism – Scandinavia. 3. Group identity – Scandinavia. 4. Scandinavians – Ethnic identity. 5. Scandinavia – Foreign relations. 6. Postcolonialism – Scandinavia.
   I. Series II. Kristín Loftsdoóttir, 1968– III. Jensen, Lars.
   305.8'395-dc23

Library of Congress Cataloging-in-Publication Data
Kristín Loftsdóttir, 1968–
   Whiteness and postcolonialism in the Nordic Region : exceptionalism, migrant others and national identities / by Kristin Loftsdottir and Lars Jensen,
      p. cm.—(Studies in migration and diaspora)
   Includes bibliographical references and index.
   ISBN 978-1-4094-4481-7 (hardback) 1. Whites—Race identity—Scandinavia. 2. National characteristics. 3. Exceptionalism—Scandinavia. 4. Postcolonialism—Scandinavia. I. Jensen, Lars. II. Title.
   HT1575.K75 2012
   305.809—dc23
                                                                            2012014351

ISBN 978-1-4094-4481-7 (hbk)
ISBN 978-1-138-26697-1 (pbk)

Transferred to Digital Printing 2014

Contents

List of Contributors		*vii*
Series Editor's Preface		*xi*
Introduction	Nordic Exceptionalism and the Nordic 'Others' *Kristín Loftsdóttir and Lars Jensen*	1
1	Colonial Discourse and Ambivalence: Norwegian Participants on the Colonial Arena in South Africa *Erlend Eidsvik*	13
2	Colonialism, Racism and Exceptionalism *Christina Petterson*	29
3	'Words That Wound': Swedish Whiteness and Its Inability to Accommodate Minority Experiences *Tobias Hübinette*	43
4	Belonging and the Icelandic Others: Situating Icelandic Identity in a Postcolonial Context *Kristín Loftsdóttir*	57
5	Transnational Influences, Gender Equality and Violence in Muslim Families *Suvi Keskinen*	73
6	Reading History through Finnish Exceptionalism *Anna Rastas*	89
7	Danishness as Whiteness in Crisis: Emerging Post-Imperial and Development Aid Anxieties *Lars Jensen*	105
8	Bodies and Boundaries *Kirsten Hvenegård-Lassen and Serena Maurer*	119

9	Intimacy with the Danish Nation State: My Partner, the Danish State and I – A Case Study of Family Reunification Policy in Denmark *Linda Lund Pedersen*	141
10	Aesthetics and Ethnicity: The Role of Boundaries in Sámi and Tornedalian Art *Anne Heith*	159

Index   *175*

List of Contributors

Anne Heith is Associate Professor of Comparative Literature at the Department of Culture and Media Studies, Umeå University, Sweden. Her latest book is *Texts, Media, Contexts* (in Swedish, 2006). Between 2008 and 2011 she was a full-time researcher in Border Poetics and Border Aesthetics at Tromsø University, Norway. Her research focuses on the ways in which discursive constructions of ethnicity, race, whiteness, gender, nation and globalization intersect in artistic representations. Her recent publications include examinations of the function of ethnification in Sámi and Swedish Tornedalian cultural mobilization.

Anna Rastas (Dr.Soc.Sc) is Research Fellow at the School of Social Sciences and Humanities at the University of Tampere, Finland. Her doctoral dissertation (2007) examined racism in the everyday life of children and young people. She has co-edited books on racism and multiculturalism and is the author of several articles and chapters on racialized relations and identities, transnational subjectivities, whiteness in Finland, representations of Africans and African diaspora in Finland. Her other research interests include literature for children, critical childhood and youth studies and ethnographic and participatory research methods.

Christina Petterson is a postdoctoral research fellow at the research project Gender as a Category of Knowledge at Humboldt University in Berlin. She has a Master of Theology degree from Copenhagen and a PhD in Cultural Studies from Macquarie University in Sydney. Her research focuses on the colonialism, missions, race, sexuality, class, and the role of Christianity in eighteenth-century Europe.

Erlend Eidsvik is a PhD candidate in the Department of Geography at the University of Bergen and a participant at the interdisciplinary research programme In the Wake of Colonialism at the same university. His research interests include Nordic encounters on the colonial arena, with a geographical emphasis on Southern Africa.

Kirsten Hvenegård-Lassen is Associate Professor at Roskilde University, Denmark. She is attached to the research group Intercultural Studies and the interdisciplinary Centre for Gender, Power and Diversity, and teaches the BA and MA programmes in Cultural Encounters. She has a PhD in Minority Studies from the University of Copenhagen. Her research focuses on migrancy with a special emphasis on intersecting mechanisms, categorizations and discourses of inclusion and exclusion.

Kristín Loftsdóttir is Professor of Anthropology at the University of Iceland. She received her PhD in anthropology from the University of Arizona (2000). She has published several books and articles internationally. Among her books are *Teaching 'Race' with a Gendered Edge* (co-editor 2012), *The Woman Who Got a Spear on Her Head: The Strangeness of Methodology* (in Icelandic, 2010). Her research focuses on Icelandic identity formation in the context of the economic crisis, in addition to a critical investigation of whiteness in relation to international development, issues relating to mobility, pastoralism and Icelandic racialized identity.

Lars Jensen is Associate Professor at Cultural Encounters, Roskilde University. He has worked and published in postcolonial studies for two decades, and is one of three editors of the *Historical Companion to Postcolonial Literatures: Continental Europe and its Empires*. He is currently finishing a manuscript on postcolonial Denmark, which examines how Denmark has dealt with its colonial history and how contemporary Denmark's post-imperial anxieties over migration reflect this broader history.

Linda Lund Pedersen is a PhD student in Gender Studies at the London School of Economics and Political Science. Her current research areas include the political/existential philosophy of Hannah Arendt in regard to debates on others and nation state in a Danish context, exemplified through family reunification policies and regulation of Muslim women's attire. She is also interested in the emergent field of postcolonialism and critical race/whiteness studies in Nordic/European contexts. She has published and edited book chapters, articles, journals and anthologies.

Serena Maurer received her PhD in Women Studies at the University of Washington in 2006, where she was a Lecturer in 2006–2007. From 2007 to 2010, she was Visiting Lecturer in Cultural Encounters in the Department of Culture and Identity at Roskilde University in Denmark as well as Affiliate Assistant Professor with the University of Washington's Women Studies Department. She is currently preparing a programme on immigration in Italy and Spain for the University of Washington Education Department and working with schools in Seattle, WA, USA to develop anti-oppressive modes of education.

Suvi Keskinen is Associate Professor in the Department of Social Research at the University of Turku, Finland. She has conducted research on gendered violence, media representations and multicultural politics. Her research interests include postcolonial feminism, politics of belonging, nationalism and racism. She has published widely in Finland and internationally. Among her publications are the co-edited book *Complying with Colonialism: Gender, Race and Ethnicity in* *the Nordic Region* (2009, Ashgate), and the articles Troublesome Differences – Dealing with Gendered Violence, Ethnicity and 'Race' in the Finnish Welfare State (2011, *Journal of Scandinavian Studies in Criminology and Crime Prevention*) and Limits to Speech? The Racialized Politics of Gendered Violence in Denmark and Finland (2012, *Journal of Intercultural Studies*).

Tobias Hübinette has a PhD in Korean Studies from Stockholm University, is a Reader in Intercultural Education at Södertörn University and works as a researcher in Migration Studies at the Multicultural Centre, Sweden. He has published within Asian studies and adoption studies, and cultural studies and postcolonial studies, and his current research concerns critical race and whiteness studies within a contemporary Swedish and Nordic context.

Series Editor's Preface

Following the publication of Edward Said's seminal work *Orientalism* in 1978, the binary study of colonialism and postcolonialism has burgeoned. In nearly all instances, postcolonialism has been perceived through the lens of the traditional Western European colonisers – Britain, France, Italy, Spain and Portugal – and their subjugates in Asia and Africa, as well as those under imperial rule in the Americas from the early 1500s. One region, in the context of both coloniser and colonised, has tended to be marginalised: that region, which comprises the countries of Norway, Sweden, Iceland, Finland and Denmark, together with the autonomous regions of the Faeroe Islands, the Aland Islands and Greenland, is the one which provides the focus for the chapters in this insightful and scholarly work. As the editors stress, '… in terms of colonial history, the Nordic countries manifest all variations of experience from colonizing powers, to colonies themselves'. And it is the geographical juxtaposition of the exploiter and the exploited and the ways in which the themes of identity and ethnicity, whiteness and gender and role reversal have played out that makes this a fascinating text.

Whilst we tend to consider the process of colonisation as one which took place between a distanced core and periphery, only one chapter in this book is located beyond the boundaries of the Nordic Region – in South Africa. All the others are positioned within the margins of the region. Thus with the above noted exception, all the tensions of the colonised/coloniser experience have taken, and are taking, place close to home. As the title of this book implies, one of the overriding themes of occidental colonisation is the superiority of whiteness and the way in which it so clearly delineates supremacy in the eyes of the coloniser, not just in terms of 'black and white' but more pertinently in the varying shades of belonging and otherness. As with the Irish and the Jews, both of which groups have been racialised in terms of physiognomy and colour, external features and whiteness come in varying forms and shades and thus various levels of acceptance. This is exemplified by the othering of Icelanders and Greenlanders/Inuit under Danish colonisation, and the residual distinctions between first- and second-class citizenship that became a characteristic of their postcolonial society.

It is significant that both the editors, together with several of the book's contributors, discuss the way in which, in the twenty-first century, traditional overt 'racism' has come to be superseded by 'cultural' racism which ranges from the subtle and covert forms of discrimination which are manifest in supposedly 'open' institutions to the overt, blatantly articulated and violent attacks on those who are different as a result of religion, politics or sexual proclivity as well as race. Countries in the Nordic region have sought to project an image of liberality and open-mindedness towards those who are other. However, the increasing number of economic immigrants, drawn to the stable economies of countries such as Norway, Denmark and Sweden, has led to increasing tensions and an erosion of that image of tolerance. The horrific massacre of 77 people – mainly teenagers – in Oslo in July 2011 by Anders Behring Breivik, a 32-year-old Norwegian right-wing extremist with a developed hatred of Islam, Marxism and, indeed, anything he perceived as anti-Nordic, catapulted Norway onto the global stage of racially motivated violence. This act emphasises the fact that the countries of northern Europe have their place in colonial and postcolonial studies. This volume, anchoring as it does the past to the present as well as looking to the future, provides an accessible and intellectually informed contribution to the study of imperialism and its manifestations in northern Europe.

Anne J. Kershen
Queen Mary University of London
Summer 2012

Introduction

Nordic Exceptionalism and the Nordic 'Others'

Kristín Loftsdóttir and Lars Jensen

In recent decades scholars have demonstrated how the formation of European national identities was deeply influenced by imperialism and colonialism. The colonized countries provided important sources of counter-identifications to the customary versions of European identities growing out of internal/domestic/national territorially defined processes. Key ideas such as modernity and nationalism – often seen as defining the European historical experience – outside these postcolonial interventions are spoken of as if they were arising in isolation from imperial and colonial contexts. The critique of this narrative has been forthcoming from a number of sources predominantly working in the field of postcolonialism (for example Dirks 1992; Young 2001; Gilroy 1993). Edward Said stressed that colonization was not only something happening in faraway places, but at the 'heart of European culture'. While the reach of colonialism was global, this does not make it a universal narrative, but a narrative with universal ramifications. To abandon the idea of the universal narrative entails the recognition of the transnational and transcontinental connections that have shaped European history, but also draws attention to the importance of analysing how these connections are played out in localized contexts, not only in the 'metropolitan centres' in Europe and its 'colonial peripheries', but also in the various regions of Europe. 'The Nordic' constitutes one such region and represents as such a particularly interesting case study, not least because of the relatively high degree of commonality in their post-war cultural historical experience. In terms of colonial history, the Nordic countries manifest all variations of experience, from colonizing powers, to colonies themselves. Yet while they were certainly peripheral to the major metropolitan cultures, they generally participated actively in the production of Europe as the global centre and profited from this experience.

This book places the Nordic in a postcolonial perspective, asking how discussions and debates in contemporary society are made meaningful or obscured by references to past events and tropes related to the practices and ideologies of colonialism and imperialism. The book responds to an interest that has been surfacing in the Nordic countries regarding their historical connections to colonialism and imperialism, but also in a more contemporary framework, how this powerful eighteenth- and nineteenth-century narrative is connected to the reactions in the Nordic countries when the 'Rest' comes to reside in the

'West' (Hall, 1992). The different contributors ask how the interwoven racial, gendered and nationalistic ideologies originating from the colonial project have formed a part of contemporary Nordic identities. As such the book engages with theorizing race, gender, multiculturalism and history in general by providing a deeper analysis of their meaning within a particular context. The book addresses how certain notions and structural inequalities that can be understood as being some sort of residue from the colonial period, become recreated or projected onto different groups in the contemporary Nordic countries and thus how borders of whiteness, and notions of Nordic-ness become more reified and, as well, contextualize them within a broader European and North American context. The book also investigates how this process is played out in power relations between the Nordic countries and within the Nordic countries themselves. Thus it draws attention to the diversification of the category Nordic, which despite its apparent homogeneity is a region composed of different populations with very different cultural histories, such as the indigenous Sámi within the Norwegian population, as well as the power relations between the Nordic states.

The idea of Nordic exceptionalism is the central theme of the book that cuts across diverse questions relating to identity and colonialisms, which we take to mean two quite different things. It can express an idea about the Nordic countries' peripheral status in relation to the broader European colonialism and to the more contemporary processes of globalization. Or it can represent the idea that Nordic self-perception is rooted intrinsically differently from the rest of Europe and that this self-perception generates different kinds of encounters from experiences elsewhere. This notion of Nordic exceptionalism has been especially spelled out in relation to research on current forms of internationalization, where it is usually taken to revolve around the notion of the Nordic countries as global 'good citizens', peace-loving, conflict-resolution orientated (DeLong 2009: 368–9) and 'rational' (Browning 2007: 27–8). Christopher Browning speaks of Nordic exceptionalism as constituting a central component in Nordic and national identities of the Nordic states, thus representing a particular form of nation branding (2007: 27–8). The Nordic countries have also actively engaged in anti-racist and anti-imperial activities since the 1970s without questioning their own involvement in colonial and racist activities (Keskinen et al. 2009). The present volume explores the legacy of this idea of Nordic exceptionalism by positioning it in the context of Nordic involvement in processes of globalization during the colonial period, the cultural encounters in which they were engaged as well as the experiences drawn from the large-scale migration after World War II. The intersection of different aspects of cultural identity is emphasized (race, gender and class) and also how these social categories are entangled with notions of religion and culture. Theories of intersectionality have gained increased importance (Phoenix and Pattynama 2006) which see identity as composed of many intersecting variables, interacting in complex ways, thus highlighting the importance of analysing the multiple positions at play (Yuval-Davis 2006; Valentine 2007).

Introduction 3

In this introduction, we contextualize the chapters in this book by giving a background to the key themes explored, which are then analysed more thoroughly in the different chapters. We start by giving a brief overview of the Nordic countries in relation to the creation of the modern world, creating an important background for the more country specific examples discussed in the different chapters of the book. We then explain in what ways postcolonial perspectives can be useful and consequently discuss racism in the past and the changes and continuities that characterize racism in the presence. By focusing on issues such as multiculturalism we also seek to draw attention the role played by the images of 'others' (transnational and indigenous peoples) within the Nordic countries as sources of counter-identification, and how domestic contestations over what constitutes acceptable identities within the nation have played out. We see the book as instrumental in creating a frame for an integration process between the diverse Nordic experiences, and of drawing out in what ways it makes sense to speak of the Nordic region as sharing particular postcolonial and intersectional interests and insights.

The Nordic Countries in the World

As earlier stated, we briefly point out the fluid relationships of the Nordic countries among themselves and with the rest of the world. The book does in some sense prioritize an analysis of Nordic nation states through its case studies while simultaneously highlighting transnational connections and fluidity. The Nordic countries encompass both independent states (Norway, Sweden, Iceland, Finland and Denmark) and autonomous regions (the Faeroe Islands, Greenland and the Aland Islands). Throughout the centuries the relationships between these countries have shifted boundaries and been contested and changed. They have involved and continue to involve the existence of people from various ethnicities, languages and areas that have upheld regional identities (Tägil 1995: 2). The Kalmar union in 1397 united Norway with Denmark and Sweden, as well as different parts of the Norwegian kingdoms, which were constituted by Iceland, Greenland the Faeroe Islands, Orkney and the Shetland islands and became parts of the combined kingdoms. Shetland and Orkney then became parts of Scotland in 1472 (due to unpaid dowry) (Oslund 2011: 12). The Kalmar union ended in 1536 and Iceland, Greenland and Faeroe Islands became subjects of the Danish Crown (Oslund 2011: 12). When Norway became a part of Sweden in 1814, the Faeroe Islands, Greenland and Iceland, were retained by the Danish King (Tägil 1995: 5). From the seventeenth until the nineteenth century, the Danish empire was quite powerful with its possessions in the North Atlantic and its tropical colonies in India, the Gold Coast (coastal Ghana), and the islands of St. Thomas, St. John and St. Croix in the Caribbean. Sweden, however, was by comparison a small colonial power with few colonies in the Caribbean and the USA, as well as possessing for a very brief time a fort in Ghana (Sawyer 2002: 17). Finland was a part of the Swedish kingdom since the early Middle Ages, but became in the early eighteenth century one of many separately administered areas in the Russian empire (Engman 1995: 181), becoming an independent state in 1917. Involvement in colonialism took various forms as this present volume elaborates further, such as business interest of Norwegians (Kjerland et al. 2009) or reproduction of colonial images in Iceland (Loftsdóttir 2010).

Diana Mulinari, Suvi Keskinen Sara Irni and Salla Tuori use the concept colonial complicity as a central metaphor to capture the multiple ways in which northern Europeans took part in these various colonial processes and continue to do so in the present (2009: 1). Simultaneously, by looking at the Nordic countries in a postcolonial context, we should keep in mind the complex relationship of these entities among themselves historically, thus avoiding turning 'names into things', as warned by Eric Wolf (1984), and recognizing the Nordic countries themselves as the result of a long history and different conflicted relationships.

Theorizing the Postcolonial

As pointed out in the introduction to *Postcolonial Studies and Beyond*, written by scholars from various disciplines, postcolonial studies is a contested field, partly because it is understood in quite diverse ways, even coming into being under different names in different disciplines. It is not regarded for example by anthropology and history as a distinctive sub-disciplinary specialty area as it is in those English departments that recognize it. The peculiarity of its position is also reflected in that it is conceptualized as either 'enormously radical' or the 'latest ideological offspring of Western Capitalism' (Loomba et al. 2005: 3). Postcolonialism, as argued by the editors, should not be seen as coming literally 'after' colonialism, as such a conception would ignore those still colonized and who are still the objects of oppression by structures created by colonialism. Rather the focus is on 'the contestation of colonial domination and the legacies of colonialism' (Loomba et al. 2005: 12).

Edward Said's *Orientalism* originally published in 1978 – often cited as one of the foundation works as the postcolonial sought to broaden its critical scope from the overt concerns with literature studies to broader concerns about the production of culture within colonialism and its aftermath – emphasizes clearly the reproduction of the past into the present when speaking of orientalism as a 'library or archive of information commonly ... held' (Said 1995: 41). As such the 'archive' created a naturalized knowledge of 'others', providing them with mentality and characteristics, constituting something real that could be acted on (Said 1995: 41–2). Ashcroft and Ahluwalia (2001) suggest that the power of Said's argument lies in its demonstration of how texts can influence the real life of people by creating a certain view of the world and informing how it is acted upon. This includes showing how the vision of certain societies is 'deeply woven into canonical European literature' (Cooper 2005: 4). In the Nordic countries one could think of Karen Blixen's *Out of Africa* as one illustrative example that has influenced generations of Nordic readers' perception of Africa and Africans. As elaborated by Stuart Hall, this colonial archive was constituted by various discourses such as the writing of classical scholars (for example Ptolemy's *Geographia* from the second century), religious and biblical sources and tales of travellers, which supplemented and drew on religious and classical works (Hall 1992). Throughout the centuries, scholars built on each other's works and helped cement stereotypes that have proven their time worn resilience in moments of contacts, whether peaceful or conflictual.

The chapters here provide analytical glimpses of the 'colonial archive' in relation to the Nordic countries, some articles focusing on how it was manifested in past engagements, while others look more at its reproduction in the present. As argued by Nicholas Dirks: 'Colonialism has not vanished from former colonial powers, where debates over nationality and multiculturalism mask increasing anxiety over the categories and identities of race, language, culture and morality' (Dirks 1992: 24). As these chapters demonstrate clearly, this is not only the case with the colonial powers but also those nation states that stood by on the sideline, but were nevertheless active in reproducing colonial perceptions of the world. Erlend Eidsvik, in his chapter in this book, engages directly with colonial history in places far from the Nordic countries by tracing the history of a particularly influential Norwegian settler family in South Africa, and through this shows how Scandinavian participation in colonialism outside their own relatively small and few colonial domains represented an important building stone in the establishment of other European empires. Colonial history has in Europe tended to be seen as a 'domestic relationship', whereas in fact the European colonial powers were both rivals, jealous of each other's possessions and depended on the recruitment of other Europeans in order to sustain their internal imperial order.

Racism in a Global and European Perspective

Racism has been instrumental in shaping our current present as well as past happenings, constituting an important reserve for the colonial archive in Said's sense. The Nordic countries were not by any means merely bystanders in the formulation of the racist theories and explanations of world difference. This is, for example, manifested in the active preoccupation of Swedish scholars with racial theories and their 'scientific' contribution. Affirming the Nordic countries long involvement in global theories of difference is the fact that the Swedish naturalist, Carl von Linné was a crucial actor in shaping Europe's consciousness of the planet through his classification system for all plants on the earth in his *Systema Naturae* (Pratt 1992). Linné put forward a classification of Human Sapiens in 1735 into six varieties (including two monster-like beings, *ferus* and *monstrosus*) (see discussion in Banton 1987: 4), which were remarkably similar to the racist typologies developed in late nineteenth century. Racist categorization of human diversity gained intense hegemonic power to interpret the world in the mid and late nineteenth century, then seen as constituting a scientific and hence as a superior way of knowing the world (Pickering 2001). As argued by Kimerlé Williams Crenshaw, 'racism helps to create an illusion of unity through the oppositional force of a symbolic other' (Crenshaw 2000: 550).

In recent years, scholars have increasingly stressed how the Europeans themselves were situated in diverse ways in relation to power, with gender and class as important variables (Stoler 1992: 321). Within Europe, certain populations were racialized and often subjected to similar stereotypes as those classified as 'black'. We have to be careful not to essentialize racial concepts, as pointed out in Matthew F. Jacobson's research on how 'whiteness' was created in a US context (1998). Instead we need to problematize current classifications of racial differences, seeing them as created within particular historical processes, and recognize that their more stabilized meaning was acquired relatively recently. Lorna Schiebinger's (1990) research on the early history of anatomy in the eighteenth century importantly reflects how a racist perception of the world is always gendered. Schiebinger points out how European anatomists and scientists, predominantly 'white' males themselves, saw 'white' women and non-white individuals as exotic. 'White' women and 'black' people were said to have a smaller brain, hence constituting a more primitive form of humans (Schiebinger 1990: 390–91), which served well to justify their domination and subordination by white educated European men. Sander Gilman's research shows quite clearly how nineteenth-century medical and popular discourses, rested on a close dialogue between descriptions of sexuality in relation to 'blackness' and women in general where deviant sexuality of white women was explained with reference to blackness (1985).

Within the Nordic countries this historical racist classification of people were used against a number of them, including anti-Semitism against the Jews in the 1930s. Yet, racist attitudes also worked in a number of different ways, depending on local situations and agendas. Christina Petterson's chapter traces one of the lesser-known cases of this, the Danish administration of Greenlanders/Inuit as a racially based system. This was common practice throughout the colonial world, but the history of trying to suppress this fact, through the invention of the benevolent colonial master, was a Danish characteristic. Furthermore, as Lars Jensen argues in his chapter, this self-image lived on beyond the end of colonialism. The Danish colonial apparatus was replaced by a modernization programme, which saw a complete transformation of Greenlandic society, but with the Danes at the top as decision-makers, while the Greenlanders remained second-class citizens in their own country as they had been during colonial rule. This way of thinking finds a parallel in Danish thinking about its role in the rise of development aid, as indeed was the experience in the other Nordic countries. Anne Heith discusses in her chapter two other Nordic indigenous populations, the Sámi and the Tornedalians. She shows how aesthetic responses to colonialism are, both an identity building project and a critical self-examination of the processes of internalization.

With the prohibition racial discrimination in various legal bodies since the mid twentieth century, racism has in some sense become more difficult to pinpoint, often – even though not always – more hidden and diversified (Harrison 2002; Balibar 1988). The focus on racism in the context of intersectionality recognizes that racism itself takes multiple forms in contemporary societies, increasingly attaching itself to other features such as religion and culture, in the process making these phenomena difficult to disentangle. 'Culture' is thus often used instead of 'race' as an explanation for the marginalized positions of certain groups, in the process objectifying and homogenizing a large group of people in a similar way as the widely repudiated discourse of biology was used before. Such cultural arguments are often embedded in the language of nationalism and ethnicity and sometimes referred to as 'new' racism (Balibar 1991, Abu-Lughod 2002), or 'cultural racism'. Racism has become more diverse in terms of visibility ranging from 'subtle, hidden subtexts to flagrant acts of hate speech' (Harrison 2002: 150), which reflects that while acts of racism and discrimination based on racial classification are generally prohibited by various legal conventions, racism often exist in institutionalized context and is expressed in more diversified ways. Nordic involvement in racism and recreation of racist symbols lives on, as Tobias Hübinette's chapter demonstrates, in various contemporary forms both at an academic level in Sweden (through the idea that in Sweden the continued existence of 'Orientalist studies' does not constitute a problem, since Sweden was not a colonial power), and at the more immediately expected popular level where the defence of a racist terminology is seen as evidence of a healthy dose of anti-PC, which has, however, also to rest on the idea that Swedes are inherently non-racist. Anna Rastas and Tobias Hübinette's chapters both focus on the importance of the legacy of a racist vocabulary in dealing with contemporary multicultural aspect of Sweden and Finland. Rastas' conclusion in relation to her analysis on Finland can probably be applied to the other Nordic countries where she importantly points out that to acknowledge racism as a part of Finish history would mean that it has to be dealt with seriously in the present.

Studies of whiteness are a part of research on racial identity in general (Hartigan 1997: 498). Whiteness is particularly interesting in a Nordic context, where limited research has been done on racial identity in relation to whiteness in the Nordic countries (see still as an example Rastas 2005, Hübinette and Lundström 2011, Sawyer 2002, Loftsdóttir 2010). As scholars have shown power rests with the normalization of certain bodies (Puwar 2004). Whiteness can be seen as including certain privileges where individuals can 'afford' to forget their own skin colour and position of power (Loftsdóttir 2003, Jensen 2011). Cultural arguments can be seen as embedded in the language of nationalism and ethnicity (Balibar 1991), as particularly important for whiteness. The book links notions of whiteness with a dynamic view of racism as not only being concerned with skin colour, but as entangled with other markers of inferiority or superiority (such as in the terms Nordic and European). Kristín Loftsdóttir shows in her chapter the ambiguities of colonial production of the Icelandic self-image, that is, the idea of a uniqueness of an Icelandic identity, in relation to the colonial exhibitions held in Copenhagen in the late nineteenth and early twentieth centuries. Her analysis shows the importance of placing notions of whiteness within a historical perspective, to see this as a shifting marker that gains importance in particular historical circumstances. As in some of the other chapters, her analysis shows the refusal to acknowledge racism as a part of Icelandic history, in addition to emphasizing that this has to be contextualized within a particular historical articulation of otherness and difference. Using theories of intersectionality can clarify and make these entanglements clearer. Hence Serena Maurer and Kirsten Hvenegård-Lassen in their chapter provide a reading of the Danish handbook for prospective migrants. They show how ideal notions of Danishness are cast against patrolled versions of acceptable migrants, based on highly gendered notions of family and kinship. Their chapter clearly shows how whiteness creates a racialized reality which can easily be unrecognized by those who are seen as 'white'. Linda Lund Pedersen outlines in her chapter the deeply personal effects of the bureaucratic ways of handling ethnic Danes who are trying to get a 'third country' spouse to the country. As in Maurer/Hvenegård-Lassen's chapter, a seemingly abstract state intervenes in profoundly personal ways in the life conditions of people, who happen to find a spouse outside the acceptable market for prospective immigrants.

Discussing racism in the present brings us to the issue of multiculturalism that as previously indicated is discussed directly or indirectly in many of the articles. 'Multiculturalism' as a term is increasingly used to capture the multiple identities characterizing modern nation states. The use of the term often implies that the multicultural society itself is a new phenomenon, thus hiding to some extent how societies have always been composed of different cultural groups, in addition to a tendency to only use the term multiculturalism to refer to the culture of 'other' people, that is, the presumed minorities within the nation states (Skaptadóttir and Loftsdóttir, 2009: 207–8). Migration in the present has to be seen as embedded in the colonial past (Ponzanesi 2002: 206, 212), even though taking various forms particular to specific histories and circumstances. Indeed, European colonialism saw an immense translocation of Europeans to the colonial world, including immigrants from the Nordic countries. Likewise, immigration history reveals migrations both temporary and permanent on a sizeable scale before the one that began with guest workers arriving in the 1960s. Suvi Keskinen deals in her chapter with two popular Finnish novels as instances of public debates over Muslims in contemporary Finland and how discussions of gendered violence often become a way to create a dualistic contrast between majority and minority viewpoints. Her discussion clearly shows the gendered aspects of how 'multiculturalism is discussed within Nordic societies (see also Holli et al. 2005; Loftsdóttir 2012; Tuori 2007), and how colonial legacies play into the articulation of these discourses. Several articles of the book discuss this dealing with the contemporary Nordic countries' difficulties in coming to terms with the global reality of which they continue to be a part, including transnational flows of people.

In spite of globalization and its accompanying complexities of interconnections, the nation state continues to be among the most important platforms of identification and identities (Ginsburg et al. 2002). While emphasizing the internal imagination of the Nordic nation states, the case studies draw out their similarities and interconnection. By deconstructing the Nordic, we seek to stress the role played by the images of 'others' (transnational and indigenous peoples) within the Nordic countries as sources of counter-identification, and how domestic contestations over what constitutes acceptable identities within the nation have played out. It is important to locate the Nordic countries in relation to the creation of the 'modern' world through various colonizing and imperialistic discourses that are reflected in the background for the more country specific examples discussed in the different chapters of the book. The book in this way is concerned with the specifics of Nordic experiences of globalization.

References

Abu-Lughod, L. 2002. Do Muslim Women Really Need Saving? Anthropological Reflections on Cultural Relativism and Its Others. *American Anthropologist*, 104(3), 783–90.

Ashcroft, B. and Ahluwalia, P. 2001. *Edward Said*. London: Routledge.

Balibar, E. 1991. Is there a 'Neoracism'? In *Race, Nation, Class: Ambiguous Identities*, edited by E. Balibar and I. Wallerstein. London and New York: Verso, 17–28.

Balibar, E. 1991. 'Class Racism'. In *Race, Nation and Class: Ambiguous Identities*, edited by E. Balibar and I. Wallerstein. London: Verso, 204–16.

Banton, M. 1987. *Racial Theories*. Cambridge: Cambridge University Press.

Browning, C. 2007. Branding Nordicity. Models, Identity and the Decline of Exceptionalism. *Cooperation and Conflict*, 42(1), 27–51.

Cooper, F. (ed.). 2005. *Colonialism in Question: Theory, Knowledge, History*. Berkeley: University of California Press.

Crenshaw, K.W. 2000. Race, Reform and Retrenchment. In *Theories of Race and Racism: A Reader*, edited by L. Back and J. Solomos. London and New York: Routledge, 549–60.

DeLong, R.D. 2009. Danish Military Involvement in the Invasion of Iraq in Light of the Scandinavian International Relations. *Scandinavian Studies*, 81(3), 367–80.

Dirks, N.B., 1992. Introduction: Colonialism and Culture. In *Colonialism and Culture*, edited by N.B. Dirks. Ann Arbor: University of Michigan Press, 1–26.

Engman, M. 1995. Finnst and Swedes in Finland. In *Ethnicity and Nation Building the Nordic World*, edited by S. Tägil. London: Hurst and Company, 179–216.

Gilman, Sander. 1985. *Difference and Pathology*. Ithaca, NY: Cornell University Press.

Gilroy, P. 1993. *The Black Atlantic: Modernity and Double Consciousness*. London and New York: Verso.

Ginsburg, F.D., Abu-Lughod, L. and Larkin, B. 2002. Introduction. In *Media Worlds: Anthropology on New Terrain*, edited by F.D. Ginsburg, L. Abu-Lughod and B. Larkin. Berkeley: University of California Press, 1–36.

Hall, S. 1992. The West and the Rest: Discourse and Power. In *Formations of Modernity*, edited by S. Hall and B. Gieben. Cambridge: Polity.

Harrison, F.V. 2002. Unraveling 'Race' for the Twenty-First Century. In *Exotic No More: Anthropology on the Front Lines*, edited by J. MacClancy. Chicago and London: University of Chicago Press, 145–66.

Hartigan J. Jr. 1997. Establishing the Fact of Whiteness. *American Anthropologist*, 99(3), 495–505.

Holli, A.M., Magnusson, E. and Rönnblom, M. 2005. Critical Studies of Nordic Discourses on Gender and Gender Equality. *Nordic Journal of Women's Studies (NORA)*, 13(3), 148–52.

Hübinette, T. and Lundström, C. 2011. Sweden after the Recent Election: The Double-Binding Power of Swedish Whiteness through the Mourning of the Loss of 'Old Sweden' and the Passing of 'Good Sweden'. *NORA – Nordic Journal of Feminist and Gender Research*, 19(1), 42–52.

Jacobson, Matthew F. 1998 *Whiteness of a Different Color: European Immigrants and the Alchemy of Race*. Cambridge: Harvard University Press.

Jensen, L. 2011. The Whiteness of Climate Change. *Journal of the European Association of Studies on Australia*, 2(2), 84–97.

Keskinen, S., Irni, S., Mulinari, D. and Tuori, S. (eds). 2009. *Complying with Colonialism*. Burlington, VT: Ashgate.

Kjerland, K. Alsaker and Rio, M.K. (eds). 2009. *Kolonitid: Nordmen på eventyr og big business I Afrika og Stillehavet*. Bergen: Scandinavian Academic Press, 5–9.

Loftsdóttir, K. 2003. Never Forgetting? Gender and Racial: Ethnic Identity during Fieldwork. *Social Anthropology*, 10(3), 303–17.

Loftsdóttir, K., 2010. 'Encountering Others in the Icelandic Schoolbooks: Images of Imperialism and Racial Diversity in the Nineteenth Century,' In *Opening the Mind or Drawing Boundaries? History Texts in Nordic Schools*, edited by Þ. Helgason and S. Lässig. Göttingen: Vandenhoeck and Ruprecht UniPress, 81–95.

Loftsdóttir, K. 2012. Whiteness Is from Another World: Gender, Development and Multiculturalism. *European Journal of Women's Studies*, 19, 41–54.

Loomba, A. 1998. *Colonialism/Postcolonialism*. Abingdon and New York: Routledge.

Loomba, A., Kaul, S., Bunzl, M., Burton, A. and Esty, J. (eds). 2005. *Postcolonial Studies and Beyond*. Durham and London: Duke University Press.

Oslund, K. 2011. *Iceland Imagined: Nature, Culture, and Storytelling in the North Atlantic*. Seattle: University of Washington Press.

Phoenix, A. and Pattynama, P. 2006. Intersectionality. *European Journal for Women's Studies*, 13, 187–92.
Pickering, M. 2001. *Stereotyping: The Politics of Representation*. Basingstoke: Palgrave.
Ponzanesi, S. 2002. Diasporic Subjects and Migration. In *Thinking Differently: A Reader in European Women Studies*, edited by G. Griffin and R. Bradoitti. London: Zed Books, 205–20.
Pratt, M.L. 1992. *Imperial Eyes: Travel Writing and Transculturation*. London and New York: Routledge.
Puwar, N. 2004. *Space Invaders: Race, Gender and Bodies out of Place*. Oxford: Berg.
Rastas, A. 2005. Racializing Categorization among Young People in Finland. *Young*, 13(2), 147–66.
Said, E.W. 1995. *Orientalism*. London: Penguin Books.
Sawyer, L. 2002. Routings: 'Race', African Diasporas, and Swedish Belongings. *Transforming Anthropology*, 11(1), 13–35.
Schiebinger, L. 1990. The Anatomy of Difference: Race and Sex in Eighteenth-Century Science. *Eighteenth-Century Studies*, 23(4), 390–91.
Sigurðsson, I. 1986. Íslensk sagnfræði frá miðri 19. öld til miðrar 20. aldar. Reykjavík: Sagnfræðistofnun Háskóla Íslands.
Skaptadóttir, U.D. and Loftsdóttir, K. 2009. Cultivating Culture? Images of Iceland, Globalization and Multicultural Society. In *Images of the North*, edited by S. Jakobsson. Reykjavík: Reykjavíkur Akademía, 201–12.
Stoler, L.A. 1992. Rethinking Colonial Categories: European Communities and the Boundaries of Rule. In *Colonialism and Culture*, edited by N.B. Dirks. Ann Arbor, Michigan: University of Michigan Press, 319–52.
Tägil, S. 1995. Introduction. In *Ethnicity and Nation Building the Nordic World*, edited by S. Tägil. London: Hurst and Company, 1–7.
Tuori, S. 2007. Cooking Nation: Gender Equality and Multiculturalism as Nation-Building Discourses. *European Journal of Women's Studies*, 14(1), 21–35.
Valentine, G. 2007. Theorizing and researching intersectionality: A Challenge for Feminist Geography. *The Professional Geographer*, 59(1), 10–21.
Wolf, E.R. 1984. *Europe and the People without History*. Berkeley: University of California Press.
Young, R. 2001. *Postcolonialism: An Historical Introduction*. Malden: Blackwell Publishers.
Yuval-Davis, N. 2006. Belonging and the Politics of Belonging. *Patterns of Prejudice*, 40(3), 197–214.

Chapter 1
Colonial Discourse and Ambivalence: Norwegian Participants on the Colonial Arena in South Africa

Erlend Eidsvik

Introduction

This chapter investigates the spaces of cultural ambivalence, when a group of Norwegian immigrants arrive on the colonial arena in Knysna in the Cape Colony in the latter half of the nineteenth century. Upon the establishment of a variety of business enterprises within shipping, forestry and trade, the immigrants – the Thesen family – became major economic participants in the region, and influential participants on the political scene. Since they did not belong to either of the dominant white immigrant groups – the British and the Boers – these immigrants utilized their ambivalent position to manoeuvre into new mercantile and social spaces.

Ambivalence is an essential analytical concept in colonial discourse, referring to the complex relations between colonizer and colonized (Bhabha 2004 [1994]). Here, discourse is understood as a system of statements within which the world can be known, derived from a Foucaualdian and Saidian tradition where discourse concerns how knowledge is produced and the influence of what we do, our social practice, and how knowledge and power are indivisible (Foucault 1972; Foucault 1981; Said 1994; Said 2003 [1978]). Such a system of statements is configured by dominant groups in society by enforcing knowledge, values and disciplines upon dominated groups. Thus colonial discourse can be understood to be the composite of *signs* and *practices* that organize social relations between colonizing and colonized people (Ashcroft et al. 2007: 37).

By investigating such signs and practices through perspectives of ambivalence, hybridity and liminality, inherently instrumental concepts within colonial discourse, I will argue that these migrants not only adhered to the colonial discourse, but also reconstituted and reinforced this discourse through explorations and exploitations of their own ambivalent position.

Non-Colonial Countries, Colonial Discourse and Mythmaking

The last few decades have seen an increased scholarly (self-)scrutiny on the European colonial projects and the interconnections between Europe and its colonies. In general, these contributions are anchored in an understanding that colonial discourses are shaped by the interactions between metropole and colony, rather than preshaped and projected into the colonial spaces (Said 1994; Viswanathan 1998; Chakrabarty 2000; Lester 2001; Cooper 2005).

However, studies of colonial discourse from a Nordic point of view have until recently been minuscule. Inspired by the emerging body of postcolonial scholarship, recent contributions have challenged the myth about Nordic exceptionalism and displayed examples of Nordic involvement in colonial projects (Brimnes, Ipsen et al. 2009; Keskinen, Tuori et al. 2009; Rio and Kjerland 2009; Maurer, Loftsdóttir and Jensen 2010). Nordic, or Scandinavian[1] encounters on foreign territories – historically as well as contemporary – are rarely discussed in a terminology that refers to colonialism. On the contrary, the Nordic self-image and self-narrative is to a large degree constructed in stark contrast to colonial activities, denying economic exploitations and cultural oppressions (Palmberg 2009; Simonsen 2010). In the case of Norway, a narrative purporting a historical legacy devoid of colonial entanglements is recalled in the contemporary political discourse.[2] This narrative inherently serves to position Norway as a neutral entity on the international arena in the construction of a self-image as a humanitarian power (Tvedt 2002; Tvedt 2003).

---

1 The regional concepts of the Nordic region and Scandinavia are often applied synonymously. A common understanding includes Denmark, Sweden and Norway as Scandinavia. The Nordic region consists of Scandinavia in addition to Finland, Iceland, and the autonomous territories of the Faeroe Islands and Greenland.

Yet, in recent use, Finland and Iceland are occasionally included in Scandinavia. Here, I will be speaking about the Nordic region, although some of the texts I refer to are speaking from a Scandinavian perspective. While the Nordic and Scandinavian regions are obviously not the same, the perspective from which I am looking invites the term Nordic countries, as the broader term which also contains all of Scandinavia.

2 See for example lecture by Norwegian Foreign Minister Jonas Gahr Støre at Oslo Military Society, 23 October 2006. Here, the Minister states: 'We do have certain advantages: we are not part of the power blocs in international politics; we do not have a colonial past; and we do not have a reputation for having a hidden agenda' (www.oslomilsamfund.no/oms_arkiv/2006/2006-10-23-Støre-engelsk.html), and former Norwegian Prime Minister Kjell Magne Bondevik New Year's speech 1 January 2000, when he addressed his vision that Norway as a nation should strive to become a humanitarian (super)power building on a tradition of (Christian) charity, solidarity and development aid, recalling a legacy of a neutral and benign bystander on the international arena (www.regjeringen.no/en/dokumentarkiv/Regjeringen-Bondevik-I/smk/Taler-og-artikler-arkivert-individuelt/2000/arsskiftet_1999–2000.html?id=264369).

The semi-peripheral status of the Nordic countries compared to the metropolitan European colonial powers calls for caution when trying to juxtapose the practices on the colonial arena performed by such different countries. However, there is a point in investigating the dynamics of Norwegian migrants – in this chapter through a case study – and challenging the myth about Norwegian exceptionalism, and instead demonstrate that Norwegians took part in the construction of colonial discourse; not in colonization or in an imperial project per se, but in maintaining and constructing colonial discourse.

Collectively, the recent studies on Nordic colonial encounters display empirical heterogeneity of economic and cultural encounters in colonial enterprises, and have contributed to develop a postcolonial theoretical framework in a Nordic context that is on the verge of emerging. However, much work still remains to be done. As for example Maurer et al. (2010: 1) state, 'Nordic postcolonialism … lacks an independent theoretical framework through which its themes and ideas can be articulated'. The recent publications mentioned above have seen analytical twists exploring the concepts of *hybridity* (Frello 2010), *provincializing* (Jensen 2010), and *complicity* (Vuorela 2009), to mention some recent contributions to the field.

Frello (2010) investigates the concept of hybridity through a focus on purity and transgression of purity. Departing from the biological origin of the concept, she extends its applicability by considering hybridity as a discursive resource, and analyses the relations between purity and hybridity and how they are articulated in a Danish TV series. Informed by Chakrabarty's work *Provincializing Europe* (Chakrabarty 2000), Jensen explores provincializing of Scandinavia through investigations of the peripheral status of Scandinavia relative to metropolitan Europe, and examines what forms of colonial modernities might be specific to Scandinavia (Jensen 2010). Vourela departs from Spivak's terminology and applies the concept of 'colonial complicity' to address how the tacit acceptance of practices is transformed into colonial complicity (Vuorela 2009: 20).

These concepts are significant contributions in the investigation and analysis of Nordic encounters on the colonial arena. Yet, the influence and impetus by the Nordic countries in colonial conquests can be considered as relatively subsidiary. The Nordic countries constitute a semi-peripheral region in a world conditioned by the imperial metropoles in their conquests of colonial territory. And as Jensen (2010: 13) remarks, the Scandinavian contribution to European thought in the colonial period is rather diminutive. However, as illustrated in these studies, encounters took place, and they had significance and consequences for the Nordic migrants, the colonizer and the colonized.

Spaces of Colonialism

Colonialism has been studied through different lenses. As Stoler and Cooper (1997: 4–5) summarize, colonialism has been approached as dominion of exploitation where European powers have extracted land, labour and produce in ways which were becoming politically impossible and economically less feasible on the domestic arena (Barratt Brown 1974). Secondly, colonies have been studied as a place beyond the inhibitions of the increasingly bourgeois cultures of Europe (Stoler 1995). Thirdly, colonies have been seen as laboratories of modernity, where Europeans could carry out experiments in social engineering on an arena without confronting resistance of the European society at home (Anderson 1995; Cooper and Stoler 1997). And fourthly, following in the tradition of Said (2003 [1978]), a scholarly focus on colonies as the *other* of whom Europeanness was expressed.

However, colonialism, as a system, should not be limited to colonies or colonial institutions. As an ideological and economic system, colonialism included encounters through exploration, missionary activities and trade. Considering colonialism beyond the metropoles, Scandinavian engagement in the colonial projects was part of a systematic European expansion (Ipsen and Fur 2009). And as Vuorela (2009) has pointed out, even if the Nordic nations were not the central driving forces behind colonial conquest, there are links to connect the non-empires to *the knowledge production* which was instrumental in promoting the colonization process, as well as direct support of the colonial projects.

This is a modest interpretation, as it is not merely knowledge and acceptance of practices on the colonial arena that are involved, but also performance of power, as some of the empirical cases presented below illuminate (Bertelsen 2009, Eidsvik 2009). Consequently, we are not merely talking of partakers and adaptors of a tacit knowledge *complying with the colonial* discourse, but also maintainers and developers of a colonial system by reconfiguring and reconstituting the colonial discourse through practices and performance of power.

Contact Zone, Semi-Periphery and Colonial Encounters

Colonial encounters, practices and performance of power can be thought of in relation to the concept of *contact zone*. This term, as conceptualized by Pratt, encompasses the social spaces, or meeting points between disparate cultures, often in highly asymmetrical relation of subordination and dominance (Pratt 1992: 4). Hence, the contact zone is the liminal space that emerges in the meeting between the colonizer and the colonized. Each encounter, or contact zone, is different and specific and should be analysed for its specific interplay.

Exploring these contact zones, the concepts of metropole and periphery (or colony) offers an idea of a spatially and power-divided relation between an imperial centre and a periphery. The metropole and the colony were connected through flows of capital, commodities, ideas and labour. Moreover, if metropole and colony – as *places* – always are products of wider contacts, as Massey (1995: 183) suggests, an emphasis on the nature of how power and knowledge are produced within transnational frames might reveal the interconnected historical geographies of the sites we study (Lester 2002: 30).

Yet, approaching colonialism in a Scandinavian context, the idea of *metropole* is hardly applicable. Politically, demographically and economically, Scandinavia was, and still is, in what can be categorized as semi-peripheral Europe. The degree of periphery is even more palpable for Norway, being in the margins of the semi-periphery during the periods of Danish and Swedish hegemonic power.[3]

Norway as a Colonial Nation?

Arguably, the Danish-Norwegian monarchy had colonial ambitions in the seventeenth century that sought to challenge the metropolitan powers in Europe (Jónsson 2009). The colonies in the West Indies, West Africa and India were small, yet they played an important role in the development of merchant capitalism in the eighteenth century (Fihl 2008). Norway, which is the focus here, was a Danish province from 1536[4] until 1814, when it was ceded to Sweden in the Treaty of Kiel as compensation for Sweden's loss of Finnish territory to Russia. Although constitutional independence and home rule were achieved in 1814, Norway was in a personal union with the Swedish king, and complied with Swedish foreign policies until the union was dissolved in 1905 and Norway became independent.[5] Being a subject of foreign rule itself, the idea of Norwegian colonial ambitions in the period prior to 1905 is somehow peculiar. However, in the period between 1814 and 1905, Norway re-entered the international arena, in particular through shipping. Concurrent with these international pursuits, the last few decades in the nineteenth century bore witness to a national awakening, which disputed foreign governance and called for full independence. On the ideological-political level, the medieval territorial expansions and occupations in the North Atlantic were brought into focus. The loss of Iceland, Greenland and the Faeroe Islands was by many seen as arrogated to Denmark in the Treaty of Kiel in 1814 without the voice of Norway being heard.[6] The backdrop for a new international orientation,

---

3 The categories of metropole (core), semi-periphery and periphery are informed by World System Theory and Wallerstein's division of the world into these three structural positions in a capitalist system – a system which he argues has been the decisive economic system since the sixteenth century (Wallerstein 1974, 2004).

4 The kingdoms of Norway and Denmark merged in a union in 1380. From 1536 Norway was considered a Danish province. See O. Riste (2005). *Norway's Foreign Relations: A History*. Oslo, Universitetsforlaget.

5 The union between Sweden and Norway was in theory a relation pertaining to international law between two independent states. However, the nations were unified under the Swedish crown, and foreign affairs were administered in the Ministry Cabinet in Sweden. See J. Nærbøvik (1993). *Norsk historie 1870– 905. Frå jordbrukssamfunn mot organizasjonssamfunn*. Oslo: Det Norske Samlaget.

6 Riste (2005) argues that the Swedish negotiators did not claim the previous North Atlantic possessions owing to a lack of knowledge that the areas were annexed prior to Danish rule.

at least partly, was moulded in the search for an imperial legacy in the old colonial possessions.

Simultaneously, shipping boomed during the nineteenth century. In 1825, Sweden-Norway and Great Britain signed a bilateral agreement allowing vessels from the involved countries to carry cargo. This caused an increase in export of Swedish timber to Great Britain, mainly carried on Norwegian ships (Nygaard 2009). The strategy of Norwegian ship-owners was to purchase second-hand ships, and strip the vessels which allowed for a smaller crew and thus increased profit. The stripped ship could not compete on speed, but for cargo where the price was decisive, pace was of lesser importance. This strategy, coupled with low freight rates and low wages, continued throughout the nineteenth century (Hodne 1981). From a modest outset in the first half of the nineteenth century, the volume of Norwegian tonnage increased significantly from the mid nineteenth century, and by the end of the century Norway had become a major player in international shipping. The new role as the cheap freighter on the seven seas enabled many Norwegian sailors to disembark on foreign shores and become involved in economic niches, and also bring material as well as non-material items back to the domestic arena.

Migrants and Complicit Colonialists?

On the African continent – the main arena for European imperialism and colonial conquests – the numbers of Nordic migrants, disembarked sailors and opportunity seekers was low compared with the emigration to North America, which reached nearly three million people in the period between 1820 and 1930.[7] Statistics are incomplete, yet the number of emigrants travelling to some African countries was proportionally significant, in particular South Africa, where approximately 5,200 residents of Scandinavian origin were registered in the 1904 census.[8] The number

---

7   From the Nordic countries together, nearly three million people left for North America between 1820 and 1930, of which almost one-third returned home. See for example H. Norman and H. Runblom (1987). *Transatlantic Connections: Nordic Migration to the New World after 1800*. Oslo: Norwegian University Press.

8   *Census of the Cape Colony 1904*, 30; *Census of the Natal Colony 1904*, 532; *Census of the Orange River Colony 1904*, 28–9; *Transvaal Census 1904*, 142. The accumulated censuses have registered 3,998 people born in Sweden-Norway, and 1,249 born in Denmark. Emigrants from Denmark, Sweden and Norway were categorized as emigrants from the Scandinavian countries, while emigrants from Finland were registered as Russian emigrants until the 1926 census, indicating a slow response time since Finland became independent in 1917. Kuparinen, compiling from multiple sources in the Nordic countries, has identified 1,462 persons from Norway, 1,454 from Sweden, 1,222 from Finland and 1,213 from Denmark leaving for South Africa in the period between 1886 and 1914. There is a significant discrepancy between the emigrants registered in the Nordic countries and the Nordic immigrants recorded in the censuses in South Africa (Kuparinen 1991: 27–30).

of Scandinavian migrants ranked them third in the decade between 1874 and 1883 behind Britain and Germany (Kuparinen 1991: 69).

Colonial encounters also took place in many regions on the African continent. For example, recent studies have illustrated how Scandinavian seamen were instrumental in maintaining the Belgian colonial apparatus in Leopoldian Congo to serve the harbours and ships along the spine of the colony, the Congo River (Wæhle 2002; Wæhle and Tygesen 2006). In Mozambique, Norwegian vested interests lay in the possession of large-scale plantations under the Portuguese colonial system. The Norwegians enforced their own jurisdiction on the 40,000 employees in what has been referred to as a totalitarian and brutal system (Bertelsen 2009). Similarly, Norwegians established farms in Kenya (Kjerland 2010) and trading companies in Zanzibar (Bang 2008). Yet, encounters on the colonial arena were not merely propelled by economic interests, but also by religious interests through missionary activities. As Engh (2009) states, in proportion to the population, Norway has sent out more missionaries than any other nation. From the mid-nineteenth century, missionaries from the Norwegian Missionary Society (NMS) went to South Africa, Madagascar and India, in particular. Skeie, in studying the Norwegian mission in Madagascar, reflects upon how the missionaries here were not detached or isolated from French colonial rule, but instead operated as what she denotes as 'a careful balancing act' between colonial rulers and the Malagasy population (Skeie 2009: 59–60). The NMS was involved in running primary schools in the Merina Kingdom,[9] prior to French colonial rule, and was still at the core of the colonial educational activities in the early phase of French colonization of the island, and had at its height as many as 30,000 pupils in NMS-run schools (Skeie 2009: 52). The concept of 'a careful balancing act' is much vaguer than 'complicity', and the missionaries are seemingly deprived of complicity with the colonial in the analysis. Yet, this 'careful balance' also reflects the specific contact zone between the French colonizers, the Norwegian missionaries and the local population, illustrating the ambivalent, in-between position held by the missionaries.

In colonial Zanzibar during the same period, Bang (2008) depicts a comparable setting and she illustrates how a Norwegian trading agent manoeuvred between agencies and traders from the two colonial rivals, Germany and Britain. She narrates how this position obtained and defined on the fringes of the colonial apparatus conditioned a liminal position – or in-betweenness – that enabled certain behaviours and a certain level of access, yet confined behaviours that would be in conflict with the dominant colonial groups.

These cases display colonial encounters by migrants from a non-colonial country and how they not only adhered to the colonial system in the spaces they operated in, but also played an active role in producing the colonial discourse by reconstituting knowledge and practices in colonial domains governed by dominant European colonial powers.

---

9   The Merina Kingdom was a Malagasy state ruling from the interior of Madagascar from 1797 until French colonization in 1897.

Migrant Ambivalent? A Case from the Cape Colony

The following case illustrates how a group of Norwegian immigrants that arrived in the Cape Colony in 1869 exploited their ambivalent position as neither British nor Boer to carve out a position for themselves, from which they took part in orchestrating the colonial discourse. The immigrants in this case, the 13 members of the Thesen family, left their bankrupt shipping business in Stavanger, Norway, after nearly three decades of shipping trade in the North Sea and the Baltic Sea. The sombre prospects for further business in Norway led the Thesens to search for alternative arenas. The British consul in Stavanger offered institutional support and issued a letter of recommendation to the Thesens to settle in a British colony (Eidsvik 2009).[10] Already here, before leaving Norway, the colonial entanglements serve as a prerequisite for their exodus. The group of migrants – sailing on their own ship repurchased from the bankrupt estate with their last family savings – planned to settle in New Zealand. But halfway, in Cape Town, their vessel needed extensive repair after being hit by storms in the dreaded waters off the shores of the southern tip of Africa. In order to raise sufficient means to continue their voyage, the Thesens sought assistance from the Swedish-Norwegian consul in Cape Town. The consul connected the migrants to his network of business partners, and arranged for shipping of goods along the southern coast of the Cape Colony. The prospects of establishing a shipping business in the Cape Colony prompted the family to settle in 1870 in the small town of Knysna, one of a few sheltered and natural harbours on the rugged southern coast between Cape Town and Port Elizabeth. Knysna was, and still is, surrounded by extensive forests. The family established Thesen & Company, whose main economic activities became forestry and timber business and shipping. The company was involved in a diversity of enterprises, and had by the beginning of the twentieth century become the major economic stakeholder in Knysna, diversifying its interests into nearly all spheres of economic – and political activities (Eidsvik 2009). The social stratification in Knysna and the Cape Colony was pronounced, classifying British at the top end of the social ladder, followed by Boers, coloureds and finally African/Blacks.[11]

---

10 A more thorough investigation of the emigration of the Thesens and the establishment of the company Thesen & Co can be found in Eidsvik (2009). The basis for the descriptions and the analysis is the business and private archive of Thesen & Co, compiled in KAB A 2605: The Thesen Collection, Western Cape Archives Repository, Cape Town, South Africa.

11 The term *coloured* is a contested term, often perceived pejorative as an imposed racial category, but accepted as a label of self-identity by others. The application of the term stems from categorization of people by British colonial rule in the Cape Colony. In general, it refers to ethnic groups with origin south of the Sahara, mixed with people with European and Malay origin. See V. Beckford-Smith (2005). 'Coloured: Southern Africa', in D. Johnson and P. Poddar, *A Historical Companion to Postcolonial Thought in English*. New York: Columbia University Press. The term African/Black is likewise a problematic category. The terminology changed from Black to African/Black for the 1996-census.

The space for economic power was a demarcated space constructed by and for the British, and the Thesens were partly absorbed into the British segment of the society. However, the family was also connected to the political Boer elite through marital bonds, and manoeuvred its position between the two major and conflicting groups within the white population. The position of liminality was utilized in pragmatic terms to avoid political tension and potential conflicts, and to make the most particularly in terms of economic advantages of the liminal position.

A shortage of freighters along the South African coast upon the arrival of the Thesens created an economic niche which they exploited. The British colonial apparatus at the time was eager to settle rural areas in the colonies in South Africa, after earlier British schemes of rural settlements in the Cape Colony and Natal had not proved too successful. To ensure the transport of people, provisions and cargo along the coast to the settlers was an important infrastructural factor for the colonial government.

The colonial government played an equally important role in shipping and in the management of forestry. From 1795 until 1876, all forest in the Cape Colony was Crown forest expropriated by the British Colonial Government. Only seven years after the arrival of the Thesens, the forests were opened for private enterprise. However, the labour practices had been established much earlier by the colonial apparatus itself. Groups of woodcutters were allowed to provide the governmental timber processing stations established in mid-eighteenth century with a certain amount of timber. The woodcutters were a marginal group consisting of European settlers of Dutch and French descent, and 'coloureds', living in what has been described as deprived conditions (Grundlingh 1992). The poverty of this group became a concern for the colonial government at the end of the nineteenth century, and specific measures were called for to address the poverty of the woodcutters. When the forests were opened for private enterprises, the labour structure that had exploited the woodcutters was passed on from the colonial forestry management practices. The private companies, and among them the largest company Thesen & Co, developed the exploitative practice further through a system of credit and dependence.[12] Grundlingh (1992: 49), for example, argues that the woodcutters were trapped in a state of poverty with limited space for social mobility through a system of suppressive dependency. The woodcutters were, in many cases, paid in coupons that could be redeemed in commodities. Such coupons were also issued on credit, which kept the woodcutter indebted, dependent and loyal to the merchants. From official levels, the district forest officer complained in 1911 about

---

Prior to that, the categories of Black, Bantu, Native and even Kafir (prior to 1911) have been applied as official categories. For an in-depth study of the South African system of demographic classification from the colonial era until the present, see A.J. Christopher (2002). 'To Define the Indefinable': Population Classification and the Census in South Africa. *Area*, 34(4), 401–8.

12 SAB FOR 58/56A. 'Woodcutters Grievances. Correspondence from 20 August 1906 to 24 April 1911'.

the paradox between the accumulation of assets among the timber merchants and the prevailing poverty of the woodcutters. The letter specifically addressed Thesen & Co, and claimed that Thesen was 'the principal member of a class which, by its absorption of the profits attending the timber industry, has been chiefly responsible for the impoverishment of the woodcutter'.[13]

Allegations of Monopoly

The economic dominance of Thesen & Co grew from a modest beginning in the 1870s. Shipping and forestry continued to be the backbone, however the company diversified into a series of enterprises, and became an omnipresent and influential participant in the economic sphere in the region from the beginning of the twentieth century.[14] From the 1880s, competing merchants in Knysna expressed discontent with the monopoly-like situation in shipping and trade. The dissatisfaction culminated in a letter addressed to Thesen & Co signed in 1913 by 15 merchants claiming that the company monopolised all mercantile activities in the town:

> We the undersigned Merchants and Storekeepers are entirely dissatisfied with the present unheard of unique conditions existing in Knysna, under which business is being conducted; and with the unfair in fact we might say suicidal competition in almost every branch of Mercantile business and Trade generally, due solely to your firm being Storekeepers as well as Ship owners, the latter being practically a monopoly, at present.[15]

The complaint addressed the ubiquitous presence of the Thesen & Co, being wholesaler and retailer as well as agents for other companies. The complainers demanded the Thesen & Co to give in to retail business to ensure fair conditions for all merchants and secure a variety of partakers in the economic sphere. Responding to the claims, the accused part offered reduced freight rates. The other allegations were discarded as incorrect claims, and no further actions were taken.[16]

---

13   SAB, FOR 58/56A.H. Ryan to Assistant Conservator Forest Knysna. 15 February 1911.

14   The company Thesen & Co existed from 1870 until 1974, when it was sold to Barlow & Rand, later to become Barloworld.

15   KAB A 2605 vol. 2/81. Complaints re monopoly of Thesen & Co Ltd. Letter from 15 merchants in Knysna, dated 19 March 1913.

16   KAB A 2605 vol. 2/81. Re: Complaints re monopoly. Letter of response signed C.W. Thesen, 10 April 1913.

Ambivalence and Appropriation of Neutral Space

An illustrating example on how the Thesens navigated through social and political spaces between British and Boers is the reburial of A.L. Thesen, the initiator of the emigration from Norway. Upon his death in 1875, he was buried at the cemetery of the Dutch Reformed Church. The family's confessional membership was later changed to the Anglican Church. In 1959, the grave had to be moved owing to alterations at the cemetery. The grave could be moved to a different site at the same cemetery; however, the family considered moving the grave to the Anglican Church.[17] 'The whole thing would be out of place', one of the Thesen descendants stated in a correspondence on the issue, referring to that such an act could be perceived as a political statement.[18] In lieu of a solution with symbolic consequences, the final decision was to rebury A.L. Thesen in a private and neutral spot in the forest a few kilometres east of Knysna, on the site where the first Thesen & Co sawmill had been built. Almost a century after the arrival of the Thesens, the position of liminality still had currency. Instead of choosing either of the two options which might conflict with each other, a new gravesite was appropriated. Negotiations with Afrikaner and Anglican strands are avoided, and the liminal position was maintained by constructing and appropriating a new neutral space.

Colonial Relations and Ambivalence

The colonial history of South Africa can be mirrored through periods where major societal shifts have taken place – periods of *social dislocations*,[19] as Lester suggests (2000: 278–9). The transition from a colonial order of forced labour to a period guided by British liberalism[20] in the early nineteenth century is one period with major social, economic and political implications. A second period constitutes the transition to industrial capitalism in late nineteenth and early twentieth century. The third period is the current transition to a post-apartheid period. The case in this paper takes place in the second period against the backdrop of the first transition.

Yet, several layers of colonial relations are involved. In the case of the Cape Colony, the indigenous Khoi and San populations were subjects of colonization first by the Dutch (1652–1795), and later the British (1795–1910), and continued to be subjects for racially stratified governance in the Union of South Africa from

---

17 KAB A 2605 vol. 1/25. Letter from Harry Thesen to Katie, Ella, Rolf, Theodor and Oscar Thesen, 23 March 1959.

18 KAB A 2605 vol. 1/25. Answer to Harry Thesen from Oscar Thesen, 2 April 1959.

19 The term *social dislocation* was first introduced by E. Laclau (1990). *New Reflections on the Revolution in Our Time*. London, Verso.

20 Forced labour was abolished in the *Slavery Abolition Act* of 1833 throughout the British Empire. In the Cape Colony, slaves became legally free in 1838 (Thompson 2001: 57).

1910 and later the Republic of South Africa from 1961. The relationship between the British colonizer and the former Dutch colonizers, or what became the Boer population, was characterized by disputes and tension throughout the nineteenth century and it culminated in the South African War 1899–1902. The Boers did not accept British hegemony, and migrated into rural areas escaping British colonial legislation and here they continued their own colonial practices. However, as Judd and Surridge have remarked, English-speaking and Afrikaans-speaking South Africans were often bound together in complex ways, facing the same challenges with drought and a harsh environment, and not least they had a common desire to keep control of the indigenous population (Judd and Surridge 2002: 1–3). This also became evident as the two dominant white groups were equally committed to sustain white supremacy in South Africa upon the establishment of the South African Union in 1910.

Taking this into consideration, colonial South Africa can be depicted as an arena inscribed in hybridity – in linguistic, ethnic and social terms. Linguistically, Afrikaans is mainly based on Dutch, but also includes elements from French, Portuguese, Malay, Bantu-languages and KhoiSan languages, and as such is a deeply hybrid construction. Further, the system of racial categories implemented by the British colonial apparatus in the nineteenth century is also a process of hybridization, even in the primordial biological meaning of the concept, as the category 'coloured' entails a hybrid classification of different ethnic groups, such as San, Khoikhoi, Malay and European.

Conclusion

It was upon this context of colonial relations that the group of Norwegian migrants, the Thesens, arrived in 1869. The colonial discourse – the signs and practices that constitute the way society is organized and reproduced within colonial relations – were established first by Dutch colonial practice and reconstructed and reconstituted by the British colonial apparatus. This system of statements constructed and maintained by a dominant group of society was recognizable, and the Thesens became within a short time after their arrival a part of the colonial discourse through their business enterprises and participation in the exploitation of existing labour practices. In addition they created for themselves a liminal position among the white dominant groups in the Cape Colony.

The concepts of ambivalence, liminality and hybridity are intimately connected in postcolonial theory. Liminality refers to a threshold area, a spatial notion of in-betweenness. Bhabha refers to the art historian Renée Green and his classification of a stairwell as a liminal space. The pathway between upper and lower levels is neither upper nor lower, but instead recognized as a liminal space of continuous interchanges and processes of movements (Bhabha 2004 [1994]: 4). For example, a colonized subject might be in a liminal space between colonial discourse and a new position of a non-colonial identity. Transcending these spatial and identity levels is, though, a continuous process of engagement and contestation (Ashcroft, Griffiths et al. 2007: 117). In this case, it is the (Norwegian) immigrant that labels herself or himself within this pathway, being neither (official) colonizer, nor colonized. Yet, the immigrants navigate into, and occupy, a position within the colonial discourse which enables them not only to accept and comply with the established discourse, but also to reproduce and even reinforce the uneven relations of power.

Hybridity, with its scholarly roots from biology and studies on race and evolutionary theory is a disputed term.[21] Yet, in the context of postcolonial studies hybridity commonly relates to how new transcultural forms emerge from the contact zone produced by colonization. Hybridization, in this understanding, entails political, linguistic, ethnic and political forms. Bhabha construes hybridity relative to the relation between colonizer and colonized. As such, all cultural statements are constructed in a space he labels 'Third Space of enunciation' (Bhabha 2004 [1994]: 54). This 'third space', according to Bhabha, implies an ambivalent space that overcomes cultural diversity. Consequently, it is in the 'in-between' space, or 'third space', where meaning of culture is constituted. The position of the migrants – in this case Norwegian migrants – invokes a new space recognized and conditioned by its ambivalent position from where colonial discourse is not only adapted, but also reinforced.

Archival Sources

KAB: Western Cape Archives Repository, Cape Town. Vol. A 2605: The Thesen Collection.
SAB: National Archive Repository, Pretoria. FOR 58/56A.

References

Anderson, W. 1995. Excremental Colonialism: Public Health and the Poetics of Pollution. *Critical Inquiry*, 21(3), 640–69.
Ashcroft, B., G. Griffiths et al. 2007. *Post-Colonial Studies: The Key Concepts*. London: Routledge.
Bang, A.K. 2008. *Zanzibar-Olsen: Norsk trelasthandel i Øst-Afrika 1895–1925*. Bergen: Fagbokforlaget Vigmostad & Bjørke.
Barratt Brown, M. 1974. *The Economics of Imperialism*. Harmondsworth: Penguin.

---

21 See for example R.J.C. Young (1995). *Colonial Desire. Hybridity in Theory, Culture and Race*. London, Routledge.

Beckford-Smith, V. 2005. Coloured: Southern Africa, in *A Historical Companion to Postcolonial Thought in English*, edited by D. Johnson and P. Poddar. New York: Columbia University Press, 105–6.

Bertelsen, B.E. 2009. Kolonialisme på portugisisk og norsk. Plantasjen Madal i Mosambik, in *Kolonitid: Nordmenn på eventyr og big business i Afrika og Stillehavet*, edited by K.A. Kjerland and K. Rio. Oslo: Scandinavian Academic Press.

Bhabha, H.K. 2004 [1994]. *The Location of Culture*. London: Routledge.

Brimnes, N., P. Ipsen et al. (eds). 2009. *Itenerario: Scandinavian Colonialism*. Leiden.

Chakrabarty, D. 2000. *Provincializing Europe: Post-Colonial Thought and Historical Difference*. Princeton: Princeton University Press.

Christopher, A.J. 2002. 'To Define the Indefinable': Population Classification and the Census in South Africa. *Area*, 34(4), 401–8.

Cooper, F. 2005. *Colonialism in Question: Theory, Knowledge, History*. Berkeley, CA: University of California Press.

Cooper, F. and A.L. Stoler (eds). 1997. *Tensions of Empire: Colonial Cultures in a Bourgeois World*. Berkeley: University of California Press.

Eidsvik, E. 2009. Thesen & Co – væreigarar i Sør-Afrika, in *Kolonitid: Nordmenn på eventyr og big business i Afrika og Stillehavet*, edited by K.A. Kjerland and K. Rio. Oslo: Scandinavian Academic Press, 45–64.

Engh, S. 2009. The Conscience of the World? Swedish and Norwegian Provision of Development Aid. *Itenerario*, 33(2), 65–82.

Fihl, E. 2008. Tropical Colonies, in *A Historical Companion to Post-colonial Literatures: Continental Europe and its Empires*, edited by P. Poddar, R.S. Patke and L. Jensen. Edinburgh: Edinburgh University Press, 97–9.

Foucault, M. 1972. *The Archaeology of Knowledge*. New York: Phanteon.

Foucault, M. 1981. The Order of Discourse, in *Untying the Text: A Poststructuralist Reader*, edited by R. Young. London: RKP, 48–78.

Frello, B. 2010. Dark Blood. *Kult*, 7 (*Special Issue: Nordic Colonial Mind*), 69–84.

Grundlingh, A. 1992. 'God het ons arm mense die houtjies gegee': Poor White Woodcutters in the Southern Cape Forest Area, c.1900–39, in *White but Poor: Essays on the History of Poor Whites in Southern Africa 1880–1940*, edited by R. Morell. Pretoria: University of South Africa, 40–56.

Ho, E. 2004. Empire through Diasporic Eyes. *Comparative Studies in Society and History*, 46, 210–46.

Hodne, F. 1981. *Norges økonomiske historie 1815–1970*. Oslo: Cappelen.

Ipsen, P. and G. Fur. 2009. Introduction. *Itinerario*, 33(2), 7–16.

Jensen, L. 2010. Provincialising Scandinavia. *Kult*, 7 (*Special Issue: Nordic Colonial Mind*), 7–21.

Jónsson, M. 2009. Denmark-Norway as a Potential World Power in the Early Seventeenth Century. *Itinerario*, 33(2), 17–27.

Judd, D. and K. Surridge. 2002. *The Boer War*. London: John Murray.

Keskinen, S., S. Tuori et al. (eds). 2009. *Complying with Colonialism: Gender, Race and Ethnicity in the Nordic Region*. Farnham: Ashgate.
Kjerland, K.A. 2010. *Nordmenn i det koloniale Kenya*. Oslo: Scandinavian Academic Press.
Kuparinen, E. 1991. *An African Alternative: Nordic Migration to South Africa, 1815–1914*. Helsinki: Finnish Historical Society.
Laclau, E. 1990. *New Reflections on the Revolution in Our Time*. London: Verso.
Lester, A. 2000. Global Capitalism, Social Dislocation and Cultural Discourse in South African History. *South African Historical Journal*, 42(1), 277–89.
Lester, A. 2001. *Imperial Networks: Creating Identities in Nineteenth-Century South Africa and Britain*. London: Routledge.
Massey, D. 1995. Places and Their Pasts. *History Workshop Journal*, (39), 182–92.
Maurer, S., K. Loftsdóttir et al. 2010. Introduction. *Kult*, 7 (*Special Issue: Nordic Colonial Mind*), 1–6.
Maurer, S., K. Loftsdóttir et al. (eds). 2010. *Kult*, 7 (*Special Issue: Nordic Colonial Mind*). Roskilde: Department of Culture and Identity.
Nærbøvik, J. 1993. *Norsk historie 1870–1905. Frå jordbrukssamfunn mot organizasjonssamfunn*. Oslo: Det Norske Samlaget.
Norman, H. and H. Runblom. 1987. *Transatlantic Connections: Nordic Migration to the New World after 1800*. Oslo: Norwegian University Press.
Nygaard, K.N. 2009. Norsk seilskipsfart på Sør-Afrika, in *Kolonitid: Nordmenn på eventyr og big business i Afrika og Stillehavet*, edited by K.A. Kjerland and K. Rio. Oslo: Scandinavian Academic Press, 11–22.
Palmberg, M. 2009. The Nordic Colonial Mind, in *Complying with Colonialism: Gender, Race and Ethnicity in the Nordic Region*, edited by S. Keskinen, S. Tuori, S. Irni and D. Mulinari. Farnham: Ashgate.
Pratt, M.L. 1992. *Imperial Eyes: Travel Writing and Transculturation*. London: Routledge.
Rio, K.M. and K.A. Kjerland. 2009. *Kolonitid: Nordmenn på Eventyr og big business i Afrika og Stillehavet*. Oslo: Scandinavian Academic Press.
Riste, O. 2005. *Norway's Foreign Relations: A History*. Oslo: Universitetsforlaget.
Said, E.W. 1994. *Culture and Imperialism*. London: Vintage.
Said, E.W. 2003 [1978]. *Orientalism*. London: Penguin Books.
Simonsen, A.H. 2010. Fantasies and Experiences. The Norwegian Press Coverage of Africa 1900–2002. *Kult*, 7 (*Special Issue: Nordic Colonial Mind*), 22–40.
Skeie, K.H. 2009. A Balancing Act: The Norwegian Lutheran Mission in French Colonial Madagascar. *Itinerario*, 33(2), 45–63.
Stoler, A.L. 1995. *Race and the Education of Desire: Foucault's History of Sexuality and the Colonial Order of Things*. Durham, NC: Duke University Press.
Stoler, A.L. and F. Cooper. 1997. Between Metropole and Colony: Rethinking a Research Agenda. *Tensions of Empire: Colonial Cultures in a Bourgeois World*. F. Cooper and A.L. Stoler. Berkeley: University of California Press.
Thompson, L. 2001. *A History of South Africa*. New Haven, CN: Yale Nota Bene.

Tvedt, T. 2002. *Verdensbilder og Selvbilder: En humanitær stormakts intellektuelle historie*. Oslo: Universitetsforlaget.
Tvedt, T. 2003. *Utviklingshjelp, utenrikspolitikk og makt: Den norske modellen*. Oslo: Gyldendal.
Viswanathan, G. 1998. *Outside the Fold: Conversion, Modernity, and Belief*. Princeton, NJ: Princeton University Press.
Vuorela, U. 2009. Colonial Complicity: The 'Post-colonial' in a Nordic Context, in *Complying with Colonialism: Gender, Race and Ethnicity in the Nordic Region*, edited by S. Keskinen, S. Tuori, S. Irni and D. Mulinari. Surrey: Ashgate.
Wæhle, E. 2002. Nordmenn i Kongofristatens tjeneste: Monganga Makazzi, Judchi og andre nordmenn under Kongo-stjernen 1885–1918, in *Nordmenn i Afrika: Afrikanere i Norge*, edited by K.A. Kjerland and A.K. Bang. Bergen: Fagbokforlaget Vigmostad & Bjørke.
Wæhle, E. and P. Tygesen. 2006. *Kongospor: Norden i Kongo – Kongo i Norden*. Copenhagen: Nationalmuseet.
Wallerstein, I. 1974. *The Modern World System: Capitalist Agriculture and the Origin of the European World-Economy in the Sixteenth Century*. New York: Academic Press.
Wallerstein, I. 2004. *World-systems Analysis: An Introduction*. Durham, NC: Duke University Press.
Young, R.J.C. 1995. *Colonial Desire: Hybridity in Theory, Culture and Race*. London: Routledge.

Chapter 2
Colonialism, Racism and Exceptionalism

Christina Petterson

In his article from 2003, 'Dansk raceantropologi i Grønland' (which translates as Danish race-anthropology in Greenland), Danish historian Poul Duedahl argued that Danish anthropology, because of its inherently apolitical and disparate nature, could not and did not legitimate Danish colonialism in Greenland. Such an argument is but one example of a larger discourse on Danish colonial exceptionalism, and not only operates with a very limited notion of colonial *violence*, but also a very limited view on *colonial* violence. I will argue that Duedahl's category of 'Danish anthropology' could not *avoid* legitimating Danish colonialism, because the social structures as well as the scientific discourse, in which anthropology had to operate in the nineteenth and twentieth centuries, were already implicated in and conditioned by colonial power structures. My reading involves several steps. First I address the perception of exceptionalism in Danish relations to Greenland more broadly and complicate this narrative by a deeper understanding of violence. I then discuss racism and its relation to whiteness. Finally I offer a number of background analyses that show the Danish racial state in Greenland, and how it was established long before Duedahl's anthropologists measured skulls.

The aim in this chapter, then, is not to present a systematic history of Danish anthropological research in or on Greenland, nor to provide an in-depth analysis of a certain period, but to address the image of benevolent Danish colonialism, as presented by various actors over several centuries, which contribute to a larger discourse on Danish exceptionalism.

Denmark, the Benevolent Colonial Master

In the early eighteenth century, Poul Egede, the son of the first missionary to the Greenlanders, Hans Egede sets the scene for Danish self-promotion as a benevolent and caring colonial power:

> There are countries under the sun, where neither ice nor snow has ever been seen, the inhabitants do not even know names for them, and yet, I would rather live in your [country] than in theirs, even though so many precious things come from there. The heat from the sun is insufferable; the days and nights are of equal length all year. But the continuous uniformity is not as pleasant as the difference here in our North. The people, who are black and need no clothes,

hunt each other there like you hunt caribou, and those who are captured they save until ships come from other countries, and sell them to the foreigners for spirits and tobacco. Are you not much happier in your country? The foreigners usually let you keep your own people and the property of the people. (Egede 1925: 114–15)

The constructed comparison between Greenlanders and other indigenous peoples shows how fortuitous the Greenlanders were to be colonised by the Danes, in that these 'foreigners' (usually) do not sell off their people to slavery and allows them to keep their property. Poul Egede's moral condemnation of those who sell their own people exonerates the Danish slave trade, which was the sixth or seventh largest in the world at the time.[1] However, the slave trade itself constitutes the economic context for this practice. This systemic violence undergirding an ostensibly humane practice demands a theoretical approach which recognises several levels of violence, which sustain and construct a peaceful state of affairs.

Cultural critic Slavoj Žižek's study on violence, *Violence: Six Sideways Reflections* (2008) presents us with such an approach. Žižek distinguishes between subjective violence and two forms of objective violence. Subjective violence is directly visible violence (crime, conflict, unrest), while he subdivides objective violence into symbolic violence, 'embodied in language and its forms' (Žižek 2008: 1), and systemic violence, which is institutionalised and state-sanctioned violence. He argues that subjective and objective violence cannot be perceived from the same standpoint, since subjective violence is always seen in relation to a 'non-violent zero-level' as an *aberration* to the peaceful and normal state of things, while objective violence is *inherent* to the status quo, this peaceful and normal state of things. As such, objective violence is invisible (Žižek 2008: 2). Determining the Danish colonisation as humane means seeing it as non-violent in a subjective sense. But if one deepens the analysis, and looks at the systemic violence enacted in the social and racial stratifications of Greenlandic society, as well as the symbolic violence of depicting the Greenlanders as children and/or savages, then the face of violence becomes much more complex than just a question of force.[2]

With this in mind, we can then return to the image of Denmark as a particularly humane and benevolent coloniser, which has been reiterated not only in media and popular culture as Kirsten Thisted has pointed out (Thisted 2008: 32–5), but also in scholarly discourse.[3] In an incisive article, Danish anthropologist Hanne Thomsen

---

1 I would like to thank Lars Jensen for this observation.

2 My targets here are not *all* analyses of Danish colonialism in Greenland; I am only questioning analyses which support the idea of Danish exceptionalism. As an example of work that engages systemic levels of violence, see historian Ole Marquardt's analyses of colonial Greenland, which draws attention to the economic consequences of Danish colonialism (for example 1998 and 1999).

3 See Kjærgaard for an example of this.

notes that this alleged humanity of the Danish colonisers in Greenland was governed by economic motives, instead of expressing some inherent benevolent cultural trait. In its colonial engagements in for example the West Indies, Denmark was as brutal as any other colonial regime. The difference in Greenland was that the colonial powers were completely reliant on the indigenous population to gain a profit (Thomsen 1998: 23). Thomsen is critiquing the claims to the Danish self-perception as humane colonisers per se, and revealing ulterior motives behind such a self-presentation. However, by relegating force and brutality to Danish practices in the West Indies, and highlighting that the Danes were humane in Greenland *because* it was in their interest; her analysis unwittingly leaves us with the image of a benevolent and humane Danish colonisation of Greenland, albeit in a slightly more fragmented version.[4] It is possible to continue this fragmentation, and by using Žižek, to draw attention to the oxymoronic nature of the notion of humane colonialism.

The Danish Racial State

Within the objective violence enacted by the Danish colonisers on the Greenlandic population, race holds a privileged position. However, there generally is a profound reluctance in Denmark to address race as a structural factor in the social politics of the Danish state. Race is, in several anthropological accounts, usually reserved either for extremes, such as Nazi eugenics and South Africa's apartheid politics, or restricted to individual attitudes. Both of these tendencies are not an uncommon step in studies dealing with state and race (Goldberg 2002: 3 and 149). Issues pertaining to skin colour and difference are usually euphemistically termed as *ethnic*. Danish research on Greenland is no exception to this rule. Anthropologist Ole Høiris (1986) has published an account of how Danish anthropologists at the turn of the twentieth century embody a general Western anthropological racist attitude to non-Europeans as well as a more particular account (1983) that relates to the view on Greenlanders before World War II. Høiris's studies – along with Duedahl's – indicate that Denmark was an active participant in racial studies from the late nineteenth century until World War II. Furthermore, these studies indicate that Greenland played a significant role in this research, in that Greenland provided the empirical data for analysis. In Høiris's works however, racism is regarded as a primarily *individual* expression of racist prejudice and thus not an expression of a larger a structural factor in the social politics of the Danish state. Duedahl represents a different way of separating Danish race research from its national and

---

4 Thisted notes a similar tension in her discussion of Johannes Brøndsted's preface to *Vore gamle Tropekolonier* from 1953: 'When it is emphasised so forcefully that Denmark's main interest was financial gain [in the preface], how can it be that one nonetheless throughout this work is confirmed in the assumption of Denmark as the small heroically fighting and basically humanitarian nation?' (Thisted 2008: 30, my translation).

historical situation, by seeing such research as part of the larger general Western anthropological racist attitude of the time, mentioned above. Such a synchronic approach in effect separates Danish race research from its own colonial history, and conveniently exempts the Danish state from any involvement in matters of race. However, the Danish state had racial policies that had drastic effects on the Greenlandic population, to which we now turn.

The *Instruction of the 19th April 1782* is a crucial document in the colonial history of Denmark and Greenland and important here because of its jurisdiction and its implications for the understanding of the Greenlanders as civil subjects. The *1782 Instruction* was not a 'Law for Greenland' in a formal sense. It dealt with rules and regulations for the employees of the Trade (primarily Danes and Greenlanders with mixed heritage); that is, those who were employed on a regular wage basis and not those who sold their products to the Trade. Its non-law status is partly determined by its jurisdiction (Gad 1976: 18). First of all, this places the Greenlanders outside any notion of rights, and thus leaves them in a 'state of nature' in which they were presumed to function well (Gad 1974: 140).[5] Furthermore, even though the 'ordinary Greenlanders' were not included in the jurisdiction of the law, it nevertheless had a profound effect on their lives and trading patterns. The item of particular interest here is the fourth post: 'Concerning the Greenlanders'. This item goes through the various ways of dealing with the Greenlanders, how to encourage them to hunt as well as how to encourage them to store food for winter.[6] This shows the subsumption of Greenlandic practice within the Danish colonial apparatus. The Greenlanders had been hunters for centuries and had developed various means of storage. In the *Instruction*, however, it is articulated as though hunting and storage is something that the Greenlanders need to be encouraged to do. Finally, the *Instruction* distinguishes between Greenlanders, according to racial 'mixing', focusing on Greenlanders, as mentioned above, who had a Danish father, worked for the Trade, and thus were subsumed under the jurisdiction of the *Instruction*. This distinction has profound effects, in that it creates and enforces a view of the non-mixed population as belonging to nature, subservient to the laws of nature, and that they should – ideally – be left alone to carry on as before. In practice they were left to live their own lives, once these had been honed to match

---

5 Gad quotes whaling assistant Peder Hanning Motzfeldt's promemoria from 1799, where Motzfeldt comments as follows: 'I dare say that the Greenlanders' simple nutrition and way of life only in very few cases make civil laws necessary, especially since they, in their mutual relationships, accord with old customs and regulations. These, (as far as I can see) are in close congruence with the laws of nature and fairness, when one excludes what their superstitious ideas of witchcraft may lead them to, as well as the matter of inebriation, which, according to the present order of the Trade, rarely takes place' (Gad 1974: 143, my translation).

6 These are examples of how the directive repeats and thus institutionalises some of the attempts by the missionaries to control the labour power of the Greenlanders. See Lauridsen and Lytthans for descriptions of how the missionaries encouraged hunting and proper food storage (Lauridsen and Lytthans 1983: 168–73).

the desires of the mission and the Royal Greenland Trading Department (KGH), as argued by Hanne Thomsen. In contrast, the mixed Greenlanders were viewed differently. Because they belonged to the jurisdiction of the *Instruction* they were included within a sphere of 'civilisation'. The main aim of the *Instruction* thus seems to be to sustain this distinction, and thus keep the sphere of nature away from the sphere of civilisation. This is primarily controlled through regulation of marriage and reproduction, which also are addressed in much detail in the second item: 'Concerning marriage'. Only when something occurred to trouble this distinction, for example theft committed by Greenlanders against Danes, was this to be punished.

As a result of the Danish reforms in the early twentieth century, separate legal spheres for Greenlanders and Danes were consolidated through the 'Law regarding the government of the colonies in Greenland' from 1908 (Sørensen 1983: 29).[7] This meant that the employees of the Trade and mission continued to be under Danish law, while the rest of the Greenlanders came under the jurisdiction of Greenlandic law. In his historical survey of developments in twentieth century Greenland, Axel Kjær Sørensen comments that while this legal distinction may be *seen* as discrimination against the Greenlanders, one would get the opposite impression if one looked at what was punishable and which punishments were handed out. I am not persuaded by such an assertion. This is systemic discrimination, which places one segment of the population under Danish law and the other segment of the population under a set of rules and practices, which were ostensibly milder. However, Sørensen is not taking the different living conditions and power dynamics into consideration. His judgement is based on the laws and not their practice, which he does acknowledge could make a difference (Sørensen 1983: 37). I will briefly relate a case which illustrates the arbitrary nature of the practice of Greenlandic law.[8]

Peter Gundel was a hunter/fisherman from the settlement of Illumiut near Jakobshavn (Ilulissat). Suffering from tuberculosis and gout, he was unable to hunt, and he used his spare time to write – sometimes novels, sometimes letters, and sometimes the doctor's reports. For these scribal activities he was paid sporadically; otherwise, he survived in relative poverty on welfare, while his

---

7 The most significant changes of this law are the separation of trade and administration, and the establishment of municipal councils and national councils (one in North Greenland and one in South). These councils replaced the local councils from the mid nineteenth century, and led to the establishment of a formal law for the Greenlanders, although Greenlanders employed by the Trade or the mission were under Danish law (Sørensen 1983: 35).

8 It is a case which Sørensen could not have known, for the case is from 1928 and the archival restriction on legal cases is 80 years. The legal documents have therefore not been available before 2008. The letters, which give us one side of the story, were in private possession until their 'discovery' in 2002. The following vignette is based on the letters, which are now published (Gundel and Tølbøl 2004).

wife made money sewing. He struck up a friendship with a Danish doctor, Jørgen Hvam, who had spent three years in Jakobshavn (Ilulissat), and it is Gundel's letters to Hvam from 1923 to 1930 which have been published. Peter Gundel died on 8 March 1931 at the age of 36.

Gundel was apparently regarded as a troublemaker and seemed to attract misfortune. The case begins with a fight between Gundel and another fisherman, Jonathan, concerning their nets which had become entwined. According to Gundel, it was Jonathan's fault, which meant that Gundel was within his right to cut Jonathan's nets to free his own (Thisted 2004: 91). This enraged Jonathan, who attacked Gundel. Gundel threatened to report Jonathan to the authorities for assault. Jonathan's stepson then stepped forward and claimed that he had seen Gundel steal some fish from the Trade, and sell them. Gundel admitted to the deed – without adding that this was quite common practice, because the Trade generally underpaid the fishermen.

Gundel now had to face the district council[9] and plead for a mild sentence. While trying to explain to the chair of the council, Knudsen, how easy it was to err, he chose the somewhat unfortunate example of Knudsen shutting himself in the stockroom with a local woman, Mariane – which Gundel witnessed. Knudsen reacted by imposing a more severe sentence: Loss of civil rights for five years; a fine (Danish Kroner – DKK 25); liability fees (DKK 10); public announcement of his guilt and a warning of deportation if he was charged again (Gundel and Tølbøl 2004: 213–14).[10] This was just the beginning of a long line of charges and accusations of rape and theft, unpaid sewing jobs, grudges flaring, fingers pointed within a very small community. Gundel was so desperate that the only way out of this network of enemies waiting to pounce was to appeal to the king of Denmark.

Thisted concludes that 'everyone already has lots of stories about everyone else, no one is impartial, and the case may serve as a cautionary example of what happens when small communities have to manage legal issues by themselves' (Thisted 2004: 94). However, it is also important to keep the deplorable material conditions in mind: the nets that were slashed, the fish that were stolen, the sewing jobs that were not paid for – indications of the poverty of the community; and the extent to which people were struggling for the same jobs, the same fish and the same money to survive. These conditions have shaped Greenlandic social fabric – or, rather, the Danish racial state in Greenland. This is what led Greenlanders

---

9 Sysselråd, a level between the municipal council and the national council, which was implemented with the revisions of the administration in 1925. The chairman was Danish and the rest of the council (two to four men), were Danish and Greenlandic in equal numbers.

10 This was his second sentence. He received the first in 1925 for illegal trade and for hosting a get-together with the crew from a ship and local girls (Thisted 2004: 92).

like Peter Gundel to state in 1923 that Greenlanders are treated like slaves by the Danes (Gundel and Tølbøll 2004: 10).[11]

I have included this vignette on Gundel to show how Danish law and its segregationist practice functions as a marker of race and class. Gundel lived 150 years after the *Instruction*, which was replaced several times with different directives, as well as the implementation of a Greenlandic law in the early twentieth century (as mentioned above). Nevertheless, I want to argue that the *Instruction* of 1782 articulated and formalised practices which laid the foundations for inequality between Danes and Greenlanders.

This juridical practice belongs to what Žižek terms systemic violence, in that it produces, upholds and naturalises an inequality between Danes/elite Greenlanders and 'ordinary' Greenlanders. This inequality, which continues to characterise Danish-Greenlandic relations, is nevertheless *not* regarded as such, which Sørensen's dismissal of the segregation practices as discrimination makes abundantly clear.

This systemic violence is undergirded by the symbolic violence enacted in portraying the Greenlanders as mentally inferior and savage, and blissfully unaware of the state of their own depravity and misery. This portrayal takes place in a constant reference to whiteness as an ideal, as we see in the following excerpt from Paul Egede's diary (1740):

> After I had led evening worship with the colonists and our followers, I was compelled to tell them about our own as well as other countries, and when they heard that black people existed, they asked: 'Are they blacker than us?' I answered that the Greenlanders were white in comparison, nothing light could be seen except teeth and eyes. The boys that heard this began laughing at this, and said, 'It must be fun to see these people laugh and stare'. (Egede 1988: 127, my translation)

Paul Egede's brother, Niels Egede, the merchant, mentions how a weathered Greenlander was ridiculed by the others, who asked Egede, whether the black moors were as black as him. To this Egede answered:

> that he was just as white in comparison with them, as I with a raven. They say: 'Then they must be worse than a troll. There certainly will not be many falling in love with their women'. Here they became almost haughty concerning the existence of a people more hideous than they. (Egede and Egede 1939: 177, my translation)

These examples reveal that skin colour was an object of discussion and that the Greenlanders compared themselves with black people, internalising an established

---

11 Gundel was in the process of translating *Uncle Tom's Cabin*, so his comparisons are founded in contemporary literature.

hierarchy of ugliness where black people took a lesser place than the Greenlanders, with whiteness at the pinnacle of aesthetic pleasure.

In his cultural study of whiteness, *White*, Richard Dyer suggests that the embodiment of whiteness is constituted by three elements: Christianity, 'race', and enterprise/imperialism. For sake of clarity, I will focus only on the aspect of race. As part of his presentation of elaborated concepts of race in the late eighteenth and nineteenth centuries, Dyer notes that there are, broadly speaking, two ways of categorising race: a genealogical approach, which draws upon origins and lineages of reproduction, and a biological approach, which is concerned with fixating difference on the body (Dyer 1997: 20).[12] To highlight the genealogical approach, I have chosen the elusive Norsemen, who settled in Greenland around the year 1000 and probably disappeared towards the end of the fifteenth century. When Hans Egede set out for Greenland in 1721, the primary stated motivation was to find the descendants of these Norsemen and then to bring the Reformation to them. In pursuing this desire of finding the Norsemen, he followed in the footsteps of many explorers before him. Worth mentioning is the explorer Dannel, who on his third journey in 1654 kidnapped four Greenlanders, three women (Kuneling, Kabelau and Sigoko) and a man (Ihiob), and brought them back on his ship (Harbsmeier 2001: 28). The women (Ihiob died on the way to Copenhagen) eventually were brought to Gottorp, in present-day Germany, where they were subjected to intense investigations by the secretary to the duke, Adam Olearius, who also happened to be an accomplished scientist of all trades. Olearius noted that one of the women,[13] had paler skin than the others, bigger eyes, a sense of humour, and, last but not least, she was clever and more perceptive. On this basis he saw a possibility that she was a descendant of the Norsemen, or as he put it, the earlier Christian settlers (Gad 1967: 295). This shows, as Dyer also points out, that the genealogical approach presupposes bodily and intellectual differences. Such differences would lay the ground for the racial politics of the Danish state as manifested in the *Instruction* and its sculpting of the Greenlandic population.

Further there is the biological categorisation, where Danish scientists have measured and collected skulls, measured bodies and collected hair. This is where Duedahl's article becomes relevant. In his assessment of Danish physical anthropology in Greenland, Duedahl argues that the divergences in Danish anthropology over the inferiority of the Greenlanders meant that Danish anthropology hardly could be seen to legitimate Danish colonialism in Greenland. This argument is based on research of archival and published sources from 1882 to 1949, which presented measurements and analyses of Greenlandic sculls and blood. He then poses the following question: Why was the number of anthropologists in

---

12 Dyer's study focuses on whiteness, and the function of race in this conceptualisation. For studies on race and racism, see Banton 1998 and Goldberg 1993 and 2002.

13 From the portraits available, it would seem to be Kabelau. Harbsmeier gives us the names of the four Greenlanders, but does not touch upon the racial issue, while Gad informs us of the racial issues without giving us the names of the four.

the great age of international science 1870–1945 comparatively small in Denmark and the tone comparatively moderated compared with anthropological literature from Germany, France, England and USA, countries where, according to Duedahl, anthropologists played an active role in the political legitimisation of colonialism? He puts forth three factors which contributed to this state of affairs. First he points to the difference in colonial ambition in 1900. While France and England were expanding, and made great profits from imperialism, Greenland no longer played a significant economic role for Denmark. At this stage in Greenlandic history, he argues, the independence movement in Greenland had led to moderate home rule. Anthropology thus became *apolitical*, he argues, because it did not legitimise colonial practice, but was focused on providing a biological explanation for the origin of the Eskimos. Second, if anyone was to be blamed for providing the scientific foundations for Danish supremacy in Denmark, it was the older ethnological tradition, which had long practised hierarchical classifications on the basis of cultural differences. Finally, he points to critiques of the craniometrical method by external experts as an important factor. Duedahl's arguments rest on a number of presuppositions, some of which are mentioned in the article and some which are not. His assumption that Danish anthropology did not play a legitimising role for state imperialism rests on the research presented in the article, which concludes that the attitudes towards Greenlandic inferiority were so diverse, so as not to make up a unified position. However, in his presentation of the anthropological research, it is stripped of any historical or political context, which makes it easy – or should I say simplistic – to assume that the research had no political significance. I will draw out one obvious example: Duedahl reports that Fr. C.C. Hansen in 1926 published an article on the degeneration and demise of the Norse settlers (Nordboerne), based on skeletal findings from an archaeological expedition to the Norse ruins in 1921. The conclusions drawn from the analysis of the 25 skeletons were that there was no sign of miscegenation. This means that the Norse settlers had died, not from being 'bred out of existence', but from malnourishment, tuberculosis and intermarriage (Duedahl 2003: 349). What Duedahl fails to mention is that during the 1920s there was a considerable struggle between Denmark and Norway over the rights to Eastern Greenland.[14] Greenland had been a Norwegian colony before entering into the union with Denmark in the fourteenth century. Between 1536 and 1814 the dual kingdom of Denmark-Norway was governed from Copenhagen. The Europeans in Greenland from 1721 thus came from both Denmark and Norway; however, they were sent by the Danish king. After the peace treaty in Kiel in 1814, Denmark lost Norway to Sweden, but retained the North Atlantic colonies (Greenland, the Faeroe Islands, and Iceland). Since the first European settlers in Greenland were Norsemen, Norway could potentially through these Norsemen claim a right over Greenland on the basis

---

14 See Erlend Eidsvik's chapter in this volume.

of first settlement.¹⁵ Thus, by claiming that the Greenlandic population is not descended from the Norsemen, but instead died from illness and malnourishment, Fr. C.C. Hansen's research pre-empts any possible Norwegian claims on that account and thereby supports Danish supremacy over Greenland. Likewise, the research of Søren Hansen, which is presented in some detail, shifts from assuming a racial hierarchy between the primitive and racially inferior Greenlanders and the white Europeans from 1886 to 1911, to suddenly emphasising the similarities between Europeans and 'Eskimos':

> The ostensibly large difference between the indigenous population of Greenland and the Danes is that big that we cannot in fairness count them as countrymen and it is no coincidence that in spite of the big difficulties presented by the conditions in that country, a possibility for a political home-rule has opened up, which would be unique in colonial history. This quite simply rests on the fact that Greenlanders intellectually are completely on line with the majority of civilised peoples. (Hansen 1922, quoted in Duedahl 2003: 348–9)

Here there is a notable shift in attitudes of racial superiority around the times of Norway's claim to Greenland. Furthermore, his main argument: the apolitical nature of Danish anthropology rests on an understanding of anthropology as generally speaking apolitical, but which could be used politically, for example to prove the racial inferiority of native people (Duedahl 2003: 335–6). When this was not stated as an explicit motive, it was consequently not political, Duedahl claims. This overlooks, or denies, the fact that in regarding the Greenlanders as mere objects of research, to be measured and weighed by Danish doctors and anthropologists, a racial hierarchical relationship is *presupposed*.¹⁶ In addition, the amount of state-funded research in Greenland by Danish scientists is in itself a claim to possession and supremacy, without it needing to be homogeneous or of one mind. The research simply supported the existing status quo, which was deeply hierarchical. In this light Duedahl's article becomes an attempt to exonerate Denmark of racial politics, by depicting anthropological research as disparate and

---

15 The Norsemen had two settlements, the Western settlement (Vesterbygden) and the Eastern settlement (Østerbygden). Both settlements are located on the West coast of Greenland. During the seventeenth century the Eastern settlement was placed on Greenland's east coast Hans Egede attempted to undertake expeditions to finding the lost settlement and its settlers, but did not succeed. While it seems to be presumed that Graah's expedition to Greenland in 1829–30 put an end to speculations about the location of Eastern Settlement on the east coast, an article from 1885 nevertheless bemoans the fact that this thesis still has its proponents, mainly due to a strip of coast which has not been investigated (Steenstrup 1885: 131).

16 Which means that it is an *unquestionable assumption* and perhaps not a conscious deliberation. Even if the research was not carried out as a conscious attempt at legitimating Danish colonialism, the power structures in place make this result unavoidable, when they are left unexamined.

apolitical. His argument builds on inadequately developed comparisons with other nations, which does not even consider the difference between imperial histories. It should also be noted that the assessment of the political insignificance of Danish racial research on an international scale does not explain the impact of the same research on the Greenlandic population,[17] nor does it indicate the self and other image that this kind of research could generate in its scholars. It also ignores the already racialised nature of European self-definition, of which it is a product.

Conclusion

From the very beginning of Danish colonialism in Greenland, the Danish colonial administration and mission intervened in Greenlandic everyday affairs and attempted to control marriage, reproduction and labour. The more formalised attempts were instituted in 1782 with the *Instruction of the 19th April 1782* that divided the population into civil subjects under Danish law and Greenlanders under the laws of nature. In 1908 the Greenlanders were placed under a law, which upheld this distinction between Greenlanders and the civil subjects under Danish law, which included Danes as well as the emerging Greenlandic elite employed by the colonial administration. Systemic discrimination between Danes and Greenlanders still persists today. This is the context in which the Danish anthropological investigations of the Greenlanders took place in the late nineteenth and early twentieth centuries. Consequently, the anthropological research supported the existing status quo, which was deeply hierarchical and racialised. Attempts, such as Duedahl's, to separate 'physical anthropology' from ethnology, Danish colonialism and the racist anthropology of other nation states is superficial and apologetic and completely overlooks the systemic and racial nature of the Danish state.

References

Banton, M. 1998. *Racial Theories*. Cambridge: Cambridge University Press.
Bertelsen, A. 1945. *Grønlænderne i Danmark: Bidrag til belysning af Grønlandsk kolonisationsarbejde fra 1605 til vor tid*. Meddelelser om Grønland 145(2). København: C.A. Reitzels Forlag.
Duedahl, P. 2003. Dansk raceantropologi i Grønland. *Historisk Tidsskrift*, 103, 335–58.
Dyer, R. 1997. *White*. London: Routledge.
Egede, H. 1925. *Relationer fra Grønland 1721–36*, edited by L. Bobé, *Meddelser om Grønland*. København: Bianco Lunos bogtrykkeri.

---

17 See Linda Tuhiwai Smith for a Maori perspective on Western research, epistemology and methodology and its connections to colonialism (Smith 1999).

Egede, P. 1988. *Efterretninger om Grønland uddragne af en journal holden fra 1721 til 1788 af Paul Egede*, edited by M. Lidegaard, Det Grønlandske Selskabs skrifter, 29. København: Det Grønlandske Selskab.

Egede, P. and N. 1939. *Continuation af Hans Egedes relationer fra Grønland*, edited by H. Ostermann, Meddelelser om Grønland 120. København: C.A. Reitzels Forlag.

Gad, F. 1967. *Grønlands historie* vol. 1: *Indtil 1700*. København: Nyt Nordisk Forlag.

Gad, F. 1974. *Fire detailkomplekser i Grønlands historie 1782–1808*. København: Nyt Nordisk Forlag Arnold Busck.

Gad, F. 1976. *Grønlands historie, vol. 3, 1782–1808*. 3 vols. København: Nyt Nordisk Forlag Arnold Busck.

Goldberg, D.T. 1993. *Racist Culture: Philosophy and the Politics of Meaning*. Oxford: Blackwell.

Goldberg, D.T. 2002. *The Racial State*. Oxford: Blackwell.

Gundel, P. and G. Tølbøl (eds). 2004. *Jeg danser af glæde: Peter Gundel. Dagbogsbreve 1923–30*. København: Det Grønlandske Selskab.

Harbsmeier, M. 2001. *Stimmen aus dem äußersten Norden: Wie die Grönländer Europa für sich entdecken*. Fremde Kulturen in alten Berichten 11. Stuttgart: Jan Thorbecke Verlag.

Høiris, O. 1983. Grønlænderne i dansk antropologi før 2. verdenskrig. *Tidsskriftet Grønland*, 1, 30–46.

Høiris, O. 1986. *Antropologien i Danmark. Museal etnografi og etnologi 1860–1960*.

Kjærgaard, K. 2008. Berømmelig i Norge, Roesværdig i Dannemark, Men Udødelig i Grønland – Hans Egede-receptionen gennem tre hundrede år med særlig henblik på kunstneriske fremstillinger, in *Fra oprører til apostel: Hans Egedes liv og kirken i Grønland*, edited by H. Brun, Kabelvåg, 126–66.

Lauridsen, T.K. and K. Lytthans. 1983. Det grønlandske kald. MA thesis. København: Københavns Universitet.

Marquardt, Ole. 1998. Indkomstspredning i Vestgrønland i anden halvdel af 1800-tallet. *Grønlandsk kultur- og samfundsforskning 1997*, 45–68.

Marquardt, Ole. 1999. Grønlænderne og Vestens civilisation. Træk af Rink-tidens grønlandspolitiske diskussion. *Grønlandsk kultur- og samfundsforskning 98/99*, 7–26.

Olsen, P.E. 1987. Disse vilde karle: Negre i Danmark indtil 1848, in *Fremmed i Danmark: 400 års fremmedpolitik*, edited by B. Blüdnikow. Odense: Odense Universitetsforlag.

Petterson, C. 2010. *The Missionary, the Catechist and the Hunter*. Governmentality and Masculinities in Greenland. PhD thesis. Sydney: Macquarie University.

Smith, L.T. 1999. *Decolonizing Methodologies. Research and Indigenous Peoples*. Dunedin: University of Otago Press.

Sørensen, A.K. 1983. *Danmark-Grønland i det 20. århundrede – En historisk oversigt*. København: Nyt Nordisk Forlag Arnold Busch.

Steenstrup, K.J.V. 1885. Om Østerbygden. *Geografisk Tidsskrift*, 8, 123–32.
Thisted, K. 2004. Peter Gundel, Dagbogsbreve til læge Jørgen Hvam. *Tidsskriftet Grønland*, 3–4, 81–128.
Thisted, K. 2008. '*Hvor Dannebrog engang har vajet i mer end 200 Aar'. Banal nationalisme, narrative skabeloner og postkolonial melankoli i skildringen af de danske tropekolonier*. Tranquebar Initiativets Skriftserie 2. København: Nationalmuseet, 1–51.
Thomsen, H. 1998. Ægte grønlændere og nye grønlændere – om forskellige opfattelser af grønlandskhed. *Den jyske historiker*, 81, 21–56.
Thuesen, S. 2007. *Fremmed blandt landsmænd. Grønlandske kateketer i kolonitiden*. Nuuk: Atuagkat.
Žižek, S. 2008. *Violence: Six Sideways Reflections*. New York: Picador.

Chapter 3
'Words That Wound': Swedish Whiteness and Its Inability to Accommodate Minority Experiences

Tobias Hübinette

During the classical colonial period and at the time of hegemonic racism from the nineteenth to the first half of the twentieth centuries, an array of words, names, expressions and terms were used to describe and denote minorities both in the colonies and within Europe itself. Categories like 'Negro', 'Redskin', 'Oriental', 'Eskimo', 'Lapp', 'Semite' and 'Gypsy' were used both within the scientific world as well as by the state apparatus, by the media, in the cultural sphere and, above all, in daily life. However, after the Holocaust, the end of formal decolonization and the social revolution of 1968, many of these words have started to fall out of use due to political activism coming from the side of minorities in countries like the US, Canada and Australia as well as in some European countries like the UK, the Netherlands and Germany. For example, the word 'Negro' and its even more denigrating version 'Nigger' is nowadays in an Anglo-American and English language context usually known as the N-word, several American baseball teams which were previously called 'Redskins' have changed their names, and in 2002 the United States Congress decided to replace the term Oriental with the word Asian in statistical and official documents (Han 2010; Kennedy 2003; Olsson 2007; Stapleton 2001). However, a public debate has also taken place in many countries with regards to colonial and racist words and expressions. Here those opposed to questioning the use of racially derogatory expressions, typically people from the white majority population, accuse the representatives from different minorities for espousing hypersensitive hysteria, extremist or conservative censorship, identity politics, 'reverse racism' and, above all, political correctness (PC). Those representing the white majority view propose the continued use of what they argue are objective and value-neutral words and expressions, which they see as deeply rooted in Western civilization.

This issue of how the majority and the minorities are relating differently to Europe's colonial and racist history and legacy has lately also come to the foreground in the Nordic countries and in Sweden. In the Nordic countries in general many of these words and terms are still being used uncritically in everyday life as well as within academia and by printed, visual and electronic media (see also Anna Rastas's contribution to this anthology). This chapter will look at three case examples of contested words and expressions in contemporary Sweden with the background of Swedish whiteness and by making use of speech act theory and the psychoanalytic concept of melancholia. The first example concerns the word 'Negro' (*neger*) and its various linguistic derivations which in a Swedish context are not considered to be racializing terms in spite of the fact that representatives from the African diaspora have protested against the 'naturalized' use of the word (Bondesson 2009; Sabuni 2005). For example, in 2009 a Swedish Facebook group called 'The name is Negro ball' (*Det heter negerboll*) was able to recruit tens of thousands of Swedes in a massive 'anti-PC' campaign in a span of a few months after a Swedish journalist had defended the continuous use of the word on public service television.[1] The second example is the biggest Asian studies department in northern Europe, which bears the name of the Department of Oriental languages and is located at Stockholm University, and its senior staff members are still today using the term Oriental Studies and names like the 'Orient' and 'Orientals' although junior members and especially those of Asian background have protested against this old-fashioned naming (Hübinette 2002). The third example was brought up in a critical way by a German woman living in Sweden in 2010 (Liljestrand 2010). She pointed out that a number of rock climbing tracks in Järfälla outside Stockholm have been named after terms associated with the Holocaust such as Zyklon B, Crematorium and Crystal Night (*Kristallnatten*), and that these names had been used for almost 20 years without anyone seemingly protesting against them. In the debate which erupted, many Swedes defended the names as a reflection of a subcultural 'twinkle in the eye'-humour and a non-political jargon among rock climbers. The empirical data for the chapter is collected from debate texts in magazines and newspapers and Internet pages related to the three examples given above.

So why do so many Swedes still want to use words and names which are considered to be hurtful by minorities as they are loaded with histories and experiences of oppression and even genocide? Why do highly educated Swedes still cling to old-fashioned academic terms like Oriental Studies, and why do so many Swedes defend the continuous use of the word 'Negro' and find words associated with the Holocaust to be funny? Can it be explained by an innocent attitude towards historical events that are seen as unrelated to Sweden, and as an expression of a sincere openness towards neutrality and objectivity concerning controversial historical issues? Or is this about a Nordic and a Swedish exceptionalism and amnesia accompanied by an inability to accommodate minority experiences on a psychic level and therefore about the reproduction of colonial and racist structures and hierarchies? By making use of Anglo-Saxon speech act theory and psychoanalytically inspired Critical Race Studies and with a particular focus on assaultive speech or hate speech, I will try to understand Swedish whiteness and its inability to accept that certain words, names and expressions have a long and

---

[1] A 'Negro ball' (*negerboll*) is in Swedish the traditional name of a Swedish pastry, which in other countries would be known as a chocolate ball.

negative history connected to the lived experiences of minorities. This connection is again and again disavowed in the name of a colour-blind white anti-racism, but, as I will argue, can be seen as an expression of a white melancholia, which works alongside the suppression of the fact that Sweden is today a postcolonial and multicultural society. In other words, the concept of white melancholia is being used to understand why many Swedes defend the continuous use of colonial and racist words and expressions.

Introducing Swedish Whiteness and White Melancholia

In contemporary Sweden, being white means being Swede and being non-white means being non-Swedish regardless if the non-white person is culturally Swedish and was born or grew up and have lived most of her life in Sweden. This means that the difference between the bodily concept of race and the cultural concept of ethnicity has collapsed in a contemporary Swedish context. This conflation of race and ethnicity is something that not only non-white immigrants and their descendants are experiencing, but also adopted and mixed Swedes of a background from South America, Africa and Asia who, in spite of being fully embedded within Swedishness of a linguistic, religious and cultural level are encountering racializing experiences caused by their non-white and therefore 'non-Swedish' bodies (Hübinette and Tigervall 2008; Lundström 2010).

The historical background to this construction of Swedishness in relation to whiteness can be traced back to the privileged position of Swedes in relation to the historical construction of the white race itself, a scientific discourse that was hegemonic for almost 200 years (Hagerman 2006; Schough 2008). Because of this image of the Swedes as being the whitest of all whites, the Swedish state founded the world's first academic institute for race science in 1922 and also implemented a sterilization programme which affected more than 60,000 Swedes before the programme was dissolved in the mid-1970s, and which was heavily racialized (Broberg 1995; Tydén 2000).

However from the 1960s and onwards, Sweden together with the other Nordic countries became the leading international supporter of decolonization and one of the world's most radical proponents of anti-racism, constructing itself as a colour-blind and non-racist country. It is this specific Swedish anti-racist whiteness which forms the principal background for this chapter, and not the pre-1968 race hygiene driven Swedish whiteness. This contemporary Swedish whiteness which views itself as anti-racist, post-racial and non-racist is in the chapter seen as the dominant discourse of being Swedish. This Swedish whiteness includes both native-born whites and immigrant whites, and non-white Swedes can also invest themselves in this discourse.

An important psychoanalytically informed concept in the chapter is white melancholia. In his discussion on postcolonial melancholy, British Cultural Studies scholar Paul Gilroy (2005) argues that this condition characterizes many

British people who cannot accommodate the fact that Britain is no longer a world power, or want to accept the presence of so many of the former empire's different subjects in Britain. The US ethnic studies scholar Ann Anlin Cheng (2001) uses the concept racial melancholy when she analyses the psychic effects of racism among racialized minorities. However, in another article which I have co-written with Catrin Lundström I argue that it is also possible to talk about a specific Swedish white melancholia which is related to the above introduced Swedish anti-racist whiteness (Hübinette and Lundström 2011). This white melancholia is obsessively and anxiously invested in keeping the image of Sweden as an anti-racist country alive and has particularly expressed itself in the anti-racist anger towards the entrance of a racist party in the Swedish parliament after the election of 2010.

Why Certain Words Wound

Beginning in the late 1980s a new research field was formulated in the US under the name of Critical Race Studies or Critical Race Theory (CRT) among scholars with a minority background. They drew attention to the fact that the anti-discrimination laws introduced in the country since the abolition of formal discrimination and segregation did not seem to overcome the persistent racial inequalities in American society (Crenshaw, Gotanda, Peller and Thomas 1995; Delgado and Stefanic 2000). At the same time, another new field of research, Critical Whiteness Studies, developed among primarily white anti-racists. This field carries out research on and critically reflects upon what it means to belong to the white majority in a racist society (Dyer 1997; Frankenberg 1993; Hill 1997; Ignatiev 1995; Roediger 1991). These two closely related fields are often put together and designated as Critical Race and Whiteness Studies. The birth of these fields owes much to emergence of the new USA that appeared after various civil rights movements among the minorities had begun to ebb away. In its wake an increasing colour-blindness had come to dominate built on many white Americans' belief that racism had simply been legislated away in the 1970s and 1980s. To them the only thing explaining the non-white populations' continued economic, political and cultural marginalization in American society came from individual shortcomings in a neoliberal post-civil rights US.

Although the twin fields do not exist within the Swedish academia in an institutionalized sense, there are a number of Swedish researchers who identify with critical whiteness studies and seek to apply its theories, models, results and perspectives on contemporary Swedish conditions (see for example Anna Lundstedt (2005), Catrin Lundström (2010), Lena Sawyer (2001, 2006), Hynek Pallas (2011), Oscar Pripp and Magnus Öhlander (2008), Ylva Habel (2008) and Katarina Mattsson (2006), and the special issue on whiteness in the gender studies journal *Tidskrift för genusvetenskap* (2010). With regard to critical race studies applied to Swedish contemporary contexts, my own and Carina Tigervall's study of the (adoptee) non-white body and its relation to Swedishness can be seen as an attempt at conducting a Swedish critical race studies research project (others include Cederberg 2005; Hübinette and Tigervall 2008; Hällgren 2005; Kalonaityté, Kawesa and Tedros 2007; Lundström 2007; Mattsson and Tesfahuney 2002; Motsieloa 2003; Osanami Törngren 2011; Pred 2000; Sawyer 2000; Schmauch 2006).

One of the research questions which CRT took on from the beginning was the relationship between power, knowledge and language. This was exemplified by the relationship between the continued use of colonial and racist words and expressions in everyday life, media, and popular culture, and the continued existence of a discriminatory majority society despite the relative success of the civil rights movements and an official anti-racist legislation and rhetoric. The CRT researchers drew inspiration from the linguistic theories developed in Anglo-Saxon analytical philosophy, and especially the everyday life-oriented part of it focusing on the everyday role of language in the creation of human culture (Austin 1986).

CRT researchers see racist expressions as falling within a certain type of utterances which are called illocutionary speech acts (Matsuda, Lawrence III, Delgado and Williams Crenshaw 1993). These types of sentences are usually followed by an expectation that the promise will be carried out. Illocutionary speech acts are also characterized by an often ceremonial and ritualized nature, that is, they derive their power from constant repetition, and are known in philosophy of language as iterative. One illustration of this could be when a white person utters a racist word or a racist opinion. This statement draws upon a long history of colonialism and racism that is activated and a contemporary segregated and discriminatory society becomes legitimized.[2]

Furthermore, CRT is also based on the understanding that race is a social construction as well as a performative act, which means that when a white person for example utters a so-called racial slur, or a derogatory racist term, directly at a non-white person, the latter becomes racialized, and the speaker is placed in a higher position and identified with whiteness while the recipient is put into a subordinate position as a lesser non-white subject (Alcoff 2005). In other words, the non-white body is neither subordinate nor non-normative in itself – instead the subordination and the non-normativity are created by language that relates to the social imaginary of the normative white majority.

---

2   But if an underprivileged non-white person would call a white person something which would allude to his or her racial categorization, that is the opposite, such utterance would most probably fail as there is neither a history nor any contemporary context to relate to when and where non-whites are oppressing whites on a structural and systemic level. Such a statement is instead perhaps met by surprise or a sneer or an aggressive counteract or maybe most probably completely ignored.

To Believe in the Orient

Northern Europe's largest institution for Asian Studies can be found at Stockholm University's Department of Oriental Languages. The department is home to teaching and research on the Middle East and North Africa, Turkey and Central Asia, India and South Asia, and China, Japan and Korea. During the colonial era, the scientific name for Asian Studies was Orientalism or Oriental Studies all over the Western world, and its practitioners were called Orientalists. At that time, in addition to being a geographically diffuse and almost imaginary place (as it still is), the Orient was associated with decadence and despotism and the 'Orientals' were represented as being cunning, untrustworthy or even evil as Edward Said demonstrated in his famous book *Orientalism* in 1978. After formal decolonization and postcolonial immigration to the West, however, this view of Asia and Asians has changed, a process accelerated by Said's book and the postcolonial scholarship that followed in its wake.

Said's book was a general attack on the Western perception of and research on Asia and Asians, and the debate that followed the publication in particularly in Anglophone Studies, has made it virtually impossible to use the terms 'Orient' and 'Orientals' without using quotation marks, while the adjective 'Oriental' today is mostly used in connection with various animal species and to designate certain objects, events and meals. Said's criticism focused on the Orientalists' intimate relationship with the colonial project where researchers intellectually and scientifically legitimized the European empires in Asia through their representations of Asians (Ahluwalia 2003; Hübinette 2003; Macfie 2000).

The debate concerning the Orientalists and Oriental Studies, however, has not been taken seriously in Sweden, as the maintaining of the department name at Stockholm University also indicates. Said's book was not translated into Swedish until 1993, and was then provided with an introductory chapter written by the author Sigrid Kahle (1993), daughter of a famous Swedish Iranist, where she defended her Swedish Asian Studies colleagues who unlike other Westerners had not, according to her, been guilty of creating an Orientalized image of Asia and Asians. Kahle's attitude towards former Swedish Asian Studies scholars has been reiterated by other contemporary Asian Studies researchers in Sweden. Together with other students and researchers, I myself tried to change the name of the department to the Department of Asian Studies in 2002 with the backing of a number of legal texts and conventions that promote a non-discriminatory stance (Hübinette 2003).

The then head of the department and all the full professors were, however, against a name change even though most of the staff members of Asian background were for it. The head and the board of the department instead stated that terms like the 'Orient' and 'Orientals' cannot possibly be seen as reflecting a colonial and racist attitude in a specific Swedish contemporary context. Northern Europe's largest institution for Asian Studies thus showed that it had completely missed the last 20 years of debate on Europe's colonial and racist past and asymmetrical relationship vis-à-vis Asia and Asians. This also has repercussions for the department's image in the future as it will receive more and more students with an Asian background who have grown up in Sweden and who perceive concepts like the 'Orient' and 'Orientals' as not only old-fashioned and 'unscientific' but also as offensive and derogatory.

The Beloved Swedish N-Word

The Swedish twin words 'Negro' (*neger*) and 'Nigger' (*nigger*) have up to present time been socially acceptable to use next to older European and domestic designations such as 'Moor' (*morian*), 'blue man' (*blåman*) and 'darky' (*svarting*) (Adelswärd 2009). The word 'Negro' is not only ascribed to Africans, but sometimes non-white people in general, while the word 'Nigger' is sometimes provided with positive associations, as in exotic children's songs and children's books and to describe and celebrate black American musicians.

Children's games like 'Nigger' and 'Who is afraid of the black man?' (*Vem är rädd för svarte man?*), songs about the 'Negro' performed by popular artists like Evert Taube, Povel Ramel and Cornelis Vreeswijk, poems about the 'Nigger' written by poets like Arthur Lundkvist, Gunnar Ekelöf and Jesper Svenbro, Pippi Longstocking's father the 'Negro king' (*negerkungen*), place names like 'Negro village' (*Negerbyn*) which can also be used as a nickname for specific neighbourhoods, nicknames such as 'Negro-Johan' and 'Negro-Anna' which many adopted and mixed Swedes with African ancestry are being called by their white relatives and friends, slang compositions as 'blue Negro' (*blåneger*) and 'Negro job' (*negerjobb*), and established names in the world of chocolates and pastries such as 'Negro kiss' (*negerkyss*) and 'Negro ball' (*negerboll*) which are both still included in the Swedish Academy's dictionary from 2006 all suggest and point to a long-time everyday and normalized use of what could be called a specific Swedish version of the N-word. It was only in 2006 that the Swedish Academy in its 13th edition of its highly esteemed dictionary added the comment 'may be perceived as derogatory' after the entry word 'Negro' (in small print and in parenthesis), and it was also in that edition that the word 'chocolate ball' for the first time was introduced as a synonym to 'Negro ball', and not until 2009 was the name of a neighbourhood called 'Negro' replaced in the city of Karlstad (Modin 2007).

It was only in the 2000s that an official debate regarding the word 'Negro' arose in Sweden after a bakery had been notified to the Ombudsman against Discrimination in 2003 for displaying written signs selling 'Negro balls'. Even though the owner was never fined, other bakeries and cafes around the country started to advertise both 'Negro balls' and 'Negro kisses' in a sort of a popular and defiant underdog-style civil disobedience campaign (Kidebäck 2004, Persson 2006). Still there are Swedish bakeries, confectioners and recipe writers who use the name 'Negro ball' or joke about 'PC censorship' by instead selling 'immigrant ball' or 'Call it whatever you want to', and it has been repeatedly reported that official representatives and particularly police officers make use of the word 'Negro' or phrases such as 'blue Negro', 'Oscar Negro' and 'Negro Niggerson' in reports, inquiries and learning material (Jonsson 2009).

It has for many Swedes become something of a radical 'anti-PC' act of resistance to continue their use of the word 'Negro' although Sweden is currently hosting an estimated number of 150,000 people with some form of African origin, including African slave descendants from the Americas and adopted and mixed Swedes. The ongoing debate on the specific Swedish N-word and whether it is a word that wounds also manifests itself in more unexpected contexts such as in the culture and art world when self-identifying anti-racist and leftist journalists, writers, artists, actors, musicians and artists use the word 'Negro' explicitly in articles, novels, poems, exhibitions, movies, lyrics and on stage to be seen as liberated and anti-bourgeois (Polite 2005). The pervasive argument for continuing to use the word expressed by Swedes as well as by the Swedish authorities, is that the word belongs to a historical heritage and is part of a Swedish vocabulary, and hence regarded as authentic and important to protect and preserve for the future (Nordberg 2009). All the public agencies that responded when being asked about the neighbourhood name 'Negro' in Karlstad in 2009, including the National Land Survey, the Nordic Museum and the county council, said that precisely because of the place name's long history it is a part of the Swedish cultural heritage. The agencies argued that it should be understood as 'imaginative' in a positive sense and of course that it cannot be seen as derogatory (Nilsson 2009).

In November 2008, the television programme leader Carin Hjulström defended in her talk show programme *Carin 21: 30* on the public service channel SVT2 the continued use of the word 'Negro' in a discussion with the author Jonas Hassen Khemiri. She illustrated this argument in a rather unsubtle way by placing a dish of chocolate balls on the table in the studio. Hjulström said that she felt more sorry for 'all children' who 'do not understand why you cannot say Negro ball' than for those who felt that the word was offensive (Wirfält 2009). The same kind of exclusivist majority perspective was also revealed when the Swedish Police Union said in a statement after new revelations that the word 'Negro' was used routinely by police officers on duty that 'all police officers' are now exposed to a 'value system panic' (*värdegrundspanik*) which can result in an 'atmosphere of fear' (*skräckstämning*) due to their fear of being reported for using derogatory names (Olsson 2010; Stiernstedt 2010).

The television programme launched a storm of sympathy on websites, blogs and discussion forums, and in the social media Facebook a group calling itself 'The name is Negro ball, and it has always been called that' (*Det heter negerboll, och det har det alltid hetat*) in record time succeeded in recruiting more members than the 'Save us from street violence' (*Rädda oss från gatuvåldet*) group, which previously could call itself the largest Swedish Facebook group. In the presentation to the approximately 60,000 members of the group during the spring of 2009 and before it was deleted by the end of the year by Facebook's headquarters in the US, the founders of the group again referred to the struggle for the Swedish cultural heritage and resistance against the 'PC mafia' and 'reverse racists' who believe they know that 'dark-skinned become hurt by the use of the word'. At the same time, several anti-racist groups were launched, but none of the dozen or so anti-racist Facebook groups ever reached over a thousand members.

Subcultural Anti-Semitic Humour

In the municipality of Järfälla outside Stockholm there is an ancient fortress situated on a rock that bears the name Gåseborg. The rock is composed of several climbing routes which according to the custom of the rock climbing community have been named by the first climber who created and marked out the trail across the rock. The roughly 40 trails at Gåseborg were created and named by various climbers from 1987 to 2001, and around 20 of them are named after historical events, phenomena and people associated with World War II. There are names such as 'Spitfire' and 'Stuka', but also a number of names that are directly associated with National Socialism and the Holocaust including 'Zyklon B', 'Himmler', 'Swastika', 'Crystal Night' (*Kristallnatten*) and 'Crematorium'.

The routes have had these names for many years and the names have been marked on different semi-official maps. Hundreds of climbers must have made use of them during this period, yet it was only in August 2010 that a woman with a German background criticized the names publicly in the main Swedish morning paper *Dagens Nyheter* for downplaying and trivializing the genocide of European Jews and for expressing disrespect for the Holocaust and World War II victims (Liljestrand 2010). In the *Dagens Nyheter* article, one of the climbers who had named one of the tracks after Hitler defended this by saying that the type of names given to the trails should be seen as an 'internal thing' among climbers, and added that he could not understand how they could be interpreted as disrespectful. The article did not lead to any closer journalistic scrutiny, let alone a debate in the Swedish media, but the story was highlighted in both American, German, Austrian, British and Israeli newspapers, where it caused a stir because of Sweden's international image as an anti-Fascist and anti-racist country.

However, an extensive internal debate followed among Swedish climbers on the Internet. An overwhelming majority of the Swedish comments claimed that the *Dagens Nyheter* article was only an expression of intolerance, abuse hysteria and prohibition zeal. Several debaters also linked it to the 'ridiculous' debate concerning the word 'Negro', and it also emerged that apparently there are plenty of routes around the country named in a similar spirit such as 'Bolted Negro' (*Bultad neger*) and 'Negro balls of steel' (*Negerbollar av stål*). Many writers had also difficulties in understanding why a humorous attitude in a subculture could be seen as offensive at all, and the main forum for the Swedish rock climber community Bloxc.com published a petition for free speech and introduced a fake competition which involved coming up with a new name for Gåseborg where proposals like 'Hess against an ethnic group' (*Hess mot folkgrupp*) and '*Klettern macht frei*' (climbing liberates) figured. The first name refers to the main Swedish law against hate speech which is named 'agitation against an ethnic group' (*hets mot folkgrupp*), and the last name is a direct reference to the sign with the text '*Arbeit macht frei*' (labour liberates) which was placed above the entrance to many concentration camps.

White Melancholia in Sweden

What connects these three contemporary Swedish examples which at first glance may seem so different from one another? They originate from three completely different spheres: the example of Orientalism is taken from the elite world of academia, the example 'Negro' appears to be localized at the more popular level of Swedish society, while the trail name example derives from a specific subcultural context. All three examples, however, are produced by the Swedish majority population, thus making it appropriate to place them within a Swedish whiteness discourse. In Anglo-American critical whiteness research, the term hegemonic whiteness is sometimes used to explain and understand that white people despite different social backgrounds and political views can still share the same privileges and perspectives on whiteness, even including racists and anti-racists (Hughey 2010). Based on the three examples, a Swedish hegemonic whiteness in this case means that many white Swedes apparently want to continue to use words and expressions which are offensive and hurtful to minorities regardless of gender, class and regional and generational differences.

Furthermore, it is highly possible that the vast majority of the white Swedes who consider themselves to be fighting for freedom of speech and the preservation of Swedish cultural heritage would not label themselves racists, but rather identify themselves as non-racists, and many would most probably call themselves anti-racists. One of the main arguments to defend the contemporary use of words like 'Oriental' and 'Negro' is that they in no way can be perceived to be racist when being used in a Swedish contemporary context. This specific Swedish context refers to a self-image which says that Sweden and the Swedes had no colonies in Asia, had no links to the slave trade and the plundering of Africa, and much less with Nazism and the Holocaust, and most importantly that Sweden of today is not a racist country. This Swedish whiteness is similar to the other Nordic countries' versions of whiteness, where it is not recognized and accepted that the Nordic people were and still are positioned above the non-Western world and participated in the colonial project just like all other Western countries.

Another important ingredient of Swedish whiteness concerns a desire to remain neutral and objective to all that has happened and happens outside the borders of Sweden to be able to feel benevolent, advanced and moral (Schough 2008: 12–24). This Swedish exceptionalism which again has many similarities and parallels to other Nordic countries' exceptionalistic attitudes as they appear in several of the other anthology articles, can also be seen as a deliberate forgetfulness grounded in a desire for not wanting to understand that minorities may feel offended and humiliated by certain words and expressions that are loaded with Europe's colonial and racist history and for not wanting to take in that Sweden today is a country marked by racial diversity.

Furthermore according to my analysis in this chapter, it is also possible to talk about a white melancholy in Sweden caused by a mourning that the Swedish population is no longer as white as before, that a Swede today can potentially be both non-white and non-Christian and perhaps above all that before non-white immigration to Sweden it was much easier to be anti-racist. This Swedish white melancholia requires that the idealized phantasm of a homogeneous and white non-racist Sweden is maintained on psychic and imaginary level, but in order for the grief to not become too overwhelming, white melancholia must manifest and articulate itself. So behind all the excited talk of a struggle for freedom of speech, of a righteous rebellion against political correctness and of a heroic defence of the Swedish language and cultural heritage, and beyond the alleged intention of being objective and neutral, one finds according to my psychoanalytically inspired analysis a white melancholia and an anger against non-whites caused by their permanent presence in the country. This presence is seen to destroy anti-racist or even non-racist Sweden, and is expressed through the continuous use of colonial and racist words, expressions and jokes in the everyday life of Sweden. It does not manifest a triumphalist whiteness, but a whiteness in crisis, and a whiteness structured by feelings of bewilderment and loss.

The preservation of Swedish whiteness as the hegemonic discourse of Swedish society is in other words a continuing denial of the idea that non-whites and non-Christians can be Swedes, a continued disregard for the experiences and perspectives of minorities, and a continued lack of and absence of a postcolonial ethic that is so necessary in the new diverse Sweden in spite of all the talk about tolerance, respect, values and ethics, and despite all official anti-racism. Through this white melancholia over the passing of white anti-racist Sweden, the Swedish majority population continues to disavow the fact that a new postcolonial Swedishness requires a reckoning with Sweden's own colonial and racist cultural heritage, and at the same time minorities are being humiliated and their histories, experiences and perspectives are being silenced and made invisible in the name of a white anti-racism. To be able to once and for all cure this white melancholia and to be able to transform and annihilate today's excluding Swedish whiteness requires that words that wound no longer are practised as illocutionary speech acts.

References

Adelswärd, Viveka. 2009. Förtryck och stolthet ryms i samma ord. *Svenska Dagbladet*, 24 January.

Ahluwalia, Pal. 2003. With words we govern men: Orientalism and the question of translation. *Stockholm Journal of East Asian Studies*, 13, 7–26.
Alcoff, Linda Martín. 2005. *Visible Identities. Race, Gender and the Self*. London: Oxford University Press.
Austin, J.L. 1986. *How to Do Things with Words: The William James Lectures Delivered at Harvard University in 1955*, edited by J.O. Urmson and Marina Sbisa. Oxford: Oxford University Press.
Bondesson, Mikael. 2009. Kvarteret Negern får nytt namn. *Dagens Nyheter*, 23 September.
Broberg, Gunnar. 1995. *Statlig rasforskning: En historik över Rasbiologiska institutet*. Stockholm: Natur & Kultur.
Cederberg, Maja. 2005. Everyday racism in Malmö, Sweden. The experiences of Bosnians and Somalis. PhD thesis. Nottingham Trent University: Department of Cultural Studies.
Cheng, Anne Anlin. 2001. *The Melancholy of Race*. Oxford: Oxford University Press.
Crenshaw, Kimberlè, Neil Gotanda, Garry Peller and Kendall Thomas (eds). 1995. *Critical Race Theory: The Key Writings That Formed the Movement*. New York: New Press.
Delgado, Richard and Jean Stefanic. 2000. *Critical Race Theory: An Introduction*. New York: New York University Press.
Delgado, Richard and Jean Stefanic. 2004. *Understanding Words That Wound*. Boulder: Westview Press.
Dyer, Richard. 1997. *White*. London: Routledge.
Frankenberg, Ruth. 1993. *White Women, Race Matters: The Social Construction of Whiteness*. Minneapolis: University of Minnesota Press.
Gilroy, Paul. 2005. *Post-Colonial Melancholia*. New York: Columbia University Press.
Habel, Ylva. 2008. Whiteness Swedish Style. *Slut*, 2, 41–51.
Hagerman, Maja. 2006. *Det rena landet: Om konsten att uppfinna sina förfäder*. Stockholm: Prisma.
Hällgren, Camilla. 2005. 'Working harder to be the same': Everyday racism among young men and women in Sweden. *Race, Ethnicity and Education*, 8(3), 319–42.
Han, Jane. 2010. Sen. Shin dedicated to making US Asians proud. *Korea Times*, 21 March.
Hill, Mike (ed.). 1997. *Whiteness: A Critical Reader*. New York: New York University Press.
Hübinette, Tobias. 2002. Orientaler finns inte längre. *Dagens Forskning*, 1(13–14), 54.
Hübinette, Tobias. 2003. Orientalism past and present: An introduction to a post-colonial critique. *Stockholm Journal of East Asian Studies*, 13, 73–80.

Hübinette, Tobias and Carina Tigervall. 2008. *Adoption med förhinder: Samtal med adopterade och adoptivföräldrar om vardagsrasism och etnisk identitet.* Tumba: Mångkulturellt centrum.
Hübinette, Tobias and Catrin Lundström. 2011. Sweden after the recent election: The double-binding power of Swedish whiteness through the mourning of the loss of 'old Sweden' and the passing of 'good Sweden'. *NORA – Nordic Journal of Feminist and Gender Research*, 19(1), 42–52.
Hughey, Matthew W. 2010. The (dis)similarities of white racial identities: The conceptual framework of 'hegemonic whiteness'. *Ethnic and Racial Studies*, 33(8), 1289–1309.
Ignatiev, Noel. 1995. *How the Irish Became White*. New York: Routledge.
Jonsson, Stefan. 2009. Nigger, nogger och neger. Varför envisas svenskar med öknamnen? *Dagens Nyheter*, 26 October.
Kahle, Sigrid. 1993. Orientalism i Sverige. Introduction in Edward Said, *Orientalism*. Stockholm: Ordfront, 7–58.
Kalonaityté, Viktorija, Victoria Kawesa and Adiam Tedros. 2007. *Upplevelser av diskriminering och rasism bland ungdomar med afrikansk bakgrund i Sverige.* Stockholm: Ombudsmannen mot etnisk diskriminering.
Kennedy, Randall. 2003. *Nigger: The Strange Career of a Troublesome Word.* New York: Vintage Books.
Kidebäck, Caroline. 2004. Negerboll är kränkande men skånskt konditori slipper skadestånd. *Sydsvenska Dagbladet*, 23 January.
Liljestrand, Jens. 2010. Nazistnamn på klätterklippa i Järfälla. *Dagens Nyheter*, 12 August.
Lundstedt, Anna. 2005. *Vit governmentalitet. 'Invandrarkvinnor' och textilhantverk – en diskursanalys.* PhD thesis. Göteborgs universitet: Etnologiska institutionen.
Lundström, Catrin. 2007. *Svenska latinas; Ras, klass och kön i svenskhetens geografi.* Göteborg: Makadam.
Lundström, Catrin. 2010. White ethnography: (Un)comfortable conveniences and shared privileges in fieldwork with Swedish migrant women. *Nordic Journal of Feminist and Gender Research*, 18(2), 70–87.
Macfie, Alexander Lyon (ed.). 2000. *Orientalism: A Reader*. New York: New York University Press.
Matsuda, Mari J., Charles R. Lawrence III, Richard Delgado and Kimberlè Williams Crenshaw. 1993. *Words That Wound: Critical Race Theory, Assaultive Speech, and the First Amendment.* Boulder: Westview Press.
Mattsson, Katarina. 2006. Fröken Sverige i folkhemmet. Ideal svensk kvinnlighet på 1950-talet, in *Feministiska interventioner: Berättelser om och från en annan värld*, edited by Kerstin Sandell and Diana Mulinari. Stockholm: Atlas, 270–303.
Mattsson, Katarina and Mekonnen Tesfahuney. 2002. Rasism i vardagen, in *Det slutna folkhemmet: Etniska klyftor och blågul självbild*, edited by I. Lindberg and M. Dahlstedt. Stockholm: Agora, 28–41.
Modin, Lina. 2007. Barnsången är kränkande. *Expressen*, 9 February.

Motsieloa, Viveca. 2003. *'Det måste vara någonting annat'; En studie om barns upplevelser av rasism i vardagen*. Stockholm: Rädda barnen.

Nilsson, David Nannini. 2009. Protester mot kvartersnamnet 'Negern'. *Aftonbladet*, 22 June.

Nordberg, Stefan. 2009. Välkommen till Kvarteret Negern. *Byggvärlden*, 8 January.

Olsson, Stefan. 2010. Polisfackets brev. *Sydsvenska Dagbladet*, 8 April.

Olsson, Tobias. 2007. Rasistiskt ord begravs i USA. *Svenska Dagbladet*, 10 July.

Osanami Törngren, Sayaka. 2011. *Love ain't got no color? Attitude toward interracial marriage in Sweden*. Malmö högskola: IMER/MIM.

Pallas, Hynek. 2011. *Vithet i svensk spelfilm 1989–2010*. Göteborg: Filmkonst.

Persson, Kjell-Åke. 2006. Rasistisk glass i Båstad? *Helsingborgs Dagblad*, 25 July.

Polite, Oivvio. 2005. Vit kvinna pratar svart med vita män. *Dagens Nyheter*, 23 April.

Pred, Allan. 2000. *Even in Sweden: Racisms, Racialized Spaces, and the Popular Geographical Imagination*. Berkeley: University of California Press.

Pripp, Oscar and Magnus Öhlander. 2008. *Fallet Nogger black: Antirasismens gränser*. Stockholm: Agora.

Roediger, David R. 1991. *The Wages of Whiteness: Race and the Making of the American Working Class*. London: Verso.

Sabuni, Nyamko. 2005. Bli kallad neger är kränkande. *Aftonbladet*, 31 August.

Sawyer, Lena. 2000. *Black and Swedish: Racialization and the Cultural Politics of Belonging in Stockholm, Sweden*. PhD thesis. University of Michigan: Department of Cultural Anthropology.

Sawyer, Lena. 2001. Första gången jag såg en neger – en svensk självbild. I *Törnroslandet. Om tillhörighet och utanförskap*. Norrköping: Integrationsverket, 133–9.

Sawyer, Lena. 2006. Makt, vithet och afrikansk dans, in *Feministiska interventioner: Berättelser om och från en annan värld*, edited by K. Sandell and D. Mulinari. Stockholm: Atlas, 175–99.

Schmauch, Ulrika. 2006. *Den osynliga vardagsrasismens realitet*. PhD thesis. Umeå Universitet: Sociologiska Institutionen.

Schough, Katarina. 2008. *Hyperboré: Föreställningen om Sveriges plats i världen*. Stockholm: Carlsson.

Stapleton, Bruce. 2001. *Redskins: Racial Slur or Symbol of Success?* Bloomington: iUniverse.

Stiernstedt, Jenny. 2010. Poliser hämmas av känsliga ordval. *Dagens Nyheter*, 8 April.

Tydén, Mattias. 2000. *Från politik till praktik; De svenska steriliseringslagarna 1935–75*. Stockholm: Fritzes.

Wirfält, Johan. 2009. Facebook-gruppen 'Det heter negerboll' är äcklig. *Newsmill*, 5 March.

Chapter 4
Belonging and the Icelandic Others: Situating Icelandic Identity in a Postcolonial Context

Kristín Loftsdóttir

> There is no less than a great danger that awaits our culture and what other countries think about it: we are being categorized along with uncivilized savage people ... and being disgraced in the eyes of the educated world. (Sveinsson 1904: 197)

When Gísli Sveinsson protested along with many other Icelandic students in Copenhagen in 1904 against the Danish colonial exhibition where the intention was to exhibit Denmark's colonies, it was driven by his belief that Iceland did not *belong* with the 'uncivilized savage' people. The danger that he spells out in regard to Icelandic 'culture' can be the possible internalization of this classification and probably of no less importance, the effects on how Icelanders would be viewed externally – by those he refers to as the 'educated' ones.

My discussion in this chapter focuses on this sense of belonging, which I perceive as helpful to tease out some of the ambiguities of colonial identity and their relationship to the postcolonial present, as well as to understand the nuances of Icelandic exceptionalism. As such notions of Icelandic exceptionalism have to be contextualized as embedded in Iceland's status in the nineteenth to early twentieth century as a subjected nation of Denmark. To illustrate this, I shift between past and present, focusing on representations of Africa in Iceland and the protest by Icelandic students against the Danish colonial exhibition, Gísli Sveinsson responds to. As I will show, simultaneously with resisting their position as a Danish dependency in the late nineteenth and early twentieth centuries, Icelanders participated in perpetrating and enforcing stereotypes of colonized people in other parts of the world, positioning themselves very carefully as belonging with the civilized Europeans, instead of the uncivilized 'others' (Loftsdóttir 2010). My discussion contextualizes the importance of this ambiguity for present day Iceland and localized notions of exceptionalism by way of two examples.

Colonialism and imperialism were essential in shaping European identities in the nineteenth century (Gilroy 1993, Dirks 1992), creating boundaries and categories of belonging, based on shifting and intersecting markers for example in relation to race and gender (McClintock 1995: 17). Belonging is, however, also generated by the exclusion of certain socially defined groups (Barth 1969) and, as stressed by Nira Yuval-Davis, particular social divisions or markers have to be recognized as being more salient in specific historical conditions than others (Yuval-Davis 2006: 201). Keeping this in mind we have to look at how sense of belonging is generated in local and historical contexts. As a category of belonging and exclusion, 'whiteness' can similarly be seen as established as a significant category of difference at a particular time. Scholars have stressed how 'whiteness' becomes a powerful category through normalization, its power embedded in its invisibility to those socially classified as 'white' (for example Hartigan 1997: 498). Critical investigations of whiteness seek as such to 'deterritorialize the territory "white" to expose, examine and disrupt' (Nakayama and Krizek 1995: 292). As a culturally constructed category 'whiteness' is thus shifting and contested (Hartigan 1997).

The emphasis on historicizing belonging is in line with Laura Ann Stoler's remark that we need to recognize better that the dichotomy of the categories 'colonized' and 'colonizer' encompass diversity and how they have emerged historically (Stoler 1992: 321). Andrea Smith, furthermore, emphasizes that the dissection of these categories is not to trivialize the horrors of colonialism but to call for a more detailed and contextual analysis of the different aspects of this categorization (Smith 2003). European identities thus have to be dissected as embedded in the colonial past (Said 1978) and, no less importantly, the more concealed involvements with colonialism made visible (Keskinen et al. 2009; Jensen 2005) while emphasizing the historical specificity of these engagements. Ann Brydon has importantly drawn attention to how the 'language of the center' was often appropriated selectively by the colonized as a way of self-inscription in a process of 'transculturation' (1995: 246), simultaneously as drawing attention to marginal areas within Europe such as Iceland in this regard. As I have pointed out earlier in my own work, Icelandic images of Africa and other colonized people were not so much concerned with constructing images of 'others' as they were with positioning Icelanders as a part of the civilized European (Loftsdóttir 2008, 2009a). Similar claim is made by Elisabeth Oxfeldt's discussion of Norway and Denmark where she points out that countries on the periphery 'imported oriental imagery to position themselves not against their colonial other but rather in relation to central European nations' (2005: 13). These insights are important to keep in mind when trying to understand Icelandic constructions of belonging and notions of exceptionalism.

I start my discussion with outlining Iceland's status within Europe, especially emphasizing Iceland's position within the European colonial and imperial landscape in the nineteenth and early twentieth century. While I see it as important to recognize Iceland's status as a Danish dependency and its influence on the evolution of Icelandic identity, Iceland's history and geopolitical position was of course quite different from the colonial experiences elsewhere where brutal violence, various dehumanizing practices and exterminations constituted a part of people's everyday lives (see for example Franey 2003). Within this ambiguous space of Iceland's status as a dependency, I seek first to outline Icelandic exceptionalism as expressed within the nationalistic movement focusing on Iceland's independence from Denmark. After this the discussion moves to focus on the contemporary discussion of diversity in Iceland where exceptionalism is used to justify and make meaningful the recycling of colonial images and ideas.

Icelandic Exceptionalism

Iceland was a Danish dependency until 1944, and had been under foreign rule from the 1300s. As scholars have stressed, Danish rule was not questioned as such until the nineteenth century (Hálfdánarson 2000), even though Icelanders seem to have maintained a separate identity long prior to that time (Karlsson 1995, Oslund 2002). As pointed out by Guðmundur Hálfdánarson (2000), the emerging nationalistic ideals in the nineteenth century fitted well with Icelanders' strong pride in their culture, reflecting a fertile ground for nationalistic ideals (Hálfdánarson 2000: 90).

Even as early as medieval times, Icelanders were greatly concerned with misconceptions that they believed foreigners had about Iceland (Durrenberger and Pálsson 1989). Arngrímur Jónsson's text *Brevis Commentarius de Islandia* published in 1593 and Oddur Einarsson's description of Iceland in 1597 were both intended to defend Iceland against unjustified claims of foreigners (Benediktsson 1971). In 1892, Þorvald Thoroddsen wrote a four-volume overview of how Iceland was represented and misrepresented (Durrenberger and Pálsson 1989), emphasizing the importance of drawing together different representations about Iceland (Thoroddsen 1892–96: iv). The renowned scholar Sigurður Norðdal published furthermore in 1942 the book 'Icelandic Culture' as a 'new Crymogea, a defense on behalf of Icelanders' (quoted in Durrenberger and Pálsson 1989: xv). These attempts were still meaningful in the context of Iceland and Icelanders being exposed to conflicting images by Europeans throughout the centuries, even as late as in the eighteenth and nineteenth centuries. Icelandic scholar Þorvald Thoroddsen (1898) quotes a description from 1492, for example, where it is said that Iceland people sell their dogs for a high price but give their children away to travelling merchants (Thoroddsen 1898: 96), and another by Andrew Boorede from 1547 where Icelanders are described as eaters of raw fish and meat, in addition to being 'animal-like beasts' dressing in the furs of wild animals without any houses (Thoroddsen 1898: 127). In the fifteenth and sixteenth century, Icelandic nature was seen as exotic and Iceland itself associated with Hell, an image which was reified in the late seventeenth century (Oslund 2002: 318). Such views did not only revolve around Iceland; the 'north' had for a long time been seen as inhabited by 'barbarians' (Lagerspetz 2003: 50). In the nineteenth century such stereotypes of Iceland were still present with Icelanders not generally represented as complete savages but neither as fully belonging with civilized peoples. The presumed laziness of the Icelanders was often remarked upon, as in a British traveller's statement that it would take an English worker only a few hours to complete a task that took Icelanders days to finish (Ísleifsson 1996: 185–93). In a similar vein an English geography book for children, published in London in 1875, claims that the hands of Icelanders are so dirty that 'you would not want them to touch you or assist with your belongings' (quoted in Ísleifsson 1996: 186). Similar views can be seen in some narratives of Icelandic immigrants to North America in the late nineteenth century. One immigrant recounted, for example, that the English had great contempt for the Icelanders (*haft hina mestu skömm á*), calling them Eskimos and even refusing to use the same towel and washbowls as them (Þorsteinsson 1940: 201).

European sources did not solely present Iceland and Icelanders in negative ways. Particularly in connection with rising nationalism, Icelanders were situated within ideas that saw peasants increasingly idealized as uncorrupted and as embodying the pure essence of the nation. Under such influences, intellectuals had a growing interest in Germanic and Celtic history (Ísleifsson 1996: 84–5; see also discussion in Loftsdóttir 2008). In Denmark, Iceland was seen as part of old Danish culture, attitudes that glorified to some extent Icelandic culture, but simultaneously located it as a part of the past and pre-modern (Karlsson 1995: 45). After Denmark's participation in the Napoleonic wars, the Danish state was close to bankruptcy and sold its tropical colonies in Africa and India to Great Britain, and then 1917 the Virgin Islands to the USA (Oslund 2002: 328). Karen Oslund (2002) stresses in this regard that it would have been rational from a purely economic standpoint to also sell Iceland, which reflects how cultural concerns were quite important in the case of Iceland, overwriting economic priorities (328).

Iceland's demands for independence were underpinned with references to the uniqueness of the Icelandic language and the medieval Icelandic literature. The Icelandic sagas constituted one of the most significant 'factors in the creation of Icelandic national identity in the nineteenth and early twentieth century' (Sigurðsson 1996: 42), being testimonies of Iceland's more glorious past of the commonwealth period. The nineteenth century nationalists tended to regard the Danish colonial government as the result of Iceland's decline from a glorious historical past, but the dependency relationship was framed as an 'unnatural' arrangement where one nation ruled another (Hálfdánarson 2000: 91). Jón Jónsson – one of the most influential persons in shaping Icelandic nationalism – reflects this notion vividly in his writing, emphasizing foreign rule as the reason for the country's poverty (Jónsson 1903: 245). While emphasizing independence as natural for themselves and protesting their spatial location as outside 'civilized' nations, the Icelanders participated in recreating and reaffirming racialized and dehumanizing images of colonized people elsewhere. The annual journal *Skírnir* was highly influential through its dissemination of news about the rest of the world, even if it was published by the Icelandic Literary Society (*Hið Íslenzka Bókmenntafélag*), founded in 1816 and based in Copenhagen. Initially, the society celebrated the importance of the Icelandic language and cultural traditions (Pálsson 1978: 71; Líndal 1969: 20), and aimed at publishing classical works and material concerned with Iceland (Sigurðsson 1986: 33–4). *Skírnir's* report on Africa and other parts of the world remote for Icelanders focused usually on the European explorations and settlements. Local populations seldom featured in these accounts – thus contributing to evoking an image of Europeans colonizing unpopulated space. The discussion focused more on progress of the colonists, future prospects for colonization and possible profit making. A few examples can be given of this. *Skírnir*'s discussion of Australia in 1827 mentions Aboriginals briefly, describing them as 'very ignorant savages' (42) and in the journal from 1852, they are emphasized as being the 'most miserable race in the world which does not know cultivation or any industry but lives on wild animals' (33). In 1852, some great compliments were also given to British colonization of the world without mentioning the colonized inhabitants (64–5). Colonizing images of subjected people were then enforced by geography books published at the end of nineteenth and beginning of twentieth century which presented classification of world populations into different racial groups in a degrading and stereotypical way (Loftsdóttir 2009a). These images of Icelanders were strongly gendered as is expressed in their focus on exploration and colonialization. Through texts speaking of colonialization in other parts of the world, Icelandic men could imagine themselves as part of the progressive, civilized Europeans, these parts of the world becoming spaces where masculinity and Europeanness were enacted and reified (see Loftsdóttir 2010).

Simultaneously with this presentation of a strongly racialized and gendered image of Iceland as belonging to 'white' European men, one can also see that it overlapped with the image of Icelanders, earlier mentioned, as different from all others, that is, a nationalistic idea that emphasizes the distinction of Icelanders from others. Such ideas must have been particularly important in justifying and making comprehensive the idea of Iceland as an independent country. Within schoolbooks used to teach Icelandic history in the early twentieth century, this image becomes clearly visible. Icelanders are represented as deriving from the 'best' part of the Norwegian population, in addition to being shaped by hardship of the country itself (Loftsdóttir 2010). Within such narratives, Icelandic exceptionalism is laid out, emphasizing Icelanders as different from anyone else. This notion is of course greatly interconnected with nationalism at that particular political period which to some extent aimed at justifying Iceland as an independent nation.

Disputes arising from the Danish colonial exhibition in Copenhagen in 1905 reflect the ambiguity of Iceland's position within the European context, as well their desire to be positioned within the 'civilized' part of the world. The exhibition was planned by the *Dansk Kunstflidforening*, which was a society whose mission was to teach applied skills to the poorer inhabitants of Denmark. There was a long tradition of such exhibitions both within Europe and in Denmark, often at the Danish amusement park, *Tivoli*. Established in 1843 in downtown Copenhagen, Tivoli hosted various amusements, concerts and games and had also since 1880 been a popular place for exhibiting people and animals from exotic places (Jörgensen 1996: 30–48). It was thus no surprise that the exhibition would be held there. The exhibition was intended to put on display colonized subjects and artefacts of Denmark in Copenhagen's Tivoli, including those from Greenland, the

Danish West Indies and Iceland (Finsen 1958) to present the Danish colonies, their main products and handicraft traditions to the largely Danish audience. In addition, there was a hope of collecting money for the association itself (Jóhannesson 2003: 137). Icelandic students in Copenhagen, the intellectual centre of Iceland during that time, were shocked and furious, when learning that Iceland would be a part of the exhibition along with other Danish colonies and protested strongly in Icelandic and Danish journals.[1] The Icelandic student association in Copenhagen demanded that the Icelanders in the committee should put a stop to Iceland's participation (Fjallkonan, 13 December 1904: 1999). When the exhibition was launched on 31 May 1905, it had cultural artefacts for display and in some cases displaying people, including a girl and a boy from the West Indian island St. Croix. The boy, Victor, later said that that he did not want to stay at the West Indian part of the exhibition where he was supposed to be but liked more to roam in the Greenlandic display. His resistance to staying in his assigned 'space' earned him a temporary exhibition in a cage (Freiesleben 1998: 37). However, in regard to Iceland, cultural artefacts were exhibited only.

The Icelanders did, however, not protest over the exhibition as such but rather the fact that Iceland was placed within it as a subjugated nation, and they were especially unhappy about their association thus with other colonized populations (Loftsdóttir 2008, 2009b). The importance of this point is reflected in the words of the Icelandic students' association in Copenhagen: 'We are aware that mostly savage ethnicities will be exhibited that are for the most part different from educated nations'[2] (Fjallkonan, 16 December 1904: 1999). The article quoted at the beginning of this chapter written by Gísli Sveinsson illustrates as well clearly the main concerns of the students. The article was entitled *Exhibition in Copenhagen from Denmark's dependencies: Iceland in great danger* and was published in the Icelandic paper *Fjallkonan* in December 1904. In the article Gísli Sveinsson vividly expresses his concern with the exhibition. He states that Iceland will be: 'exhibited along with uncultured savage ethnicities (*siðlausum villiþjóðum*) ... to disgrace us in the eyes of the cultivated world', furthermore as stressing that 'people are being taught that we should be observed as belonging to the same stage of culture and progress as the Greenlanders' (*skrælingjar*) and blacks' (my translation: quoted in Sveinsson 1904: 197).

The students also were particularly concerned about the role of Icelandic women, which can be explained with reference to nationalistic discourses often emphasizing women as symbolizing the nation (Yuval-Davis 1997, Pratt 1992). Within nationalistic discourses in Iceland, the country itself was often metaphorically referred to as a woman with an emphasis on her purity and beauty (Björnsdóttir 1994). Sveinsson clearly visualizes Icelandic women as symbolizing

---

1 According to Vilhjálmur Finsen's account, a student in Copenhagen, there were around 100 Icelandic students in Copenhagen during 1904 (Finsen 1958: 20).

2 In Icelandic: Er oss það kunnugt, að þar eru einkum sýndir villtir þjóðflokkar, sem að einhverju leyti eru frábrugnir menntuðum þjóðum.

Iceland when he asks: 'Must Iceland be known for its participation in such an exhibition, where Icelandic women in national costumes are posed next to Eskimo and Negro women?' (my translation: quoted in Sveinsson 1904: 169).

The voices of these students are of course caught up in the struggle for independence and the need to show Iceland as a nation that deserved to become an independent nation state. The students' comments reflect their emphasis on differentiating between those they saw as 'true' nations and the nature people or nature nations (Jóhannesson 2003).

Multiculturalism in Iceland and the Colonial Past

My discussion moves now toward looking at the 'political life of imperial debris' in the present, as phrased by Laura Ann Stoler (2008: 193), to focus on how the ideas of exceptionalism are expressed in contemporary Iceland. Icelandic society is characterized by accelerating global participation, even though it was certainly a part of an interconnected world in early the nineteenth century as I indicated in the previous discussion. Increased global participation took place in the mid-1990s, especially in the wake of Iceland's enrolment in the European Economic Area in 1994 and the Schengen area in 2001. Increased international engagement has both been expressed in higher numbers of immigrants in Iceland, and in more involvement of Icelanders in international affairs, for example in international development and peacekeeping, even though the engagements were greatly diminished after the economic crash in 2008. The number of foreign nationals rose from 1.8 per cent of the population in 1995 to more than 8 per cent in 2009 (Statistics Iceland 2009). Even though the plurality of the country has probably been underestimated in the past, the increased number of immigrants has caused a significant change in the small and relatively homogeneous population. Issues relating to increased 'multiculturalism' of Iceland were growing points of public discussions due to increased visibility of immigrants in Iceland but discourses in other European countries have probably also stimulated such discussions Iceland (Skaptadóttir and Loftsdóttir 2009: 211). Some public discussions about multiculturalism celebrate cultural plurality in Iceland while others express concern over the effects on Icelandic culture and society (Skaptadóttir and Loftsdóttir 2009). Parts of these discussions are similar to debates in other countries, for example the concern over the Muslim presence (Loftsdóttir 2011, 2012), which is startling given Iceland's quite different immigration history. Hence to take one obvious example, extensive immigration started much later in Iceland than in other Nordic countries. These discourses are multilayered and often contradictory but what I want to try to tease out here is how they involve certain reconfigurations of the past where Iceland is exempted from the general history of racism and simultaneously places Icelanders firmly as belonging in the category 'white' and 'Western'. I take two examples from very different directions: one has to do with public debate in regard to republication of a racist nursery rhyme in Iceland, and the other revolves around governmental discourse of Iceland's engagement with the outside world.

The republication of the children's nursery rhyme 'Ten little negroes' (called *Negrastrákarnir* or the Negroboys in Icelandic) in 2007 (it was originally published in 1922) can be seen as reflecting notions of whiteness but the republication was followed by one of the most heated debates about multiculturalism in Iceland, making it an particularly interesting phenomenon for gaining a deeper understanding of racial conceptions in Iceland. Over a short period, different forms of media were filled with people telling their opinions about the republication, some claiming that this book should not have been republished due to its racist images while others objected to the very claim that there was racism in the book. Many of those claims that defended the republication of the rhyme stressed the uniqueness of Iceland in relation to racism, claiming that in an Icelandic context the book could not been racist; that is, they saw the book as an important part of Icelandic heritage which was not racist and by association the book could not be racist (Loftsdóttir 2011). In an example from a blog discussion the book is positioned as alien and thus racist and as due to its racist character it should not be seen as a part of an Icelandic tradition:

> it is a misunderstanding that the Icelandic version of this infamous children book is made milder or changed in some way from the foreign text [of the same book] and by that made Icelandic and without racism ... So there is nothing Icelandic about this text and it is not a part of our cultural heritage, we were not oppressing dark skinned people during this period.[3]

Unlike many others who saw the book as emerging from an Icelandic 'culture', this writer sees the book as non-Icelandic. He still reaches the same conclusion; that Iceland has nothing to do with racism. The wilful separation of the republication from racism and colonialism was also secured by other less direct means, thus making the links between Iceland and racism either invisible or irrelevant. This is reflected in claims that it was just a 'coincidence' that the characters in the book were 'black', and there was nothing racist about the book as such. Another person wrote when commenting on one blog page where the republication of the book was debated:

> That's why, from my point of view, it is not an attack on anyone when a children's book is published about blacks, whites, clumsy people, redheads, dwarfs or whatever we all are. On the whole this spreads out pretty evenly and

---

3 það er misskilningur að íslenska útgáfan af hinni alræmdri barnabók 'sé á einhvern hátt milduð eða breytt frá erlendum texta og þannig gerð íslensk og án kynþáttahyggju. (::: Þannig að það er ekkert íslenskt við þetta ritverk og það er enginn hluti af okkar menningararfi enda vorum við ekki að kúga hörundsdökkt fólk á þessum tíma' (comment við: htt://eyjan.is/silfuregills/2007/10/31/um-fordoma-og-fleira/).

I actually think that it is most degrading to white people when we are looking at books about clumsiness or stupidity. Does anyone want to ban the book about Clumsy Hans?[4]

The social classification of blackness is positioned as any other classification and thus safely removed from any uncomfortable association with racism and historical and present stereotypes of blackness where people are reduced to nothing but a colour term. As Ruth Frankenberg (1993) pointed out in her monumental study of whiteness in the USA, there is a tendency to engage with racism in a way that when it is mentioned it is simultaneously diminished by conflating race with multiple colours (149). Thus, socially meaningful categorization of colour is reduced into 'meaningless one' (Frankenberg 149). Racism itself is similarly in the quotation above reduced to prejudice that can be directed against any physical markers, and thus removed from any historical contextualization. Such ideas can also be seen expressed in statements that see 'blackness' similarly as a blank natural fact, again completely removing the book and the social classification from racism:

> ... of course the pictures in the books are of black boys. What is so dangerous about children knowing that all people don't have the same color? Most people from Africa are black and when this story was written black people were called negroes and they still are. There are no white negroes and thus the illustrations in the book are of black children.[5]

The author is possibly trying to be funny when speaking of 'white negroes' but his point is still to reposition the book as having nothing to do with racism by focusing on 'blackness' as blank signifier and a natural fact. Critique of racism is thus seen as an unnecessary exercise. As Anna Rastas has pointed out, when individuals are confronted with racial categorization, they 'negotiate their positioning in racialized social relations' (2005: 148). These statements and others defending the book can also be seen to be embedded in underlying notions of whiteness, because by seeing the book as non-racist in Icelandic context, a secure space of whiteness is created which has no connection to racism. These links with whiteness are even more intensified by the lack of engagement by those entering the debate in regard

---

4   Þessvegna er, að mínu viti enginn árás á einn eða neinn, þótt gefin sé út barnabók um svarta, hvíta, klaufa, rauðhærða, dverga og hvernig við nú erum öll. Þetta dreifist á heildina nokkuð jafnt og reyndar held ég að mest sé gert lítið úr hvíti fólki þegar kemur að bókum um klaufaskap eða heimsku. Vill einhver banna bókina um Hans klaufa? (http://skessa.blog.is/blog/skessa /entry/349598/, comment við færsluna endalaus pirringur hugsandi flóns).

5   '... auðvitað eru myndirnar í bókinni af svörtum strákum. Hvað er hættulegt við það að börn viti að allt fók er ekki eins á litinn? Flest allt fólk frá Afríku er svart og á þeim tíma sem sagna er skrifuð var svart fók kallað negrar og er svo enn í dag. Það eru ekki til hvítir negrar og þess vegna eru myndirnar í bókinn af svörtum börnum.' (http://jakobk.blog.is/blog/jakobk/entry/349984/ færslan Tíu litlir negrastrákar).

to their own racialized identity. Some of the comments defending the republication refer to their individual intentions and perception of the book or to the collective *'we'* which I assume from the content refers to 'white' and even to Icelanders assumed to be all white. As this entry at a blog page reflects 'we' would not be offended if this book was about 'white' people: 'This is a children's book which is meant for fun. It could just as well be ten little "pink noses". *We* would laugh at it ...'[6] (my emphasis in the text). Closely linked are personal statements where it is claimed that 'I' have decided not to see this book as racist or that this book did not make 'me' prejudiced. Again, it is not possible to state with certainty the skin colour of those writing but from the content it is often clear that they see themselves as white. The simplification of racism to a personal intention of the speaker, is as Jane Hill (2007) has pointed out, a common theme in racial talk in the USA (Hill 2007: 80–91). This reduction of racism to personal intentions ignores, furthermore, the structural aspects of racism as beyond thoughts and intentions of individuals (Blauner 1992).

Claims about Iceland's exceptionalism in relation to racism and colonialism have, however, not only been limited to public discussions of multicultural Iceland. It can also be seen in governmental discourses as expressed in the words of key public persons representing the government. Discourse surrounding the application of Iceland for a seat in the UN Security Council for the period 2009–10 interestingly reflects similar notions of Icelandic exceptionalism. The Icelandic government did not place strong emphasis on direct involvement in international institutions until the mid 1990s (Þórhallsson 2006), where there was much more interest in more global engagement for example expressed in the growth in allocation of resources to Iceland's participation in international development. In justifying the application a strong emphasis was placed on the role that Iceland had to play internationally. The Minister of Foreign Affairs in 2007 stated, for example, in relation to the application that: 'It is unique in the West that a country as wealthy as Iceland does not want to take responsibility'[13] (Gísladóttir 2007). Interestingly, the application for the Security Council seat was often referred to in official speeches by key public figures, who connected the application to Iceland's status as an independent country and as a former colony. The president of Iceland and the Minister of Foreign Affairs said that the seat in the council was the last step in the country's independence (RUV 2008; Gísladóttir 2007). The president of Iceland said for example:

> Although Iceland was once the poorest country in Europe, a colony without economic or political rights, my nation has succeeded within the lifetime of one generation in achieving the highest standard in the world. (Grímsson 2007)

---

6   Þetta er barnabók sem ætluð er til skemmtunar. Þetta gæti allt eins verið tíu litlir bleiknefjar. Við mundum hlægja af því ... http://oliha.blog.is/blog/oliha/entry/348454/).

He continued to state that this could make Icelanders better suited to understand the situation of other colonized countries, presenting Iceland as the 'only European country, which can sympathize in the light of its own experience with the fate of Africa' (Grímsson 2007). This interplay of reference to Iceland's independence through participation in the UN Security Council and its unique role in assisting other colonized people to gain prosperity, moves between boundary maintenance of 'us' and 'others' but also to some extent the blurring of those boundaries. By acknowledging that 'we' once were a colony, the affinity with the racialized 'others' is acknowledged, but simultaneously it serves to absolve Iceland from any share in colonialism as a producer of it, positioning the country firmly as a non-participant in European racism and colonialism. By highlighting the connection of the application to the country's independence and its moral duty toward others less fortunate, Iceland positioned itself squarely in the camp of the civilized *and consequently* more prosperous countries in the world.

As in the case of the republishing of the Negro boys rhyme, the example from the world of international politics can also be seen as reflecting very clearly the persistent notion of Iceland as existing outside colonialism and imperialism in the past, simultaneously as belonging with the 'white' and 'civilized' Europeans that have moral duty toward those less fortunate.

Discussion and Final Points

In my discussion here, I have used belonging as a way to draw out the particularities of Icelandic exceptionalism. Icelanders did not only construct exotic notions of 'others' but seemed often more concerned with creating through these notions a sense of belonging with those nations seen as masculine, white and civilized in the late nineteenth and early twentieth century. As Nira Yuval-Davis (2006) points out, belonging becomes particularly 'articulated and politicized only when it is threatened in some way' (Yuval-Davis 2006: 197), which was especially pronounced in relation to the Danish colonial exhibition. However, this sense of belonging can be seen as lingering as well within present discussions of Iceland's engagement with the outside world. Icelandic exceptionalism is multilayered, constituted by several overlapping discourses. One of them is that Iceland had nothing to with colonialism and thus is also exempted from the legacy of racism. Such claims are not innocent but indicate a failure of many Icelanders to critically engage with the privileges historically associated with being classified as 'white'. The particular expression of Icelandic exceptionalism that I have mostly focused on here, which stresses the geographically insular nature of Icelanders, continues to be recreated and shaped in different contexts. It emphasizes Icelanders as unique and different from everyone else, overlapping with the view that Iceland, as the other Nordic countries, had nothing to do with colonialism.

References

Barth, Fredrik. 1969. Introduction, in *Ethnic Groups and Boundaries: The Social Organization of Culture Difference*, edited by Fredrik Barth. Boston: Little, Brown and Company.

Benediktsson, J. 1971. Formáli. Íslandslýsing: *Qualiscunque descriptio Islandiae. Sveinn Pálsson sneri á íslenzku*, edited by Oddur Einarsson. Reykjavík: Bókaútgáfa Menningarsjóðs.

Björnsdóttir, Inga Dóra. 1994. 'Þeir áttu sér móður': Kvenkenndir þættir í mótun íslenskrar þjóðernisvitundar, in *Fléttur: Rit Rannsóknastofu í kvennafræðum*, edited by R. Richter and Þ. Sigurðardótti. Reykjavík, Háskóli Íslands: Háskólaútgáfan, 65–85.

Blauner, B. 1992. Talking past Each Other: Black and White Languages of Race. *The American Prospect*, 10, 55–64.

Brydon, Ann. 1995. Inscriptions of Self: The Construction of Icelandic Landscape in Nineteenth-Century British Travel Writings. *Ethnos*, 60(3–4), 243–63.

Dirks, N.B. 1992. Introduction: Colonialism and culture, in *Colonialism and Culture*, edited by B. Dirks. Ann Arbor: University of Michigan Press, 1–25.

Durrenberger, P. and Pálsson, G. 1989. Introduction, in *The Anthropology of Iceland*, edited by P. Durrenberger and G. Pálsson. Iowa: University of Iowa Press, ix–xxvii.

Finsen, Vilhjálmur. 1958 *Hvað landinn sagði erlendis*. Akureyri: Norðri.

Fjallkonan, 13 December 1904, 199.

Franey, L.E. 2003. *Victorian Travel Writing and Imperial Violence: British Travel Writing on Africa, 1855–1902*. New York: Palgrave Macmillan.

Frankenberg, R., 1993. *White Women, Race Matters: The Social Construction of Whiteness*. Minneapolis, University of Minnesota Press.

Freiesleben, B. 1998. *Fra St Croix til Tivoli: En historisk beretning om to vestindisk børns lange rejse*. Ballerup: Acer.

Gilroy, P. 1993. *The Black Atlantic: Modernity and Double Consciousness*. London, New York: Verso.

Gísladóttir, I.S. 2007. Ræða Ingibjargar Sólrúnar Gísladóttur, utanríkisráðherra, um utanríkismál. [Online]. Available from: http://www.utanrikisraduneyti.is/frettaefni/raedurISG/nr/3960 [accessed: 5 October 2010].

Grímsson, Ó.R. 2007. Útrásin: Uppruni – einkenni – framtíðarsýn. Public presentation for the Sagnfræðingafélagið, 10 January 2006. [Online]. Available from: http://forseti.is/media/files/06.01.10.Sagnfrfel.pdf [accessed: 17 December 2007].

Hálfdánarson, G. 2000. Iceland: A Peaceful Secession. *Scandinavian Journal of History*, 25(1–2), 87–100.

Hartigan, J. Jr. 1997. Establishing the Fact of Whiteness. *American Anthropologist*, 99(3), 495–505.

Hill, J. 2007. Language, Race and White Public Space. *American Anthropologist*, 100(3), 680–89.

Ísleifsson, S.R. 1996. Ísland: Framandi land. Reykjavík: Mál og menning.
Jacobson, M. 1998. Whiteness of a Different Color: European Immigration and the Alchemy of Race. Harvard: Harvard University Press.
Jensen, L. 2005. De danske tropekolonier og den nationale forankring [Danish Colonies and Nationalism], in På sporet af imperiet: Danske tropefantasier [Tracking Down the Empire: Danish Fantasies], edited by L.B. Christiansen, L. Jensen, P.K. Johansen, S. Kok and K.H. Petersen. Roskilde: Institute for Sprog og Kultur, 65–77.
Jóhannesson, Jón Yngvi. 2003. Af reiðum Íslendingum: Deilur um Nýlendusýninguna 1905, in Þjóðerni í þúsund ár?, edited by J.Y. Jóhannsson, K.Ó. Proppé and S. Jakobsson. Reykjavík: Háskólaútgáfan.
Jónsson Aðils, Jón. 1903. Íslenzkt þjóðerni. Reykjavík: Sigurður Kristinsson.
Jörgensen, C. 1996. Köbenhavn för og nu – og aldrig. Bind 15. Vest fro Raduhuspladsen. Cöbenhavn: Fogtdal.
Karlsson, G. 1995. The Emergence of Nationalism in Iceland, in Ethnicity and Nation Building in the Nordic World, edited by S. Tägil. Carbondale and Edwardsville: Southern Illinois University Press, 33–62.
Keskinen, S., Irni, S., Mulinari, D. and Tuori, S. (eds). 2009. Complying with Colonialism. Burlington, VT: Ashgate.
Lagerspetz, M. 2003. How Many Nordic Countries?: Possibilities and Limits of Geopolitical Identity Construction. Cooperation and Conflict: Journal of the Nordic International Studies Association, 38(1), 49–61.
Líndal, S. 1969. Hið Íslenzka Bókmenntafélag – Söguágrip. Reykjavík: Hið Íslenzka Bókmenntafélag.
Loftsdóttir, K. 2008. Shades of Otherness: Representations of Africa in 19th-Century Iceland. Social Anthropology, 16(2), 172–86.
Loftsdóttir, K. 2009. 'Pure Manliness': The Colonial Project and Africa's Image in Nineteenth Century Iceland. Identities: Global Studies in Culture and Power, 16(3), 271–93.
Loftsdóttir, K. 2010. Encountering Others in the Icelandic Schoolbooks: Images of Imperialism and Racial Diversity in the Nineteenth Century, in Opening the Mind or Drawing Boundaries? History Texts in Nordic Schools, edited by Þ. Helgason and S. Lässig. Göttingen: Vandenhoeck & Ruprecht UniPress, 81–105.
Loftsdóttir, K. 2011. 'Racist Caricatures in Iceland in the 19th and the 20th Century', in Iceland and Images of the North, edited by S.R. Ísleifsson. Québec: Prologue Inc, 187–204.
Loftsdóttir, K. 2012. Whiteness is from Another World: Gender, Icelandic International Development and Multiculturalism. European Journal of Women's Studies, 19(1), 41–54.
McClintock, A. 1995. Imperial Leather: Race, Gender, and Sexuality in the Colonial Contest. New York: Routledge.
Nakayama, T.K. and Krizek, R.L. 1995. Whiteness: A Strategic Rhetoric. Quarterly Journal of Speech, 81, 291–309.

Oslund, K. 2002. Imagining Iceland: Narratives of Nature and History in the North Atlantic. *The British Journal for the History of Science*, 35, 313–34.
Oxfeldt, Elisabeth. 2005. *Nordic Orientalism: Paris and the Cosmopolitian Imagination 1800–1900*. Copenhagen: Museum Tusculanum Press.
Pálsson, H. 1978. *Straumar og stefnur í íslenskum bókmenntum frá 1550*. Reykjavík: Iðunn.
Pratt, Mary Louise. 1992. *Imperial Eyes: Travel Writing and Transculturation*. London and New York: Routledge.
Rastas, A. 2005. Racializing Categorization Among Young People in Finland. *Young*, 13(2): 147–166.
RUV (2008, 12 Mars). Morgunvaktin, interview by Sveinn Helgason with Ólafur Ragnar Grímsson. *Ríkisútvarpið*. [Online]. Available at: http://www.ruv.is/heim/frettir/frett/store64/item196388/ [accessed: 20 May 2009].
Said, E.W. 1978. *Orientalism*. New York: Vintage Books.
Sigurðsson, G. 1996. Icelandic National Identity: From Romanticism to Tourism, in *Making Europe in Nordic Contexts*, edited by P.J. Anttonen. Nordic Institute of Folklore: University of Turku, 41–75.
Sigurðsson, I. 1986. *Íslensk sagnfræði frá miðri 19. öld til miðrar 20. aldar*. Reykjavík: Sagnfræðistofnun Háskóla Íslands.
Skaptadóttir, U.D. and Loftsdóttir, K. 2009. Cultivating Culture? Images of Iceland, Globalization and Multicultural Society, in *Images of the North*, edited by S. Jakobsson. Reykjavík: Reykjavíkur Akademía, 201–12.
Smith, A. 2003. Introduction: Europe's Invisible Migrants, in *Europe's Invisible Migrants*, edited by A. Smith. Amsterdam: Amsterdam University Press, 9–31.
Statistical Series. 2009. Immigrants and Persons with Foreign Background 1996–2008. *Statistical Series*, 9(4), 1–24. [Online]. Available at: http://www.statice.is/Pages/452?itemid=7c416da9–3596–4dd3–93c9-e07ba2ed2886 [accessed: 20 June 2009].
Stoler, L.A. 1992. Rethinking Colonial Categories: European Communities and the Boundaries of Rule. In *Colonialism and Culture*, edited by N.B. Dirks. Ann Arbor, Michigan: University of Michigan Press, 319–52.
Stoler, L.A. 2008. Imperial Debris: Reflections on Ruin and Ruination. *Cultural Anthropology*, 23(2), 191–219.
Sveinsson, G. 1904. Sýning í Kaupmannahöfn frá hjáleigum Danaveldis. Íslandi stórhætta búinn. *Fjallkonan*, 16 December, no 50, 197–8.
Sveinsson, K. 1994. Viðhorf Íslendinga til Grænlands á 18. 19., og 20. öld. *Saga*, 159–210.
Þórhallsson, Baldur. 2006. Iceland's Involvement in Global Affairs since the mid 1990s: What Features Determine the Size of a State. *Stjórnmál og stjórnsýsla*, 2(2), 197–223.
Thoroddsen, Þorvaldur. 1898. *Landfræðissaga Íslands: Hugmyndir manna um Ísland, náttúrskoðun og rannsóknir, fyrr og síðar*. Kaupmannahöfn: S.L. Möller.

Þorsteinsson, Þorsteinn J. 1940. *Saga Íslendinga í Vesturheimi*. vol. I. Reykjavík: Þjóðræknisfélag Íslendinga í Vesturheimi.
Yuval-Davis, N. 1997. *Gender and Nation*. London: Sage Publications.
Yuval-Davis, N. 2006. Belonging and the Politics of Belonging. *Patterns of Prejudice*, 40(3), 197–214.

Chapter 5
Transnational Influences, Gender Equality and Violence in Muslim Families

Suvi Keskinen

In recent years public debates about social control and gendered violence in ethnic minority families, for example forced marriages, honour-related violence and female genital cutting, have flourished in several European countries (for example, Korteweg and Yurdakul 2009; Phillips and Saharso 2008; Teigen and Langvasbråten 2009). The Nordic countries are no exception to this trend. In fact, they seem overtly preoccupied with such questions (Keskinen 2009a). Debates about gendered violence in minority families have also played a central role in the politics of immigration and multiculturalism, providing arguments for those who want to reduce immigration and demand assimilation of especially non-Western and Muslim immigrants. Gendered violence has continuously featured in the public discussions that focus on the problematic effects of multiculturalism and its perceived role in promoting segregation, terrorism and 'illiberal' life styles (Grillo 2007; Vertovec and Wessendorf 2010). While demands on migrants to integrate better and to adopt the 'national values' of the country of settlement have been on the agenda of the right-wing populist parties for long, the rhetoric has more recently spread throughout the political field, and is now routinely used in political debates and the media (Hervik 2006; Joppke 2010, 137–42; Lentin and Titley 2011).

In the debates, issues like honour-related violence are often used to exemplify and (re)produce dichotomous divisions between the (allegedly) 'gender equal majorities' and the 'patriarchal immigrants' (Andreassen 2005; Bredström 2003; de los Reyes, Molina and Mulinari 2002). In such constructions, colonial imaginaries and representations are re-evoked and adapted to current societal settings and postcolonial migrations. The Nordic countries construct their national self-images on a perceived record as world champions in gender equality (Keskinen et al. 2009; Magnusson, Rönnblom and Silius 2008). In the postcolonial setting, gender equality has become a marker of difference that is used to construct divisions between those presented as the modern, civilized Nordic people and those described as pre-modern and tradition-bound, notably migrants from Middle Eastern and African countries.

This chapter analyses public discussions about Muslim girls and families in the Finnish media during summer 2010, triggered by two best-selling novels. I examine how violence in Muslim families was discussed in Finnish media and how colonial legacies are embedded in the representations that circulated in the public sphere. I argue that these public discussions represent a process of adopting, rearticulating and domesticating discourses of the Muslim 'other' from the more centrally located areas in postcolonial Europe. Participating in the multicultural problematics becomes a sign of belonging to the West and having achieved an unquestionable position among the modern European nations. I also show how the dichotomous divisions based on gender equality characterize the discussions, even though some debaters wish to question such understandings. However, the presence of the postcolonial 'others' in the discussions provides possibilities for criticism of such othering representations.

The studied books, *Parvekejumalat* (*Balcony gods*) and *Minne tytöt kadonneet?* (*Where have all the young girls gone?*), focus on young Muslim women who are controlled and treated violently by their family members, but also highlight the responses of the Finnish society and its authorities to violence and ethnic/racial differences. The authors, Anja Snellman and Leena Lehtolainen, are the two most famous and successful feminist novelists in Finland. They have both published around 20 books, focusing usually on timely topics related to gender and sexuality. Having been listed among the most popular Finnish novelists for two decades, it was no surprise that the authors gained broad publicity for their new books. The books also sold well: in the list of most sold Finnish novels in 2010 *Minne tytöt kadonneet* came seventh (with 35,100 copies), while *Parvekejumalat* came ninth (with 25,000 copies).[1]

Immigration Debates in Finland

Finland has a history of being a border zone between the East and the West (Lehtonen, Löytty and Ruuska 2004). For centuries Finland was under Swedish rule until it became a grand duchy of Russia in 1809, before gaining independence in 1917. After the Second World War, the country has shifted between liaisons to the East, notably Soviet Union/Russia, and to the West, represented especially by Sweden and the other Nordic countries and, more recently, the European Union. Having been an emigration country, with large-scale emigration to Sweden in the 1960s and 1970s, Finland has experienced growing immigration rates since the beginning of the 1990s. Nevertheless, the share of foreign-born population is still relatively small: in 2009, inhabitants whose native language was other than Finnish, Swedish or Sámi constituted 3.9 per cent of the total population.[2] The

---

1 Otava on ykkönen, Teos nousee. Helsingin Sanomat 27 January 2011, C1.
2 Statistics Finland. [Online]. Available at: http://www.stat.fi/til/vaerak/2009/vaerak_2009_2010-03-19_tie_001_en.html [accessed: 10 January 2012].

largest migrant communities are the Russians, Estonians, Swedes and Somalis, followed by the Iraqis, Iranians and ex-Yugoslavians.[3]

The discussions the two studied books raised must be understood in relation to the changing political climate and intensifying debates about immigration in the last few years in Finland. Until autumn 2008 questions related to immigration and multiculturalism were rather marginal issues in Finnish politics. They were discussed in public mainly by authorities and responsible ministers, less so by other politicians, NGOs or immigrants themselves (Raittila 2002; Raittila 2009, 70–71). In the political field there was a widely accepted consensus about a strict refugee policy, especially in relation to asylum seekers, but also a discourse with growing support for the need for work-related immigration.

However, in the municipal elections in October 2008 the radical right populist party, the True Finns, enjoyed a clearly growing support and in several municipalities, elected candidates included individuals with an anti-immigration agenda (Keskinen 2009b). Many of these had found their support by blogging or taking actively part in Internet discussions. In the parliamentary elections in April 2011 the support for the True Finns grew considerably, resulting in a position as the third biggest party in the Parliament with 19 per cent of the vote.

Since the autumn of 2008, immigration has become a debated topic in the media and the political arena, giving public space also to anti-immigration activists and racist expressions. Anti-immigration arguments gained foothold not only amongst the True Finns, but also among politicians of other parties, notably the conservative National Coalition party and the Finnish Centre party. Even the Finnish Social Democratic party has argued for a policy of 'adopting the customs of the country where you live' (*maassa maan tavalla*) which has traditionally been connected only to nationalist and anti-immigration agendas and bears clear racist undertones. When the two books analysed in this chapter were published in 2010, immigration issues were intensively debated in media and politics. Although it might not have been the aim of the authors to take a stand in such debates, their books were read in this context and discussed in relation to the 'topical' nature of the issues.

Material and Methods

The empirical data consists of the two books, as well as reviews[4] and articles published about the books and the authors in Finnish newspapers and women's magazines between May and September 2010, altogether 27 items. Furthermore, I have collected advertisements for the books in newspapers. The data also includes

---

3 Migration Institute. [Online]. Available at: www.migrationinstitute.fi/db/stat/img/ef_06.jpg [accessed: 3 July 2009].

4 Most book reviews have been found through an internet site Kritiikkiportti (www.kritiikkiportti.fi) that collects reviews published in newspapers and magazines.

interviews with the author of *Parvekejumalat*, Anja Snellman, in a literary TV programme[5] and on the Internet, as well as Internet discussions[6] concerning the books on two websites, *Kaksplus.fi* and *Hommaforum*. The website *Kaksplus.fi* is established by a magazine for families with small children, thus it mainly functions as a forum for young mothers to discuss issues related to children, family life and partnership. *Hommaforum* is a website that connects Finnish anti-immigration activists for whom the Internet is a central form of organizing and promoting their political agenda. The Internet discussions have been used to highlight how the books were read and interpreted by (parts of) the audience.

In the analysis I have focused on how gender, race and ethnicity are (co-) constructed in the texts, drawing on narrative analysis (Lacey 2000; Lothe 2000) and discourse analysis (Jørgensen and Phillips 2002; Wetherell, Taylor and Yates 2001). The narrative approach, designed to analyse stories, has influenced my reading of the two books. I have focused on the description of the main characters and settings, the presentation of central events and their connections, as well as the main themes and metaphors in the texts. The analysis of the media discussions has detected how gender, migrant families, Islam and Finnishness are described in the texts; who are the speakers and how are they presented in the texts; and what kind of distinctions and hierarchies are the descriptions based on.

Othering Narratives and Racial Hierarchies

Both novels build on the narrative of a Muslim girl being treated violently by her family. *Minne tytöt kadonneet?* is a detective novel that follows the investigation of a murder of one Muslim girl and the disappearances of three other Muslim girls. The girls are found to be victims of honour-related violence. *Parvekejumalat* tells the story of a Finnish-Somali girl who is beaten and finally thrown over the balcony by her father and brothers, because of a sexual relationship with a white Finnish boy. The information about the forbidden relationship is disclosed by another young Muslim woman, a white Finnish convert.

The main character of *Parvekejumalat*, the 15-year-old Somali-born Anis, wants to live the life of a Finnish/Western teenager. That includes, for example, going to a Madonna concert, engaging in environmental activism, using make-up and falling in love with a white Finnish boy. The narrative thus presents white Westerners and their way of life as the norm for 'others' to follow and to be evaluated against (Mohanty 2003: 53). In the book, the promises of the white Western life are posed in strong contrast to the authoritarian, closed and fundamentalist circles of Anis's family, notably the father, but also the surrounding Somali community.

---

5   *Ykkösen aamutv: Aamun kirja* 11 November 2010. [Online]. Available at: http://areena.yle.fi/video/1435344 [accessed: 29 April 2011].

6   The internet discussions were located while searching for information about the books in the internet.

A large part of the book is devoted to following Anis's brave but tragic struggle between these two polarized positions. She is presented as the heroic victim, oppressed by her family and religion but at the same time struggling to be part of 'us', the white Westerners, and thus worthy of the sympathy of white readers (cf. Keskinen 2009a). The description of Anis's family and the Somali community is characterized by several kinds of violence (both female genital cutting and honour killing), demands of women's subordination and strict control by brothers and other male members of the community. The portrayal of Anis's family and the situation of Somali women is so negative and full of oppression that at times it feels like the text turns into a grotesque parody. For example, when Anis has been pushed down from the balcony and lies in the hospital a Somali nurse sneaks in and conducts the genital cutting Anis has managed to escape earlier.

So far the book can be said to follow a dichotomous, othering representation (Said 1995) of Muslim and Somali lives. However, the author connects this narrative with one of a young Muslim convert, a white Finnish woman, thereby introducing a more complex set of themes. Alla-Zahra, the other main character in the book, has grown up in a bohemian, extremely liberal artist family where she has lacked both attention and discipline by her parents. She has been an anarchist environmental activist and a victim of gang rape by skinheads. Her mutilated body finds rest and freedom in the cover of the Muslim dress and headscarf. Through the story of Alla-Zahra the author shows that women's oppression and gendered violence is not restricted to Muslims, but crosses ethnic, racial and religious borders. Nevertheless, the violence Alla-Zahra has experienced is not given much space in the narrative and the neglect of her family can by no means be compared with the oppression that characterizes the Somali family and community in the text. Alla-Zahra is a devoted, bordering on fanatic, Muslim who organizes meetings for those interested in converting to Islam. She has fallen in love with the same boy as Anis, and the events leading to the tragic death of Anis are initiated by Alla-Zahra who informs Anis's father about the secret intimate relationship. The converted Muslim is thus the ultimate 'traitor' that allies herself with the patriarchal men.

In the book, Anis becomes friends with Alla-Zahra's younger sister and mother. This white woman eventually becomes the trusted person and the 'real' mother of Anis – in the sense that she listens to, cares and understands Anis in a way that her biological mother never has, nor has Alla-Zahra ever received such love from her mother.[7] The way that these relations are described in the book further emphasizes that hope and support can only be found in the white Finnish family and society, not in the Muslim.

The balcony as a metaphor has a central role in the book, as can be seen in the title that translates into 'balcony gods'. The balcony refers to the place where one wishes to show oneself to others or, as is the case with the described Somali family, wishes to block out the outer world with heavy curtains in front of the window. It is both the place where Anis can feel the free wind blowing in her hair

---

7   This is a theme that the author Anja Snellman herself refers to in the TV interview.

and where her father can set up the satellite television – a symbol of the 'parallel societies' that migrant neighbourhoods are claimed to stand for in the critique of multiculturalism circulating in the European societies (Grillo 2007). The balcony is the place where the gods of different religions watch and discuss people's lives. And finally it is the place where Anis faces her death.

Minne tytöt kadonneet?, which translates as 'where have all the young girls gone' refers to the well-known anti-war song from the 1960s. The female police chief, Maria Kallio, familiar to many readers from previous novels, tries to solve a homicide and disappearances of Muslim girls with her team. The book follows the genre conventions of detective novels, thus the narrative structure is simple. There are less allegories and open-ended threads to hint towards different interpretative options. Several of the disappearances are discovered to be murders by the men in the girls' families. What makes the book different from *Parvekejumalat*, and from most public discussions about the topic, is that the author links this to the question of racism. The plot can be considered somewhat clumsy and unconvincing because the end solution frames the murders as a plot by racist groups who have 'provoked' the fathers and brothers to kill the young Muslim women. This choice, however, enables the author to discuss racist activities and anti-immigration debates on the Internet in a way that differs radically from *Parvekejumalat*. In *Minne tytöt kadonneet?* the murders of the young Muslim women are used to highlight the Finnish society with a focus on its racial hierarchies, rather than simply describe the power relations among the racialized 'others'. As the name suggests, the book signals an anti-violence agenda and raises the topics of gender and race simultaneously. It is narrated from the perspective of the white female/ feminist police chief, featuring her as the main figure, in contrast to *Parvekejumalat* which tells the story from the perspective of the young Muslim women, especially through the voice of the Somalian Anis.

Transnational Influences and the Symbolism of the Veil

The books and the public discussions they raised, in many ways cite broader European and Western discourses about gender, sexuality and Islam. The narratives of victimized Muslim girls, described in the previous section, closely resemble those to be found in books, newspapers and TV programmes in other European countries (for example, Andreassen 2005; Korteweg and Yurdakul 2009). Furthermore, several European countries, among those France, Denmark and Belgium (for example, Scott 2007; Kilic et al. 2008), have recently introduced legislation to prohibit the wearing of headscarves or full coverage, or are considering this possibility. These events evoke and rearticulate in different ways the multiple meanings and symbolism that the veil carries from its (post)colonial histories. In the West, the veil has been presented a marker of profound differences, for example when signifying oppression of Muslim women, but also a symbol of fascination and desire towards the 'other' (Macdonald 2006; Young 2003, 80–85).

The veil also has a long history as a symbol of resistance to colonial powers and many studies on the current use of the Muslim headscarf in Europe show that it signals self-proclaimed identities and resistance (for example, Afshar, Aitken and Franks 2005; Woodhull 2003).

The placement of the veil (*Parvekejumalat*) or a veiled woman (*Minne tytöt kadonneet?*) on the covers of the books strongly suggests that the headscarf is the central symbol for the reading and interpretation of the texts (see Figures 5.1 and 5.2).

Figure 5.1

The cover of *Parvekejumalat* shows a veil waving in the air – opening up for interpretations ranging from the blowing of the free wind to the fatal fall from the balcony. The cover of *Minne tytöt kadonneet?*, on the other hand, contrasts the image of the 'other' woman with the Finnish coat of arms, a nationalist symbol that is also used in the extreme-right iconography. Thus, it introduces differences not only in the form of patriarchal oppression among the racialized 'others', but also produced by nationalist and racist groups in the Finnish society.

Figure 5.2

My reading of the books and their reception in the media emphasizes the view that they represent an adoption and rearticulation of the discourses and narratives about the veiled and oppressed Muslim women widely circulating in the other Western countries. However, at the same time they negotiate how such discourses and imageries can be adapted to the Finnish context. It is a process in which discourses, featuring victimized Muslim girls and violence by family members, are 'domesticated' in a country like Finland, with a relatively low immigrant and Muslim population and a recent migration history in relation to migrants from non-Western countries. Although the biggest migrant groups in Finland are the Russians and Estonians, the focus of the immigration debates has been on the asylum seekers and refugees especially from Somalia and Middle Eastern countries, and the narrative of the oppressed Muslim women fits particularly well to this context.

The figure of the violently treated and mutilated Muslim woman is well known from books by Ayaan Hirsi Ali (*Infidel*), Waris Dirie (*Desert Flower*) and numerous others. One could say that there is a whole literary industry focusing on such topics. While many works of this genre are (auto)biographical texts, there are also more literary orientated texts, such as *A Thousand Suns* by Khaled Hosseini.

The two books analysed in this article can be seen as building on and partly citing this tradition, but in a subtle and creative way that introduces a variation of themes.

The transnational influences and the porous borders that allow cultural elements (discourses, narratives, imageries) to travel from one country to another are visible for example in the closure of *Parvekejumalat*, which culminates with the fall from the balcony. This ending hints at the murders of young women in Sweden where the families are suspected of having thrown the girls off the balcony and framed the cases as accidents. No similar cases have been detected, or even suspected, in Finland. The reference is clearly to the Swedish events, which reflects the centrality of the Swedish discourses to the discussions about honour-related violence in Finland. The discourse of honour-related violence arrived in Finland in the aftermath of the murder of Fadime Sahindal, a young Kurdish-Swedish woman who was killed by her father in Sweden in 2002 (Keskinen 2009a). Therefore the ways of conceptualizing and making sense of such violent acts to a large extent follow the Swedish formulations that emphasize cultural explanations of violence. As a result of this genealogy, public discussions in Finland often introduce the extreme form of violence, honour killing, although agencies working with such issues point out that adolescents mainly experience control, coercion and non-lethal violence. The media constantly raises the question whether there have been honour killings in Finland, implying that this is the main issue of concern in relation to violence in migrant families.

Also the book reviews and articles about the books refer to the experiences of other countries, for example when writing about the honour killings that have taken place in Sweden. The book reviews also refer to Finland's position as a follower of other European countries in relation to multicultural issues: 'Now when we would finally need a melting pot of nationalities in Finland too, we can't find one. It hasn't been invented yet' (*Helsingin Sanomat* 10 June 2010). The review states that Finland has finally taken its place among the (Western) multicultural nations, but regards this situation as problem-filled and finds few solutions. Thus, it makes reference to the critical debates on multiculturalism common in the European context, linking Finland to these. The role of Sweden is central here as an intermediate, since in Finland Sweden is often used as an example of multicultural societies and policies in Europe.

Gender Equality and Muslim Girls 'Breaking Their Chains'

The dichotomy of the 'patriarchal' Muslim culture and the 'gender equal' Western culture is visible not only in the narratives of the mentioned books, but also in the public discussions and media coverage about them. In the book reviews and articles published in newspapers and magazines, the contrast between the two 'different' cultures and life styles is cited, commented on and, at times, questioned. However, it is the distinction that characterizes the discussion and the departing point for most debaters – even for many of those who wish to question it.

In the magazine articles, there are both descriptions of the 'patriarchal others' and attempts to engage in dialogue across ethnic and religious borders. The othering and dichotomous divisions are most visible in the headlines of the articles and the crystallizations picked from the text. The embedded assumptions of the oppressed Muslim women figure in titles like: 'Muslim girls break their chains' (*Iltasanomat* 28 August 2010, 30), 'The subordinated need to be defended' (*Seura* 12 August 2010, 12) and 'In support of a will of one's own' (*Me Naiset* 12 August 2010, 30). While the texts may introduce a more nuanced discussion of similarities and differences between what is described as the Finnish and migrant women/ cultures, the crystallizations that have been picked to highlight the text focus on extremities and (cultural and generational) difference: 'It was just my good luck that I was born in a country in which I won't be stoned to death' (*Seura* 12 August 2010, 14), 'In our culture we first marry and then fall in love' and 'I will not be the kind of wife my mother was' (*Me Naiset* 12 August 2010, 31). At times the texts also connect gendered violence to the ordinary: 'The detective novelist Leena Lehtolainen and the everyday life of a Muslim girl in Finland' (cover of *Me Naiset* 12 August 2010). Instead of emphasizing violence as a specific and more rarely occurring phenomenon, the title creates the idea that gendered violence is part of the everyday lives of Muslim families.

There is some space for a critical evaluation of the representations of Muslims in the books, but this is mainly restricted to media coverage in which the postcolonial 'others' are actively present. A few articles introduce dialogues between the white female authors and women who are addressed as Muslims or representatives of an ethnic minority. For example, the converted Isra Lehtinen and the Somali-born nurse Saido Mohamed are asked about their views on the representations of Muslim and Somalian life in *Parvekejumalat* of which both are highly critical (*Iltasanomat* 28 August 2010, 30). When the author of *Minne tytöt kadonneet?* is interviewed together with the Afghan born Nasima Razmyar, Refugee Woman of 2010, their dialogue touches upon unemployment, racism in the Finnish society and many other societal questions. The critical views are also given space in an interview with Saido Mohamed who questions the dichotomous divisions between Finnish and Somali violence, as well as the representation of Finnish Somalis with a clearly more critical title: 'The prejudices are only strengthened' (*Hufvudstadsbladet* 10 June 2010).

On the other hand, the dichotomous distinction between Finnish and Muslim ways of living is largely taken for granted in the book reviews and the interviews where the participants are all white ethnic Finns. Many reviews interpret the books as a description of a 'clash of cultures' (*Lapin Kansa* 19 August 2010; *Turun Ylioppilaslehti* 30 September 2010; *Etelä-Saimaa* 11 November 2010). The topics and the narratives in the books are considered 'timely' (*Savon Sanomat* 10 June 2010; *Keskipohjanmaa* 8 August 2010), 'brave' (*Kansan Uutiset verkkolehti* 9 July 2010) and 'touching' (Yle.fi/uutiset/kulttuuri 28 May 2010) insights to the 'closed' world of migrants. *Minne tytöt kadonneet?* is presented as a book discussing the 'cultural clash that immigrants experience when they come from a totally different environment to Finnish conditions' (*Lapin Kansa* 19 August 2010) and 'explaining through the disappearances of three Muslim girls the basic values and practices of Muslims, and their differences to traditional Finnish ways of thinking and acting' (*Pohjalainen* 11 November 2010). *Parvekejumalat* again 'discusses with strength the use of power, oppression and the legitimation of human rights crimes with cultural explanations' (*Keskisuomalainen* 9 June 2010).

Many literary critics were fascinated by *Parvekejumalat*, its literary style and language, and praised its ability to evoke smells, feelings and visions. They also valued its 'balanced' treatment of Islam and that it avoided falling into the 'us' and 'them' dichotomy. Only two book reviews criticized the representations of Muslims and the Somali community as did the interviewed Muslim women, cited earlier in this chapter. The themes of racism and racial hierarchies in the Finnish society that *Minne tytöt kadonneet?* introduced were very seldom discussed by the reviewers. They took the 'cultural differences' as the starting point and largely bypassed the othering and racializing traits in the books. The more overwhelming the hegemony of whiteness is, unaware or undisturbed by the presence of the postcolonial 'others', the more space there seems to be for the bypassing of the racializing and othering representations. It seems to be easy to treat whiteness as the unquestioned norm and naturalise this view (Dyer 1997) when all the participants in the discussion are (expected to be) white. Instead, the presence of the critical migrant 'other' disturbs, at least to some extent, the unquestioned normativity of whiteness and destabilizes hegemonic representations.

Between Fiction and Reality

The fact that the texts initiating the public discussion about Muslim families are fictional brings a specific angle to the debates. On the one hand, the reviews and articles emphasize the topicality of the theme in the books and regard them as statements in the immigration debate. The authors are given, and to some extent they also take up, an expert position in the issue of honour-related violence. For example, Anja Snellman referred to the fictional character of her book, but was nevertheless interviewed about the topic and lectured in a seminar about honour-related violence. On the other hand, the debaters who try to criticize the representations of Muslim families and the Somali community are often confronted by those who argue that the books are fictional and should not be read as a description of existing reality.

Nearly all book reviews and articles comment on the relationship between fiction and reality – either in the way that they consider the books a reflection of the real lives of Muslim girls, or by explicitly raising the question about the relationship between facts and fiction. The reviews point out that *Parvekejumalat* 'tells about people we see every day in the streets, but don't know at all' (*Helsingin Sanomat* 10 June 2010), 'deals with things going on in the very real world' (*Turun Sanomat* 11 June 2010) and its 'meaning is to be found in the fact that it makes visible the gendered oppression, violence and cruelty that girls and women experience' (*Keskipohjanmaa* 8 August 2010). It seems that especially the narrative of *Parvekejumalat* which is told to a large extent from the perspective of the 15-year-old Anis is read in relation to 'real Muslim lives'. The genre of the detective novel and the perspective of the white police woman in *Minne tytöt kadonneet?* does not give as much space for identifications, affective readings and fascination verging on disgust as does *Parvekejumalat*.

Some reviews openly problematize the relationship between the narratives and real life: 'One doesn't read the book for the depth of its style or the richness of the form, but for the topic and its moral passion. At this point the reason-oriented reader needs to remind her/himself of the fact that this is not a report about a typical Somali or Muslim family, but a novel about a dysfunctional family' (*Hufvudstadsbladet* 10 June 2010). One of the reviews strongly criticizes the reading of *Parvekejumalat* as a description of reality and argues that the book is based on a culturalist narrative that reproduces colonial and Orientalist discourses. This long review can better be understood as a thorough investigation and development of postcolonial and anti-racist arguments in relation to current discussions about gender, sexuality, migration and multicultural politics. The reviewer notes that 'This is perhaps the biggest deficiency in the novel: it enabled just as stereotypic reception as the narrative structure of the book gives ground to. A Somali girl who suffers from domestic violence and an unstable Finnish woman who converts to Islam produce as unsurprising results in the novel as in its reception' (*Voima* August 2010, 38–40).[8]

The fictional character of the books is also used to argue against those who criticize the othering and racializing discourses on Muslim families and Somali communities. This is especially visible in the Internet discussions where attempts to silence critical voices are made through claims that the books are fiction and that criticizing the representations that they create is therefore not relevant. For example, when the Somali-born nurse Saido Mohamed and the book reviewer criticized *Parvekejumalat* for reinforcing negative stereotypes about Somalis (*Hufvudstadsbladet* 10 June 2010), they soon got somewhat ridiculing responses from writers on the website *Hommaforum* that gathers anti-immigration activists: 'since when has a novel been a report? Why should it be evaluated as a report or even mentioned that it is not a report? The Harry Potters can hardly be considered detailed reports about a wizard school either.'[9]

Yet, many people read the books in relation to reality and they were also marketed in such a way. One bookshop marketed *Minne tytöt kadonneet?* with the text: 'Maria Kallio [the detective] examines the disappearances of Muslim girls. The book tells in a compelling way about the current multicultural Finland

---

8 The interpretations of this chapter are to a certain extent congruent with those of the review (Kuusela 2010).

9 [Online]. Available at: http://hommaforum.org/index.php?topic=29936.0 [accessed: 28 February 2010].

and of the clash of traditions' (*Suuri Suomalainen Kirjakerho* December 2011). When the participants in the website *Kaksplus.fi* discussed Parvekejumalat, one message started: 'I read the book and now when seeing Somali girls I wonder whether they are all oppressed, mutilated and unhappy.'[10] In the following discussion, some participants argued that the book presented a realistic view of Muslim lives, whereas others emphasized the fictional nature of the book and the narrow perspective that it provided on Muslim lives. The tendency to shift from the narrative of the book to discuss multicultural lives and gendered inequalities is characteristic of the whole data.

Fiction and public debates about books play a specific role in the processes in which understandings of migration and multiculturalism are created. Affective narratives and characters that one can identify with make the audiences relate emotionally to what is perceived to be Muslim lives, in this case (re)producing problem-filled understandings. Narratives and imaginaries are often very powerful and difficult to detect, therefore also hard to question. The circulation of discourses, narratives and imaginaries in different cultural arenas from fiction to newspapers, TV programmes and films creates a routine-like naturalness through the constant repetition (cf. Butler 1993). Thus, for example the dichotomy of the 'patriarchal others' and the 'gender-equal Westerners' can become a fact that 'everyone knows'. It can be reiterated, commented and questioned, as do the book reviews, articles and Internet discussions studied in this chapter, but it is extremely difficult to move beyond such dichotomies.

Gender, Nation and Race in the Postcolonial Finland

Gender and sexual relations have become the cornerstones of national identities in current Europe, marking out those perceived as different. The fact that Muslim families have become the object of scrutiny even in a country like Finland with a relatively small Muslim population and no clearly documented scope of the problem is, I argue, a result of transnational influences and identification with normative whiteness. The analysed books and the public discussions cite in many ways gendered and racialized representations common to several European countries. Since the post-World War immigration flows occurred later than in most other European countries, Finland has looked to the countries with a longer history of postcolonial migration and immigration policies in order to 'learn' from those experiences, with the result of transnational influences gaining significant impact. This trend has not been typical only of immigration debates and policies, but also for example the welfare state was built on ideas and models adopted from the other Nordic countries, notably Sweden (for example, Alestalo 2010).

---

10 [Online]. Available at: http://kaksplus.fi/keskustelu/plussalaiset/mitas-nyt/1924965-luin-parvekejumalat-ja-nyt-mietin-kun-naen-somalityttoja/ [accessed: 28 February 2011].

The tendency of countries, with a more marginal position in postcolonial Europe, to search for inspiration and follow the trajectories of the more centrally located countries has also been identified in Ireland (Titley 2009) and Iceland (Loftsdóttir 2011). These countries have, due to their marginal and at times subordinated position, been compelled to demonstrate and convince others of their place in the European (Western) cultural sphere. The Finns were, for example, in the typologies of scientific racism considered as non-Europeans and placed as part of the 'Mongolian' race (Isaksson and Jokisalo 1999). In the post-Cold War era the country has also struggled to show its loyalties and liaisons to the West European sphere, in order to balance the close connections to the 'East' (Soviet Union) during the Cold War. Such histories and present relations provide a specific environment for domesticating transnational discourses and narratives – a setting in which the adoption of European imaginaries and ideals becomes a sign and a proof of the nation's belonging to the Western world, thus showing ability to take part in its power and cultural heritage (cf. Vuorela 2009).

It is against this background that we should see the comments by the book reviewers about Finland having 'finally' become a multicultural society among other (Western) societies. Even participating in the problem-filled experiments of this cultural sphere, as the now much criticized multiculturalism, is a way of ensuring one's place among the modern European nations. The successful achievements in gender equality are signs of this belonging and the distinctions between the Muslim 'others' and the white Finnish 'us' function as a way to confirm such belongings. At the same time, this means endorsing the racial hierarchies embedded in the imaginaries of European modernity.

References

Afshar, H., Aitken, R. and Franks, M. 2005. Feminisms, Islamophobia and Identities. *Political Studies*, 53(2), 262–83.

Alestalo, M. 2010. Pohjoismainen malli ja Suomi. *Sosiologia*, 47(4), 300–309.

Andreassen, R. 2005. *The Mass Media's Construction of Gender, Race, Sexuality and Nationality*. Toronto: University of Toronto.

Bredström, A. 2003. Gendered Racism and the Production of Cultural Difference: Media Representations and Identity Work among 'Immigrant Youth' in Contemporary Sweden. *NORA (Nordic Journal of Women's Studies)*, 11(2), 78–88.

Butler, J. 1993. *Bodies That Matter*. New York: Routledge.

de los Reyes, P., Molina, I., and Mulinari, D. (eds). 2002. *Maktens (o)lika förklädnader: Kön, klass and etnicitet i det postkoloniala Sverige*. Stockholm: Atlas.

Dyer, R. 1997. *White*. London: Routledge.

Grillo, R. 2007. An Excess of Alterity? Debating Difference in a Multicultural Society. *Ethnic and Racial Studies*, 30(6), 979–98.

Hervik, P. 2006. The Emergence of Neo-Nationalism in Denmark, 1992–2001, in *Neo-Nationalism in Europe and Beyond*, edited by A. Gingrich and M. Banks. New York: Berghahn Books.
Isaksson, P. and Jokisalo, J. 1999. *Kallonmittaajia ja skinejä*. Helsinki: Like.
Joppke, C. 2010. *Citizenship and Immigration*. Cambridge: Polity.
Jørgensen, M.W. and Phillips, L. 2002. *Discourse as Theory and Method*. London: Sage.
Keskinen, S. 2009a. Honour-Related Violence and Nordic Nation-Building, in *Complying with Colonialism: Gender, Race and Ethnicity in the Nordic Region*, edited by S. Keskinen et al. Farnham: Ashgate.
Keskinen, S. 2009b. Pelkkiä ongelmia? Maahanmuutto poliittisen keskustelun kohteena, in *En ole rasisti, mutta ... Maahanmuutosta, monikulttuurisuudesta ja kritiikistä*, edited by S. Keskinen, A. Rastas and S. Tuori. Tampere: Vastapaino.
Keskinen, S. et al. (eds). 2009. *Complying with Colonialism: Gender, Race and Ethnicity in the Nordic Region*. Farnham: Ashgate.
Kilic, S. et al. 2008. Introduction: The Veil: Debating Citizenship, Gender and Religious Diversity. *Social Politics*, 15(4), 397–410.
Korteweg, A. and Yurdakul, G. 2009. Gender, Islam and Immigrant Integration: Boundary Drawing on Honour Killing in the Netherlands and Germany. *Ethnic and Racial Studies*, 32(2), 218–38.
Lacey, N. 2000. *Narrative and Genre*. Basingstoke: Palgrave.
Lehtolainen, L. 2010. *Minne tytöt kadonneet?* Helsinki: Tammi.
Lehtonen, M., Löytty, O. and Ruuska, P. 2004. *Suomi toisin sanoen*. Tampere: Vastapaino.
Lentin, A. and Titley, G. 2011. *The Crises of Multiculturalism*. London: Zed Books.
Loftsdóttir, K. 2011. Negotiating White Icelandic Identity: Multiculturalism and Colonial Identity Formations. *Social Identities*, 17(1), 11–25.
Lothe, J. 2000. *Narrative in Fiction and Film*. Oxford: Oxford University Press.
Macdonald, M. 2006. Muslim Women and the Veil: Problems of Image and Voice in Media Representations. *Feminist Media Studies*, 6(1), 7–23.
Magnusson, E., Rönnblom, M. and Silius, H. 2008. *Critical Studies of Gender Equality: Nordic Dislocations, Dilemmas and Contradictions*. Göteborg: Makadam.
Mohanty, C.T. 2003. Under Western Eyes: Feminist Scholarship and Colonial Discourses, in *Feminist Postcolonial Theory*, edited by R. Lewis and S. Mills. Edinburgh: Edinburgh University Press.
Phillips, A. and Saharso, S. 2008. The Rights of Women and the Crisis of Multiculturalism. *Ethnicities*, 8(3), 291–301.
Raittila, P. (ed.). 2002. *Etnisyys ja rasismi journalismissa*. Tampere: Tampere University Press.
Raittila, P. 2009. Journalismin maahanmuuttokeskustelu: hymistelyä, kriittisyyttä vai rasismin tukemista?, in *En ole rasisti, mutta ... Maahanmuutosta,*

monikulttuurisuudesta ja kritiikistä, edited by S. Keskinen, A. Rastas and S. Tuori. Tampere: Vastapaino.
Said, E. 1995. *Orientalism*. Harmondsworth: Penguin.
Scott, J. 2007. *The Politics of the Veil*. Princeton: Princeton University Press.
Snellman, A. 2010. *Parvekejumalat*. Helsinki: Otava.
Teigen, M. and Langvasbråten, T. 2009. The 'Crisis' of Gender Equality: The Norwegian Newspaper Debate on Female Genital Cutting. *NORA (Nordic Journal of Feminist and Gender Research)*, 17(4), 256–72.
Titley, G. 2009. Pleasing the Crisis: Anxiety and Recited Multiculturalism in the European Communicative Space, in *Manufacturing Europe: Spaces of Democracy, Diversity and Communication*, edited by Salovaara Möring. Göteborg: Nordicom.
Tuori, S. 2007. Cooking Nation: Gender Equality and Multiculturalism as Nation-Building Discourses. *European Journal of Women's Studies*, 14(1), 21–35.
Vertovec, S. and Wessendorf, S. 2010. *The Multiculturalism Backlash*. London: Routledge.
Vuorela, U. 2009. Colonial Complicity. The 'Postcolonial' in a Nordic Context, in *Complying with Colonialism: Gender, Race and Ethnicity in the Nordic Region*, edited by S. Keskinen et al. Farnham: Ashgate.
Wetherell, M., Taylor, S. and Yates, S. (eds). 2001. *Discourse Theory and Practice*. London: Sage.
Woodhull, W. 2003. Unveiling Algeria, in *Feminist Postcolonial Theory*, edited by R. Lewis and S. Mills. Edinburgh: Edinburgh University Press.
Young, R. 2003. *Postcolonialism: A Very Short Introduction*. Oxford: Oxford University Press.

Chapter 6
Reading History through Finnish Exceptionalism

Anna Rastas

This chapter examines different articulations of Finnish exceptionalism in the imaginations of encounters between Finns and Africans. Exceptionalism generally refers to an idea that some people or countries – or some phenomena – are entitled to exceptional treatment, as if 'one set of rules or behaviours is acceptable for an individual or country but that a different set should be used for the rest of the world' (Cairns 2001: 33). In my previous ethnographic studies on racism in Finland, as well as in my recent projects on textual representations of Africans, I have identified various articulations of a discourse, in which particular self-perceptions of Finns and interpretations of 'our history' are employed. Differentiating Finland and Finnish people from other nations and the moral superiority included in this discourse that I have termed *Finnish exceptionalism*, appears frequently in public discussions on multicultural Finland and in common perceptions of earlier encounters between Finns and particular others.

I suggest that in research the potentialities of the notion of exceptionalism lie in its utility for describing how particular interpretations of histories and 'our' (national or Nordic) involvements in specific developments are constructed and employed for strategic purposes: for 'selective amnesias' and for avoiding moral and ethical judgements related to our responsibilities towards those who are not included in the national (Nordic or European) 'us'.

I will first clarify why I talk about Finnish exceptionalism instead of, for example, Nordic exceptionalism. Then, I will illustrate some of the articulations and workings of Finnish exceptionalism by summarizing findings of my previous studies (Rastas 2005, 2007) on racism and on Finnish discussions concerning the N-word ('*neekeri*'). I will continue by giving more examples from my recent studies on the representations of Africa, Africans and encounters between Finns and Africans in Finnish non-fiction.[1] School books have an important role in how history is taught and how national identities are understood. I will present articulations of Finnish exceptionalism in current textbooks for upper secondary

---

1 In the three-year (2008–2010) research programme *Africa(ns) in Finnish non-fiction* various genres of non-fiction were analysed, for example scholarly texts, media texts, travelogues, autobiographies and school books. For an overview of these analyses, see Löytty and Rastas 2011, Rastas 2011.

school, and after that, as an example of how exceptionalism works in recent readings of older texts, I will use discussions on a book about the famous Finnish artist Akseli Gallen-Kallela and the time he spent in Africa with his family in 1909–10.

Finnish – or Nordic – Exceptionalism?

Finnish exceptionalism does not refer to the idea that the phenomena described exist solely in Finland, but rather to the fact that the context of my studies is Finnish society. Whether the matters I have discovered in my analysis of current discussions and discourses in Finland, and of the uses of the past in them, could be described as Nordic exceptionalism or not, is a matter of investigation. That means taking a comparative and transnational approach to the questions which are of interest to us.[2]

Mai Palmberg (2009: 46) reminds us that we should avoid seeing a deterministic line of influence between colonial enterprise and the colonial mind. The idea that Finland is innocent in relation to colonialism is largely built on the fact that Finns never established any colonies for themselves. But how could they (we) have done that? Finland was part of the Swedish realm until 1809, and after that, a Grand Duchy of Finland in the Russian Empire before becoming an independent state in 1917. Being dominated by other powers clearly influenced some critics of imperialism in Finland at the turn of the century (for example, Rantanen and Ruuska 2009). Nevertheless, Finns also gained economically from colonialism, and many Finns took part in the colonial enterprise, for example as settlers of Swedish colonies in Delaware in North America and together with other Scandinavians in the Congo (Palmberg 2009). Furthermore, Finns were subject to racialist stereotyping by Swedes and assigned a lower status in racial hierarchies also by some scholars in other European countries, but instead of questioning those ideologies Finns engaged in pseudo-scientific studies in order to produce counter arguments of 'Finns as White Europeans' (see Rastas 2004: 97–9). Consequently, racist ideologies (which linked race with nationhood) were also established in Finland.

Talking about Finnish exceptionalism does not mean that the ideas and national self-images, and the act of employing them as strategies for particular purposes, are exclusively Finnish. Similar discourses built on 'cultural non-memory and ignorance' (Blaagaard 2010: 118) have been identified also in research on the involvements of Scandinavian countries in colonialism (for example, Jensen 2010) and in studies of racism and minorities in Sweden (for example, Sawyer 2002, Hübinette and Tigervall 2009), Norway (Gullestad 2004), Iceland (Loftsdóttir

---

2 For discussions of Nordic exceptionalism, see for example Browning 2007; for more discussion on the uses of the past and the Nordic historical cultures in a comparative perspective, see for example Aronsson 2010.

2008) and Denmark (Marselis 2008: 448). Nor should any phenomenon be declared as uniquely Nordic, even though some phenomena are common among all, or at least most of, the Nordic countries. In Ireland, for example, both the absence of colonial connections and the myth of the homogeneity of the Irish population have been employed to explain the specificities of Irish racism (Lentin 2004: 150–51). Even in some of the European countries with strong imperial involvement, for example in Spain and Italy, 'the public debate about the consequences of imperial involvement in Africa is very rare and usually only concerns other colonial powers' (Brancato 2009: 25). In his article on racial Europeanization and the European racial denial David Theo Goldberg writes 'Race is a problem everywhere else but Europe' (2006: 341), and talks, among other things, about 'British assertive exceptionalism' (2006: 351).

The comparative approach becomes problematic if we attempt to employ the notion of exceptionalism in the descriptions of how the involvements in colonialism have affected national self-images in different countries. As the examples above suggest, exceptionalism as a discourse can be identified in many European societies regardless of what their real involvements and participation in the colonial enterprise were. However, exploring commonalities and differences in articulations of history and our colonial complicities (Vuorela 2009: 19)[3] in different locations may help us examine when, how, and for what purposes particular ideas and discourses – (Finnish or Nordic) exceptionalisms – are employed.

Identifying discourses that can be characterized as exceptionalism may also help us avoid some of the problems included in methodological nationalism (see for example, Wimmer and Glick Schiller 2002), whether they emerge in the form of taking national discourses and histories for granted when we rather should question nationalist imaginaries, or in the form of ignoring the importance of nationalist discourses in our analyses of transnational phenomena. While studying racism, I have, for example, discovered that many things are explained as if they were uniquely Finnish phenomena: as if Finns are, if not the only then the most colour-blind people; as if the existence of racism is denied only in Finland; as if only Finns see themselves as totally innocent in terms of the European colonial project(s) and their consequences.[4]

---

3 Anthropologist Ulla Vuorela uses the notion of 'colonial complicity' to describe a situation 'in which a country, in this case, Finland, has neither been historically situated as one of the colonial centres in Europe nor has it been an "innocent victim" or mere outsider of the colonial projects' (Vuorela 2009: 19).

4 In her analysis of the uses of the N-word ('*neger*') in Norway anthropologist Marianne Gullestad writes: 'The debaters who defended the neutrality of the word neger … defended the implicit definition of the public space as white, and the maintenance of a specific collective memory and national self-image' (Gullestad 2005: 44). The innocent national self-image has been discussed and contested also in Sweden, in studies focusing on non-White Swedes' experiences of racism, including their experiences of being called

The Politics of the N-Word

I used the notion of 'Finnish exceptionalism' for the first time in my ethnographic study on children's experiences of racism in Finland. In light of the data (field notes and interviews) that I had collected among non-white children and young people the most common racist insult among school-aged children was the N-word, '*neekeri*' (Rastas 2005). In addition to the narratives of how the N-word had been used for intentional racism directed towards young people, my data also contained dozens of accounts about encounters in which they had been told both by their peers and by grown-ups that they 'should not mind'. Negotiating these encounters seemed to be very frustrating for the young non-white Finns. Their personal experiences of the word were experiences of both intentional and unintentional racism, but many white Finns with a majority background repeatedly tried to assure them that in Finland this word is a 'neutral', not a racist word. The most common argument they faced was: 'The N-word can be used since, unlike in some other countries, it has never been a racist and pejorative word in Finland.' Due to immigration in general and the growing number of Africans and black people in Finland in particular, the appropriateness of the N-word had been contested in the 1990s (for example, Rastas and Päivärinta 2010), and the early 2000s there was considerable public discourse in Finland concerning its usage. Along with the knowledge of how much this particular word offends some people, these discussions led me to examine the meanings and individuals' explanations for their usage of this word.

The data for my analysis consisted both on ethnographic interviews among young people who had been labelled by that word and on media texts and other documents where the N-word appeared and where its meanings were discussed (see Rastas 2007).[5] The project of tracing the occurrence of the word in the Finnish language, and exploring its use in different times, resulted in the construction of a considerable amount of data: scholarly texts; old texts from the 1800s; newspaper articles and other media texts; pages from Internet websites; official documents; lists of music recordings; films and other artworks; interviews and private correspondence. Analysis of this data was based on the idea of multi-sited ethnography (Marcus 1995).[6] I was interested in how the many meanings of the

---

'*neger*' (for example Sawyer 2002, Motsieloa 2003: 27–9). Both the way in which the N-word has been used in these countries and the public debates concerning the meanings and the use of the word suggest that what I have called Finnish exceptionalism could also be understood as Nordic exceptionalism.

5 My analysis of the politics of the N-word was first presented at the National Conference on Cultural Studies (Kulttuurintutkimuksen päivät, Helsinki) in December 2003. For a detailed analysis with references to my Finnish-language data see Rastas 2007. All translations of textual data from Finnish to English are mine.

6 George Marcus describes the nature of this approach as 'tracing the cultural formation across and within multiple sites of activity'. According to Marcus '(j)ust as this mode investigates and ethnographically constructs the lifeworlds of variously situated

N-word were constructed, how they travelled between different fields and between discourses, how they have changed, and how these discourses were interrelated and interdependent.

In the Finnish language there are two versions of the N-word: '*neekeri*' and '*nekru*'. Many people in Finland try to justify the use of the Finnish word '*neekeri*' by saying that in Finland (in Finnish) only one version of the N-word ('*nekru*') is a racist expression. However, the argument is false. My analysis (Rastas 2007) demonstrates that even though the most common translation for the indisputably racist term 'nigger' is '*nekru*', the word '*nekru*' is rarely used in Finnish language, and instead in everyday language '*neekeri*' is frequently used for intentional racism.[7]

An analysis of old texts, like travelogues, dictionaries and newspaper articles, revealed that those negative and derogatory depictions of Africans that are nowadays understood as products of colonial knowledge (for example, Spurr 1993, Hall 1997), and as racist according to any possible criteria, are typical for texts in which people are called the N-word (Rastas 2007: 126–9). These representations were 'normal' and approved as correct at the time they were published, because in the eighteenth and nineteenth centuries, racism – in form of ideas about differences and hierarchies between people and between different cultures or civilizations – was considered right and 'normal' in Europe, including in Finland. Instead of insisting that these imaginations were 'neutral' and not racist they should rather be interpreted as a proof of racist thinking also in earlier times.

Racist representations combined with the N-word begin to decrease from 1970s onwards. After that, the N-word appears more often in texts in which old racist texts and representations (like advertisements with gollywog figures) are recycled in order to show how 'things have changed'. This kind of use of the N-word can be found in many texts in 1980s, along with stories of Finns who 'long ago' have used the word.[8] The intended message on these stories usually is that this kind of behaviour is no longer accepted in Finland (Rastas 2007: 129–33).

In my data the most common context of use for the N-word ('*neekeri*') was racist websites on the Internet. This 'finding' alone proves that in Finland this word has a strong connection to racism. However, a longitudinal analysis of the commonness of the word, especially in media texts, and an analyses of the contexts in which the word has appeared, also revealed changes in Finnish society and culture. After the early 1990s when the number of people of African descent

---

subjects, it also ethnographically constructs aspects of the system itself through the associations and connections it suggests among sites' (Marcus 1995: 96).

7 In the English-speaking countries the N-word usually refers to the word 'nigger', which is a racist and pejorative word, while the word 'negro' typically refers to earlier times. For a discussion of the word in the English-speaking world, and especially in the US, see for example Kennedy 2003.

8 These stories often tell about the author her/himself, how s/he encountered a black person for the first time.

in Finland rapidly increased, the N-word disappeared from formal contexts and could no longer be found in official documents. From the 1990s onwards (apart from texts easily categorized as overtly racist), most of the discussions in which the N-word appeared concerned the meanings and (in)appropriateness of the word. (Rastas 2007: 122–33). In the media texts that I analysed there were numerous examples of discussions, in which those Finns who use the N-word were the objects of disapproval, and sometimes pity (see Rastas 2007: 131–2).

It is indisputable that this particular word, introduced to Finns as a part of the colonial discourses, is nowadays considered a pejorative expression which offends the people who are addressed in this manner. In her article on colonial complicity anthropologist Ulla Vuorela quotes a radio interview with Peter Kariuki, a Kenyan-born Finnish African, according to whom 'it was only with increasing transnationalism and the need to accommodate refugees and migrants from formerly colonized countries that Finland had to wake up to the postcolonial critique' (Vuorela 2009: 25). Peter Kariuki has spoken about racism in Finland in many public forums as a civil servant and an anti-racism activist. Years ago, when I asked him to comment on the manuscript of my article on the politics of the N-word in Finland, he said: 'I often run out of arguments when I try to talk about this word with Finns, because they just repeat that in Finland this word does not mean anything bad, that it is meant to describe a black person.' In a more recent discussion about the same topic, he expressed his view on this argument as follows: 'The word embeds undertones of racially superior ideas and thoughts in whatever context it is used.' According to him justifying the use of the N-word is a simple attempt to neutralize its derogatory nature and not listen to the minority.[9]

If an educated, well-integrated person who is a good speaker with a lot of experience in public discussions on racism, as Peter Kariuki, feels powerless in front of what is here named as Finnish exceptionalism, it must be a strong weapon with which the average immigrant, or any non-white person in Finland, is denied his/her knowledge and rights. Another Finn of African descent, a black Finnish-born actress and an anti-racism activist Kaisla Löyttyjärvi, has summed up her knowledge of the meanings of this word in a television interview: 'All (white) Finns' ideas and feelings of superiority are condensed in this particular word.'[10]

Why, then, do some people still use the word in everyday interaction? Why do they refuse to listen to all the arguments against the use of this word, and dismiss or ignore them instead? In my field notes naïve claims of the necessity of using the word to describe some individuals' phenotypes were common. Another typical argument, both in my field notes and in media texts, was: 'what matters is the etymology of the word'. Interestingly, although the etymologies of the word, as

---

9 Since my old field notes were not available, I asked Peter Kariuki to check the old quotation concerning his feedback to me to make sure that I recalled his comments correctly. In our email correspondence and discussions on the phone (30 March 2011), he affirmed that the quotation was correct, and complemented his earlier account.

10 *Jos*, YLE TV 1, 18 September 2004. My translation.

explained in these discussions, were numerous and conflicting, they all usually included the assumption that 'originally' (regardless of where and to which language the origin of the word was traced by the speakers) the N-word was 'a neutral word only referring to the skin colour of some people and their origins in Africa'. However, those expressing these views admitted that pejorative meanings have been and sometimes still are attached to this word in other societies, outside Finland. According to many Finns, the word that in other countries is known as racist and pejorative, is in Finland 'neutral' and 'harmless' and, according to the speakers, therefore, legitimate. They sometimes defended the usage of the word by saying 'I can use the word if I do not mean to offend people.' When this kind of reasoning was contested, for example in Internet debates, by others who argued that the word offends people also in Finland, and that we should focus on the consequences of our behaviour instead of our (alleged) intentions, new arguments arose. Many people who participated in these debates began to criticize the 'ridiculous demands of political correctness' and defend their rights to 'speak the way we want to speak in our own country' (Rastas 2007: 122, 137–9).

Two themes that can be identified in these discussions are of interest here: the claims concerning the exceptional nature of Finnish society as a country with no history of racism, and a kind of ignorance of the presence and the well-being of the African and black populations in Finland. The only explanation I could find for many Finns' reactions towards the demands to stop using this racist and pejorative word, and for ignoring historical and other facts in their statements concerning the meanings of this word, is that the discourse of exceptionalism is used as a strategy for ignoring the existence of some (non-white) people, and, as a consequence for maintaining the situation in which 'they' are excluded from 'us'. The discourse of exceptionalism serves to deny the racialized 'others' their legitimate claim to exercise their rights as residents and citizens of Finland.

Finnish Exceptionalism in School Books

School books have an important role in the formation of national identities and in terms of promoting and reproducing representations of 'us and others' (Schissler and Soysal 2005, Palmberg 2009). In current school textbooks Finns are portrayed not only as a nation called Finns but also as Europeans, or, in reading material for the course on 'Europeans and European Union' in the upper secondary school (for example, Arola et al. 2007), primarily as Europeans and citizens of the European Union. According to the National Core Curriculum for Basic Education, children in Finnish schools are supposed to learn about 'imperialism and its impacts on the great European powers and the colonies' (Finnish National Board of Education 2004: 223), which gives an impression that imperialism had no impacts on Finns or other (smaller) European nations who were not colonial powers. In light of our analyses this idea is reproduced in current textbooks for history and social sciences in upper secondary school: Only the other Europeans are portrayed as active agents during the colonial rule.[11] When colonialism is dealt with, imperial powers are sometimes presented in a critical tone but the involvements of Finns in colonial enterprises are never discussed.

Finns were involved in various ways with European colonial regimes. Many Finns went to the colonial world for example as missionaries in Namibia, and as migrants to South Africa. Even if some of them criticized the way in which the other Europeans treated the local people, the Finns also benefited from privileges provided for White Europeans. While it is true that not everything can be included in the textbooks, a pattern can be detected in the systematic avoidance of references to topics that would include the complicity of Finns in the injustices that took place for example in South Africa. According to Olavi Koivukangas (1998: 68), those Finns and descendants of Finns who lived in South Africa during the apartheid 'did not agree with the view criticizing the South African racial policy but stated that any White person in South Africa would act in the same way'.[12]

In the text books that were included in our data there are only a few examples – pictures of advertisements published in old Finnish newspapers and magazines (for example, Kohi et al. 2008: 27, 100–101) – of how colonial thinking can be identified also in the Finnish history. Racism is dealt with as if it merely happened elsewhere: References are made to racism in South Africa, in the US and in many European countries during the Second World War, but not really in Finland. It is not surprising, that when concerns are raised about xenophobia and racism in Finland, and about the increasingly hostile and aggressive nature of the public debates, these are often met by statements about Finland's exceptional history as a country with no colonial involvements and with no historical burden of racism. This idea has been presented in public also by some Finnish intellectuals (for example, Kangasniemi 2009).

Historian Bo Stråth reminds us that due to the great number of immigrants in Europe they should be incorporated in concepts expressing community and belonging, and according to him 'ambivalence, transition and being more historically informed are some key elements' in projects in which 'a new conceptualization of culture and feelings of belonging could be elaborated'. He claims that the concept of European identity does not mediate these elements very well (Stråth 2002: 399). Emphasizing Nordic or European identities instead of national identities may change our means of defining who belong to 'us' and who are 'the others', but it does not necessarily change the way 'the others', and our histories and relations with them, are imagined and narrated. The way in which,

---

11 During the *African(ns) in Finnish non-fiction* project Toni Ahvenainen, Jenni Laulumaa and Heidi Nikula participated the analysis of the current Finnish upper secondary school text books. The most common textbooks for history and social sciences that were used in 2009 in 13 upper secondary schools in Finland's biggest cities were analysed by using content analysis and discourse analysis.

12 My translation.

for example, 'Nordic identity' (see for example, Browning 2007) is understood and defined can be as restricted and biased as our portrayals of national identities.

Exceptionalism and National Treasure

It is less surprising that racism – in the forms of white supremacy and racist depictions of especially Africans – can easily be identified in old books (see for example, Löytty and Rastas 2011). Finland represents no exception when compared to other Nordic (or European) countries. What is more pertinent to my interests here is how some of these old texts are read and interpreted in Finland today. One example of this is a book which recalls the memories of the Finnish artist Akseli Gallen-Kallela (1865–1931) from the time he spent in Africa with his family in 1909–10, and which has gained a lot of attention in Finland.

Of all Finnish painters Gallen-Kallela can be considered as a 'national icon', whose reputation has reached almost mythical proportions (Helin 2002: 51) and whose works have been seen to contribute significantly to the construction of the national self-image of Finns. The book titled *Afrikka-kirja* [*The Africa Book*] is based on Gallen-Kallela's stories about Africa, written down by his friend Martti Raitio. Gallen-Kallela's son, Jorma Gallen-Kallela, edited the book, and it was first published, soon after Gallen-Kallela's death, in 1931. The latest edition was published in 2005. The book displays beautiful pictures of the paintings that Akseli Gallen-Kallela made during their time in Africa. It is not only a story of a famous painter, and a family man who took his wife and children along on this long journey, but also a story of a hunter, a white conqueror. The works that he painted during his stay in Africa were at that time, and even long after that, underrated and regarded as 'escapades' or 'indiscretions' (Helin 2002, see also Kohi et al. 2008: 106) rather than important contributions to the national art canon. However, since the beginning of the 2000s, both the art he made in Africa and *The Africa Book* which presents the works have attracted considerable attention in Finland. The paintings have been presented at various exhibitions, and they have inspired many contemporary artists. In 2009 the Finnish Broadcasting Company broadcast a 38-piece radio play titled *Akseli Afrikassa* [*Akseli in Africa*], in which the book was read aloud by a professional actor.

In August 2009, a Finnish jazz musician Jukka Perko gave a concert with the same title, 'Akseli Afrikassa'. Perko talks about his motives for using pictures of Gallen-Kallela's 'Africa paintings' as part of his performance in a number of newspaper articles about this concert. In those articles, some of which are concert reviews, very little is mentioned about the book itself. However, the preface to the book written by Gallen-Kallela's son, is quoted in one of the texts. In the quotation, Jorma Gallen-Kallela explains the reason why his father wanted to return to Finland from East Africa: 'He was afraid that his children would become rootless English colonialists.'[13] This quotation seems somewhat odd to include in a concert review. Originally, due to the nationalistic political climate of that time, this sentence was probably included to reassure Finnish readers that even though this celebrated artist and national icon spent a long period abroad, he wanted his children to become people who cherish their Finnish roots. Nonetheless, the motives for including this quotation in a concert review written for present-day Finns may be different. The presence of people of African descent in Finland, along with discussions influenced by postcolonial critique, makes the presence of a national icon in the colonial world an issue that has repercussions for the reading of Finns' non-involvement in colonialist enterprises. Here, the message should rather be interpreted as a kind of hopeful reassurance: while living in Africa in places under the British rule Gallen-Kallela was as privileged as any white European, but he did not want to be labelled as a colonialist, and therefore we should not position him as such, nor should we judge him. Hence, Gallen-Kallela and the national iconography surrounding him can be rescued from being tainted by colonialism.

In the review of the above mentioned radio play, published in Finland's major newspaper Helsingin Sanomat (6 October 2009), the Finnish journalist Matti Ripatti writes how already in the second act of the play the listeners will learn that Gallen-Kallela was a 'child of his time in his slightly patronizing attitude towards Africans'. According to Ripatti, 'We cannot, however, call Gallen-Kallela a racist; on the contrary, even though he, for example, talks about negroes, which was typical at that time.'[14] Gallen-Kallela obviously questioned some ideas that were common those days (for example, Gallen-Kallela-Sirén 2001: 353–4). In the book he criticizes the way Africans were at times treated by British and other colonialists, and his paintings included in *The Africa Book* cannot be considered to be racist representations of Africans. Most of the Africans are presented as dignified human beings, and Gallen-Kallela named his works after the tribes of the portrayed people and often also told their names instead of just calling them Africans or 'Negroes', as many of his contemporaries had done. Nevertheless, the book also includes other, very negative and pejorative characterizations of Africans. There is also, for example, a story in which Gallen-Kallela reveals how he abused a Kikuju man who had denied him the rights to his prey, claiming that it had been hunted on Kikuju land. Gallen-Kallela (2005/1931: 156) describes how 'I had hunted it by right of the white man, and he [the Kikuju] was supposed to leave. A couple of blows with the butt of the rifle made the matter even clearer to him.'[15]

What bothers me is that even though there has been so much discussion of this book, the Finnish readers have closed their eyes and refused to see and discuss these parts of the book and the personal history of this national icon. I had never come across any critical readings of *The Africa Book* by Gallen-Kallela until I met Sasha

---

13 Virtanen 2009. My translation.
14 My translation.
15 My translation.

Huber, a Swiss-born artist of African (Haitian) descent who has lived in Finland for many years. On her website there is a short text about her artwork *Trophy I*:

> *Trophy I* is the first of a series of works portraying the journeys of exploration made by the Finn Akseli Gallen-Kallela (1865–1931) in British East Africa (present-day Kenya) between 1909 and 1911. It is an investigation of the impassioned hunting trips that he and his young son Jorma (1898–1939) made. Using the staple gun as a symbol of the deadly rifle shots, Sasha Huber has turned the killing into portraits of the animals. The first 'Trophy' is a rhino skull that was shot by Jorma. The original is in: *Afrikka-kirja: Kallela-kirja II*, 1931 (edited by Jorma Gallen-Kallela).[16]

This piece could be interpreted merely as a statement against animal rights violations, but both Sasha Huber's personal history as a European of African descent, and the fact that most of her artwork can without a doubt be interpreted as postcolonial suggest that a more extensive reading is possible. Her works have dealt with, for example, Louis Agassiz, a famous Swiss scientist who also was an influential racist and a pioneering thinker of apartheid. Seen in that light it is interesting to see how many Finns have reacted to her art work inspired by *The Africa Book*. Sasha Huber told me that already when she was planning the project some people advised her to 'be careful', because anything that can be interpreted as criticism towards Gallen-Kallela would probably arouse anger among the Finnish audience.[17] When she presented her work *Trophy I* and told about her project on the book on Finnish TV, the Finnish journalist who was interviewing her first asked if she could make a comparison between Agassiz and Gallen-Kallela, and then, with a friendly voice that expressed amusement, warned her not to provoke the Finnish audience.[18]

> SS (Sanna Stellan): So you could now make a sort of comparison between Agassiz and Gallen-Kallela?
>
> SH (Sasha Huber): Yes, umm, it … it will go a little bit into that direction but not, not that much.
>
> SS: You know, now …
>
> SH: Yeah.
>
> SS: He's very important in Finland.

---

16 Sasha Huber's homepage available at: www.sashahuber.com/?cat=31&lang=fi&mstr=4.
17 Discussion with Sasha Huber, 16 December 2011.
18 Strada, YLE TV 1, 7 January 2011.

SH: I know, yes.

SS: You be careful now.

SH: Yeah.

The journalist sums up their discussion by saying: 'So, that [referring to the art work Trophy I] tells us something about Gallen-Kallela that we might not realize.'

Especially because of immigrants like Sasha Huber, or Peter Kariuki, who identify with the historically oppressed groups, Finns, like the other Europeans, are forced to face the postcolonial criticism, and the new readings of history included in it. As Andreas Wimmer and Nina Glick Schiller have stated, immigrants 'represent a renewed challenge to the nation-building project and point to the fragility of its achievements' (Wimmer and Glick Schiller 2002: 310). In the world governed by 'the national order of things' (Malkki 1995) these nation-building projects are ongoing endeavours. An 'outsider' who may see something 'that we might not realize', or that we may not want to discuss, must be warned not to tamper with the national icons and national treasures. When these warnings are not heeded, their claims and arguments have to be dismissed.

Immigrants from former colonized countries, and their non-white descendants whose lives are overshadowed by the collective memory of subordination and its present-day implications, question our knowledge about ourselves. Losing the power to define what 'we' are like is understood as a threat to the national identity, instead of an invitation to self-reflection and new interpretations of history. Finnish exceptionalism constructs and maintains the differences between 'us' and 'others', and the superiority which not only positions 'us' above others, but also allows 'us' to maintain power to define the order of things and to 'be the way we want to be in our home'. To rethink 'our history', or to make 'us' a more inclusive category, would mean losing that power.

Finnish exceptionalism, the moral superiority that has enabled us to judge others and keep ourselves free of any ethical and moral judgements, is employed to keep control: to retain the power to stop others (especially 'them', immigrants) from saying what 'we' are like (or what we have been like), and from dictating what 'we' can and cannot say. Paradoxically, while this discourse is built on denying the impact of colonial knowledge on our thinking, some of its articulations (reactions to change), resemble colonial nostalgia, feelings of loss and longing for something that is now taken from us: power over the other (see for example, Bissell 2005). Andreas Huyssen (quoted in Bissell 2005: 240) argues that we turn to the past precisely to secure what the future can no longer supply. No matter how inconsistent our arguments and interpretations of history are, or how blind we may seem in the eyes of other people. We keep on repeating these 'truths' about Finns and Finland (or the Nordic countries); if we do not, we give away our power to define not just others but also 'ourselves'. Clinging to the national self-image of innocence (cf. Gullestad 2004), which I see as the core of (Finnish and for that matter Nordic) exceptionalism is a strategy to avoid those moral and ethical judgements that could be used to demand change. To admit that also in Finland racism is part of 'our history' would mean that we can no longer ignore it; instead, we would have to address it.

References

Arola, P., Aromaa, V., Hentilä, S. and Kauppinen, S. 2007. *Kansalainen ja Eurooppa*, 3. Painos. Helsinki: Edita.
Aronsson, P. 2010. Uses of the past: Nordic historical cultures in a comparative perspective. *Culture Unbound. Journal of Current Cultural Research*, 2, 553–63.
Bissell, W.C. 2005. Engaging colonial nostalgia. *Cultural Anthropology*, 20(2), 215–48.
Blaagaard, B.B. 2010. Remembering Nordic colonialism: Danish cultural memory in journalistic practice. *Kult – Special Issue Nordic Colonial Mind*, 7, 101–21.
Brancato, S. 2009. *Afro-Europe: Texts and Contexts*. Berlin: Trafo.
Browning, C.S. 2007. Branding nordicity: models, identity and the decline of exceptionalism. *Cooperation and Conflict: Journal of the Nordic International Studies Association*, 42(1), 27–52.
Cairns, J. 2001. Exceptionalism and globalism. Editorial. *Ethics in Science and Environmental Politics (ESEP)*, 1, 33–7.
Finnish National Board of Education. 2004. *National core curriculum 2004: national core curriculum for basic education intended for pupils in compulsory education*. [Online: Finnish National Board of Education]. Available at: http://www.oph.fi/download/47671_core_curricula_basic_education_1.pdf [accessed: 29 November 2011].
Gallen-Kallela, A. 2005. *Afrikka-kirja*. 2nd Edition. Helsinki: WSOY.
Gallen-Kallela-Sirén, J. 2001. *Minä palaan jalanjäljilleni*. Helsinki: Otava.
Goldberg, D.T. 2006. Racial Europeanization. *Ethnic and Racial Studies*, 29(2), 331–64.
Gullestad, M. 2004. Blind slaves of our prejudices: debating 'culture' and 'race' in Norway. *Ethnos*, 69(2), 177–203.
Gullestad, M. 2005. Normalizing racial boundaries: the Norwegian dispute about the term neger. *Social Anthropology*, 13(1), 27–46.
Hall, S. 1997. The Spectacle of the 'Other', in *Representation*, edited by S. Hall. London: Sage and Open University, 223–90.
Helin, P. 2002. Akseli Gallen-Kallela, in *Vieraan katse: kansalliset vähemmistöt ja vieraat kulttuurit suomalaisten kuvataiteilijoiden silmin 1850–1945: Tampereen taidemuseon julkaisuja 101*, edited by T. Pennanen, H. Sinisalo and P. Helin. Tampere: Tampereen taidemuseo, 50–51.

Hübinette, T. and Tigervall, C. 2009. To be non-white in a colour-blind society: conversations with adoptees and adoptive parents in Sweden on everyday racism. *Journal of Intercultural Studies*, 30(4), 335–53.

Jensen, L. 2010. Provincialising Scandinavia. *Kult – Special Issue Nordic Colonial Mind*, 7, 7–21.

Jos 2004, television programme, YLE TV 1, 18 September 2004.

Kangasniemi, S. 2009. Laura Kolbe ja Maria Veitola: Helsinki on Tukholmaa edellä. *Helsingin Sanomat*, 21 November.

Kennedy, R. 2003. *Nigger: The Strange Career of a Troublesome Word*. New York: Vintage Books.

Kohi, A., Palo, H., Päivärinta, K. and Vihervä, V. 2008. *Forum VI: kulttuurien kohtaaminen*. Helsinki: Otava.

Koivukangas, O. 1998. *Kaukomaiden kaipuu. Suomalaiset Afrikassa, Australiassa, Uudessa-Seelannissa ja Latinalaisessa Amerikassa*. Turku: Siirtolaisinstituutti.

Lentin, A. 2004. *Racism and Anti-Racism in Europe*. London: Pluto Press.

Loftsdóttir, K. 2008. Shades of otherness: representations of Africa in 19th-century Iceland. *Social Anthropology*, 16(2), 172–86.

Löytty, O. and Rastas, A. 2011. Afrikka Suomesta katsottuna, in *Afrikan aika: näkökulmia Saharan eteläpuoliseen Afrikkaan*, edited by A. Teppo. Helsinki: Gaudeamus Helsinki University Press, 23–37.

Malkki, L. 1995. Refugees and exile: from 'refugee studies' to the national order of things. *Annual Review of Anthropology*, 24, 495–523.

Marcus, G.E. 1995. Ethnography in/of the world system: the emergence of multi-sited ethnography. *Annual Review of Anthropology*, 24, 95–117.

Marselis, R. 2008. Descendants of slaves: the articulation of mixed racial ancestry in a Danish television documentary series. *European Journal of Cultural Studies*, 11(4), 447–69.

Motsieloa, V. 2003. *'Det måste vara någonting annat': en studie om barns upplevelser av rasism i vardagen*. Stockholm: Rädda Barnen.

Palmberg, M. 2009. The Nordic Colonial Mind, in *Complying with Colonialism: Gender, Race and Ethnicity in the Nordic Region*, edited by S. Keskinen et al. Aldershot: Ashgate, 35–50.

Rantanen, P. and Ruuska, P. 2009. Alistetun viisaus, in *Kuriton kansa. Poliitinen mielikuvitus vuoden 1905 suurlakon ajan Suomessa*, edited by A.H. Anttila et al. Tampere: Vastapaino, 33–56.

Rastas, A. 2004. Am I still White? Dealing with the colour trouble. *Balayi: Culture, Law and Colonialism*, 6, 94–106.

Rastas, A. 2005. Racialising categorization among young people in Finland, *YOUNG – Nordic Journal of Youth Research*, 13(2), 147–66.

Rastas, A. 2007. Neutraalisti rasistinen? Erään sanan politiikkaa (Neutrally racist? The politics of the N-word), in *Kolonialismin jäljet: keskustat, periferiat ja Suomi*, (Traces of Colonialism. Centers, Peripheries and Finland), edited by J. Kuortti, M. Lehtonen and O. Löytty. Helsinki: Gaudeamus Helsinki University Press, 119–41. Available at: http://acta.uta.fi/pdf/Rastas_A6.pdf.

Rastas, A. 2011. Writing Our Future History Together: Applying Participatory Methods in Research on African Diaspora in Finland, in *Afroeurope@an Configurations: Readings and Projects*, edited by S. Brancato. Newcastle upon Tyne: Cambridge Scholars Publishing, 98–120.

Rastas, A. and Päivärinta. J. 2010. Vastapuhetta afrikkalaisten diasporasta Suomessa. *Kulttuurintutkimus*, 27(4), 45–63.

Ripatti, M. 2009. *Helsingin Sanomat*, TV ja radio, 6 October.

Sawyer, L. 2002. Routings: 'race', African diasporas, and Swedish belonging. *Transforming Anthropology*, 11(1), 13–29.

Schissler, H. and Soysal, Y.N. 2005. *The Nation, Europe, and the World: Textbooks and Curricula in Transition*. New York and Oxford: Berghahn Books.

Spurr, D. 1993. *The Rhetoric of Empire: Colonial Discourse in Journalism, Travel Writing and Imperial Administration*. Durham and London: Duke University Press.

Strada 2011, television programme, YLE TV 1, 7 January 2011.

Stråth, B. 2002. A European identity: to the historical limits of a concept. *European Journal of Social Theory*, 5(4), 387–401.

Virtanen, H. 2009. Akseli Gallen-Kallela maalasi Afrikassa. *Alueviesti*, 29 July 2009.

Vuorela, U. 2009. Colonial Complicity: The 'Post-Colonial' in a Nordic Context, in *Complying with Colonialism: Gender, Race and Ethnicity in the Nordic Region*, edited by S. Keskinen et al. Aldershot: Ashgate, 19–33.

Wimmer, A. and Glick Schiller, N. 2002. Methodological nationalism and beyond: nation-state building, migration and the social sciences. *Global Networks*, 2(4), 301–34.

Chapter 7
Danishness as Whiteness in Crisis: Emerging Post-Imperial and Development Aid Anxieties

Lars Jensen

Research on Danish national identity formation has, as in other Western societies, focused on national identity evolution as a largely domestic process. Even if it has drawn upon influences, typically European, most overtly in the period in which national-liberal revolutions swept through mid nineteenth-century Europe, which produced in Denmark the beginnings of a democratic evolution through the end of absolutist rule, such international influences are rendered peripheral in relation to seeing the process as a domestic affair. This would be a trivial observation, were it not for the link between such watershed events and the narration of the nation as a naturally cultural-territorial circumscribed space. National historiography is inevitably an exercise in explaining the contemporary nation through the orchestration of and selective interpretations of historical events understood as operating inside the territorial integrity of the nation, as Benedict Anderson has demonstrated in his seminal text on nationalism, *Imagined Communities*. Disagreements over the precise meaning of certain pivotal events in the nation's history are of course common, but they are understood as 'domestic arguments'. Yet, the narration of the nation, as Homi Bhabha has discussed it, also operates as a narrative of inclusion and exclusion, that is, as a way of patrolling the limits of how the nation's story can be told, where the liminality of the nation becomes pivotal to the conceptualisation of the nation (Bhabha 1994: 148–9). His assertion that the nation defines itself through its processes of marginalisation begins at the theoretical level to engage both with what is dismissed from the perimeters of the nation's field of vision, and how the act of dismissal betrays pivotal concerns at the nation's 'core'. The geography of the nation state in this way becomes simultaneously the imaginary and the patrolled space of the nation. While the nation remains an important site for articulating sameness based on shared aspirational ideas, it also becomes a space premised on the identification of absolute, unacceptable, difference. As such the national space gives voice to an idealised perception of the self, at the same time as it excludes 'alien' influences from beyond and inside the national space. In this chapter, I wish to take point of departure in this theoretical insight and look at what this means in a specific, or localised, context. I will look at Denmark and how its national narrative ignores influences beyond the territorially bounded nation space, even when such influences have helped shaped Danish self-understanding in important ways. Two examples have been chosen, namely the modernisation of Greenland from the late 1940s through the 1960s, and the building of a Danish development aid programme in the same period.

To select an entire nation space across time and space provides a wide range of foci, from identifying international/external influences on the nation's evolution, over comparative studies, to studies which highlight the porous nature of the nation's liminality/boundary/border/periphery. To again invoke Bhabha the nation's territorial and mental hegemony is constantly subverted by destabilising efforts on its margins, but also by its own corrosive nature. The most obvious point of developing this critique in relation to Western nation spaces has come from what Stuart Hall (1996) has so aptly named the presence of the rest in the West, where the very presence of the migrant other disrupts the nation's narrative of its own cohesive nature, and exposes the actual differentiating nature of how the nation operates and in particular how it enables differential treatment of its inhabitants. This is not an unusual analytical framework to establish, but the choice of nation over state, and inhabitant over citizen, is my deliberate choice meant to create a different approach to the conceptualisation of how Danish national identity can be seen, since citizen and state, although pivotal to understanding how power relations are operationalised, are also limited in the sense that they become preoccupied with the state as an oppressive structure – that oppresses all. While this creates an important platform for recognising the state as a regulatory apparatus, it is less useful when recognising less formal, but very powerful, processes of exclusion, and inclusion, as well as important alternative hierarchies premised on the idea of centrality to the nation, rather than the state. Here national identity becomes the pivotal form for recognising sameness and difference. It is these less formalised forms of identity formation that I will discuss in relation to the two examples, modernisation in Greenland and the rise of development aid, which interestingly enough unfolded simultaneously within the Danish state apparatus, but both of which represent processes of 'self' and 'other' identifications that reach beyond the imagined space of national cohesion.

The idea is not to situate them in their historical context, but instead to ask about the extent to which the mentality that drove these interventionist practices at the time (both of which have subsequently been dismissed as a craze for modernisation), has in fact been replaced by a different, and more reflective approach to what 'development' is and should do. Modernisation and development aid went hand in hand with a particular attitude (see for example Butcher, 2007: 26), where the West/ Denmark was supposed to deliver to the Third World/Greenland the development they were seen as unable to create for themselves. This conceptualisation of the situation of underdeveloped nations was completely dehistoricised, because it left out of the equation the fact of colonialism as a hugely destructive force and presence. It was dehistoricised, rather than ahistorical, because colonialism had to be written out of the contact zone between the West and the Rest, in order to pave the way for a new engagement that would otherwise simply have been seen as neo-colonialism (for a discussion on the links between colonialism, imperialism and development discourse see Escobar 1995). Yet far from being an history-less narrative of a new global relationship, development aid rested on a historical premise that saw the evolution of successful Western societies, including the Danish welfare based nation state, as internal[1] developments, divorced from the reality of the wealth in the West as at the very least partly created through the exploitation of the Rest. The logical conclusion to this assumption was that the Rest's failure to develop was similarly the result of internal processes divorced from its colonial relationship with the West and this was in fact a continuity of colonialism's thought paradigm of the civilising mission.

The construction of the new global narrative took place at the same time as colonial states were substituted by 'independent' postcolonial states in the 'Third World' post-1945. The destructiveness of the European presence in the colonial world, which the European powers sought to ignore during formal colonialism,[2] vanished from the narratives of the newly emerged postcolonial nations to be replaced by a narrative of domestic entrepreneurship paving the way for industrialisation with the aid of Western capital. Interestingly enough while much attention has been devoted to the notion of nation-building in the wake of formal colonialism in the decolonised world, little attention has been dedicated to the nation rebuilding process in Europe after the Second World War. Here the reconstructed national narratives could no longer continue as tales of national grandeur produced through the possession of colonies. The post-war narratives instead developed an acute focus on the cultural-territorial integrity of the post-imperial nation, as it lost its remaining colonies. These narratives not only ignored the embarrassment of the oppressive nature of colonial rule and the painful process of decolonisation, but also avoided references to embarrassing recent racialised discourses at home, such as the recognition of eugenics as science, the flirt with Fascism and Nazism, and the collaboration with the Nazi regime in Germany. To this general list can be added in the specific case of Denmark the expulsion of

---

1 'Internal' is used instead of 'domestic' here, because the success of the West is both seen as a common trait and the result of parallel unique evolutions in each of the Western nation states.

2 The term 'formal colonialism' is used to signal that colonialism exists both as a more narrowly defined administrative and cultural practice in the colonial societies, and as the far more generalising concept of colonialism, or even coloniality as a continual form of domination, or hegemony, which exists beyond the societal structure of the colonial and postcolonial state.

Jews and communists before any German requests for extradition of Jews before the German occupation.³

The Danish 'modernisation' of Greenland and participation in the development aid project represented opportunities to showcase the rebuilding of Denmark's image, both as a benevolent coloniser,⁴ and as an internationally conscientious nation state. Yet, while the literature produced at the time shows the awareness about the similarities and overlaps between the Danish contribution to development aid and Greenlandic modernisation,⁵ subsequent scholarly attention has not connected the two fields.⁶ Yet when placed alongside each other their shared preoccupations are revealed in their mutual staging of a Danish self-image, which inevitably raise questions beyond seeing them as responses to immediate and separate concerns. Not only are they connected, collectively they form a particular form of thinking that reflects a perception of selfhood that has a far longer and broader history than merely the specific form it took in the welfare thought paradigm in Denmark in the 1950s and 1960s. While the welfare state (or society) is part of a broader narrative of growing post-war affluenza in the West, it follows a very specific trajectory in Denmark and, in relation to development aid, the other Nordic countries. As such it led to the still hegemonic Nordic narrative of a seemingly innate desire for equality regardless of race, gender or class, despite a reality of continued demonstrable inequality on all three fronts. Hegemonic here refers both to the way in which the state acts and regulates according to this narrative, but also to the way in which the majority societies in the Nordic countries subscribed to this

---

3 There are a few studies (all in Danish though) which look at the role broadly of racism in Denmark in the inter-war period, for example, L. Koch, 1996, *Racehygiejne i Danmark 1920–56*. Copenhagen: Information; and L. Rünitz, 2000. *Danmark og de jødiske flygtninge 1933–40 En bog om flygtninge og menneskerettigheder.* Copenhagen: Museum Tusculanum.

4 The modernisation programme in Greenland was developed in the dying years of Danish colonial rule in Greenland, and was a response to the threat of decolonisation that spread through in particular the UN. The argument is unfolded in greater depth in a forthcoming book that has a chapter dedicated to the overlaps between the discourse on modernisation in Greenland and modernisation thoughts in Danish development aid discourse.

5 Not only are there similarities; in fact chief advisory civil servants in public administration at the time worked in both fields, most notably Mogens Boserup, who also wrote, albeit briefly, on the overlaps between 'development' in Greenland and the Third World.

6 The tome on Danish development aid history is C.F. Bach, T.B. Olesen, S. Kaur-Pedersen, J. Pedersen, 2008, *Idealer og realiteter: Dansk udviklingspolitiks historie 1945–2005*. Copenhagen: Gyldendal. The most critical engagement with development aid is K. Jørgensen. 1977. *Hjælp fra Danmark: En studie i dansk u-landspolitik 1960–71*. Odense: Odense Universitetsforlag. Two useful reading of post-war Greenland is M. Lidegaard. 1973. *Ligestilling uden lighed*. Copenhagen: Schultz Forlag, and J. Dahl. 1986. *Arktisk selvstyre*. Copenhagen: Akademisk Forlag.

perception, and identified it as an ideal, and a cause worthy of universalisation, even as they failed to work consistently, if at all, for its actual implementation.

While the idealisation of the welfare state and its potential as an international (role) model was fairly universal within Danish society, this was not reflected in a general push for internationalisation. In fact Denmark postponed its large-scale financial contribution to development aid, in contrast to Sweden, by referring to its heavy investment in Greenlandic modernisation (see the quotation towards the end of this chapter). Furthermore, there was a paradox in the relationship between the Danish welfare society as an export role model on the one side, and the account of the rise of welfare as an exclusively domestic process on the other, premised on a national racialised immaculateness. To begin to speak of a Danish relevance in the Third World, now that the fact of historical possession of tropical colonies was written out of the national cultural archives, with the exception of a few nostalgic works in the 1940s and 1950s, and, of course, Thorkild Hansen's critique of the Danish slave trade in the 1960s, required an interesting balancing act between on the one hand not contextualising too deeply, lest embarrassing facts should be uncovered, while on the other hand drawing on a long history of intervention that showed the Danish international entrepreneurship as an inherently Danish quality. In relation to Greenland, the situation was equally delicate.

With the end of the Second World War Denmark, like other European colonial powers, discovered that its situation in the remaining colonies had irrevocably changed. Those European powers who failed to realise the altered conditions paid with the embarrassing defeats at the hands of the supposed colonial inferiors, the Netherlands in Indonesia, Britain in East Africa and South Asia, France in Indochina and North Africa and Portugal in Africa. The long history of the European debacle[7] from 1945 to 1975 shows how painful and costly this process was for both empires and colonies. The peaceful demise of the Danish empire was not the result of a Denmark that was more insightful or humanitarian than the other European colonial powers.[8] The situation was simply different, partly because the remaining

---

7   I choose 'debacle' over 'decline' here, since decline indicates a regrettable fall from a higher position, whereas 'debacle' emphasises the rigid, clumsy and authoritarian European efforts to retain their power. The recent attention brought to British atrocities committed during the Kenyan Mau Mau uprising in the 1950s is one example of how these efforts spilled over into violence against colonial subjects. The example also shows the reluctance with which Europeans more than half a century later address atrocities committed in the name of preserving the colonial state.

8   To argue that Denmark was in fact more humanitarian inclined immediately runs into the problem of how to defend this in the light of its slave trading record, which given the size of the country was substantial. Nor is the argument that most of the colonies were abolished relatively early particularly persuasive. Denmark could not for economic and political reasons stay on in Africa and India as a colonial power in the 1840s, and similar reasons led to the sale of the Virgin Islands to the US in 1917. In both cases the interests of the colonial subjects were unceremoniously dismissed in favour of Denmark's national interests.

colonies, Greenland and the Faeroe Islands, with their limited populations were never going to be able to mount anything like an effective guerrilla campaign, or other physical forms of anti-colonial resistance. This was realised on both sides. But there is nothing to suggest the Danish desire to re-establish its power position in both territories after the war was less ardent than that of the Dutch in Indonesia, the French in Indochina, and so forth. And similar to the colonies in Asia and Africa the Faeroese and Greenlandic desires to change the relationship with Denmark after the war were pronounced, now that they had discovered opportunities outside the control of a stale Danish administration during the years Denmark had been cut-off by the German occupation. While Greenlandic and Faeroese nationalism can be traced back to the nineteenth century, it gained a new and decisive impetus during the years of the war.[9]

Denmark's compromised position during the war created international obstacles for its desire to reinvent itself as a dependable participant in the post-war global order. International aid and sovereignty over Greenland, in particular Thule, provided the key to the initial Danish rehabilitation of its international image.[10] But if Denmark was to maintain its grip on Greenland (the US offered to buy Greenland), it required a Danish presence on the island on an unprecedented scale, after decades of relative neglect. This, together with the growing demands in the UN for decolonisation raised by recently independent countries, paved the way for a Danish policy of modernisation on a massive scale, solving both the problem of UN accusations of neglect,[11] and of avoiding future embarrassing American offers

---

9 On Faeroese nationalism see H.J. Debes, 2001, *Færingernes land*. Torshavn: Multivers; and T. Nauerby, 1995, *No Nation Is an Island*. Aarhus: Aarhus University Press. Greenlandic nationalism tends to be discussed in the literature as a twentieth-century phenomenon, yet it is possible to identify Greenlandic complaints against the lack of recognition of them as equals in the mid-nineteenth century which coincides with the Danish administrator, Hinrich Rink's, thoughts about Greenlanders eventually becoming in charge of their own society. See for example, K.J.V. Steenstrup's article, Dr Phil. Hinrich Johannes Rink, in *Geografisk Tidsskrift*, Bind 12, 1893–94, 165. For a recent discussion of Rink, see O. Marquardt, 2009, H.J. Rink, in *Grønland – en refleksiv udfordring*, edited by O. Høiris. Aarhus: AAUF, 129–154.

10 The grassroots organisations involved in the early stages of international aid immediately after the end of the war were Dansk Røde Kors (The Danish Red Cross), Mellemfolkeligt Samvirke (Actionaid Denmark) and Red Barnet (Save the Child), the latter two organisations were also active in Greenland. See Friis-Bach et al., 33. See also T. Krogh, 1989, Humanitet og politik i det danske efterkrigshjælpearbejde 1945–51 for a more critical account of the motives behind Danish international aid, in *Historie/Jyske Samlinger*, Bind ny række, 18(2), www.tidsskrift.dk/visning.jsp?markup=andprint=noand id=73418. The connection between the Danish rehabilitation efforts after the war and its Greenland policy is described in *Grønland under den kolde krig: Dansk og amerikansk sikkerhedspolitik 1945–68*. Copenhagen: Dansk Udenrigspolitisk Institut, 1997, 50.

11 Even the leading mid-twentieth-century civil servant in Greenlandic affairs, Eske Brun, in his autobiography, *Mit grønlandsliv*, draws attention to the Greenlandic mortality

to buy Greenland. It furthermore solidified the Danish membership of NATO, and it enabled the projection of a new interventionist, but 'humanitarian', Denmark on the global stage.

The modernisation programme was orchestrated by Danish politicians and top civil servants, so it wasn't caused by the nation rising to the occasion. However, as a platform for invitation to share a more positive vision for Denmark than the loss of territory, influence and international standing over the previous 150 years, it was the perfect set-up for a new more international identification that received its popular breakthrough with the campaign to modernise Greenland (from the 1950s) and the evolution of 'Third World' development aid (from the 1960s). Both campaigns started slowly. During its long held monopoly on Greenland, Denmark had put in place severe restrictions on travel to Greenland. This had the added bonus of protecting the colonial administration from critical international attention or local scrutiny by the Danish media. The modernisation of Greenland, although designed to be carried through by Danes, forced the opening up of Greenland, which led to Danish media accounts of at times appalling Greenlandic living conditions, and criticism of specific Danish strategies in Greenland, but not to a critique of Danish colonialism per se. This materialised only when parts of the Greenlandic intelligentsia went to Denmark for educational purposes. Greenlanders in Copenhagen found strategic alliance partners among the growing anti-establishment circles of the 1960s and early 1970s and became acquainted with the anti-imperialist critique, which they used to politically mobilise the dissatisfaction with their classification as second class citizens in their own country. The modernisation of Greenland albeit destructive to certain aspects of Greenlandic society, also led the path to rising demands for, initially, recognition, then influence, then home rule, and finally in 2009, self-rule. However, this should not be seen as the fruition of an evolving Danish policy. For contrary to the prevalent Danish version of this history, the Greenlanders fought a Danish recalcitrant administration and government every inch of the way for increased levels of self-determination (see Lidegaard 1973, Viemose 1977 and Thorleifsen 2003).[12] While it is clear that modernisation involves a massive investment instead of the slow, inert colonial

---

rate being higher than the Canadian, which receives, as his says, a lot of criticism (Brun 112).

12   The Faeroese and Icelandic historical relationship with Danish colonialism follow a similar path. Having unceremoniously been dismissed as undeserving of the local parliament (whereas Iceland successfully pushed for a local parliament) in connection with the Danish democratic constitution in 1849, the Faeroese established a nationalist movement among the educated elite in Copenhagen towards the end of the nineteenth century. The initial stages of this culminated and folded at the beginning of the twentieth century, where the Danish government managed to avoid a situation similar to the one, which unfolded in Iceland, that led to the eventual separation of Denmark and Iceland in 1918, and Iceland's unilateral declaration of independence in 1944. The Faeroese nationalist movement gained new momentum, during the separation years during the war, and in a shock referendum result in 1946 voted very narrowly for independence. The Danish government refused to

administration, the Danish government sought to preserve its power base during the modernisation decades through a carefully restricted delegation of influence to the Greenlanders. This is clear from the secrecy and lies[13] that surrounded the Thule Air Base and the enforced removal of the local community, as well as, from the actions of the Danish government's representatives at the UN, who positioned themselves centrally in the committee overseeing the successful decolonisation of the remaining colonies. In violation of the principle in article 73 of the UN covenant, which stipulated colonial powers must work towards ensuring independence for its colonial subjects, the Danish government integrated Greenland (and the Faeroe Islands) into the Danish Commonwealth (Rigsfællesskabet), reducing both of them to the position of shires (amter) in Denmark, and as such with no specific entitlements despite their obviously completely different situation.[14]

Modernisation in relation to development followed a different trajectory, albeit some of the ingredients were the same. What later became development aid began immediately after the war as food aid to the Netherlands, which had been hit hard during the German occupation. However, the Danish international aid quickly became associated with the pursuit of more local national interests. Hence the second place to receive aid was Northern Germany, and here food was deliberately distributed through the Danish-speaking community. Officially, the prioritisation of the Danish minority in Germany was justified with reference to the Danish population's reluctance to help the slain enemy. Underneath the official rhetoric, however, lay a nationalistic agenda. Influential circles, including the Danish PM, thought the slain German enemy might enable a renegotiation of the border settlement after the First World War. The Danes were soon forced to change their policy when the British pointed out that if they could help their enemy as active participants in the war, why could not the Danish 'neutral' state do the same?[15] Danish aid changed from its close neighbour orientation to a global involvement in medical campaigns in the decolonising world. By the early 1960s, partly through American pressure, Danish aid grew dramatically in size, and in the 1970s it joined the UN call for developed countries to contribute 0.7 per cent of their BNP to development aid.

The relationship between development aid and modernisation is clearly detected in the idea of material improvement, thought to be caused simply by the allocation of technical assistance as well as technology itself. But modernisation

---

recognise this, absolved the local parliament, and offered home rule which was installed in 1948. Incidentally this also became the model for the Greenlandic home rule of 1979.

13 See J. Brøsted og M. Fægteborg, 1985, *Thule – fangerfolk og militæranlæg*. Copenhagen: Jurist- og Økonomforbundets Forlag; and A. Lynge et al., 2000, *The Right to Return: Fifty Years of Struggle by Relocated Inughuit in Greenland*. Nuuk: Atuagkat.

14 While Denmark has recognised Greenlanders and the Faeroese as peoples, it has not granted them official status as a minority with the rights that accompany this position.

15 For a more detailed analysis of this period see Krogh.

was also present in the idea that the 'Third World' citizen would be transformed from a 'traditional' farmer to a 'modern' worker. Industrialisation narrated as an internal process in the West, and hence disconnected from the exploitation of the colonies, could now be seen as an internal process in the 'Rest' helped along by those Westerners who had successfully been through the process. Here, the exploitation history of the colonies, that is, their impoverishment seen as a direct product of colonialism was simply absent. Modernisation had in it the built-in precondition that history had no role to play, which also meant that when the modernisation programme failed, and since the West could not be at fault, after all it had proven the move from tradition to modernity could be made, the flaw had to rest with the Rest itself. The argument was endemic corruption and other forms of irrational blockings that could be reduced to two words, 'cultural difference' understood as cultural inadequacies, or the inability to shift from being too cultural to being modern and culture less. The West operated as a cultureless norm, the West simply *was* modernity and quite literally fully developed.[16]

Connecting Danish Attitudes to Greenland and Development Aid

> After a series of TV programmes about Greenland, the chairman of the governing board Poul Nyboe Andersen on January 22 1966 wrote in a feature article in the newspaper *Kristeligt Dagblad*: 'You cannot on the one hand claim that Greenland is part of the Danish realm, and therefore reject the control by the UN's trusteeship council for supervision of our Greenland policy, and then, on the other hand argue that our expenses in connection with Greenland's development have to be seen as if Greenland was not part of Denmark, but an independent developing nation.' That is the reason Greenland was designated as a regional development problem which corresponded to regional conditions in other rich nations, whereas development aid was associated with particular foreign political and business interests. (Jørgensen 1977: 80–81, my translation)

> In the Danish debate the capability of the developing countries to absorb aid played no role ... There was, however, no lack of sceptical reservations, most often they referred to Greenlandic conditions, and warned against force through development aid in such a way, that the citizens of these countries became spectators to the development process in their own country and influenced by impulses from outside to such a degree and with such speed that it resulted in alienation and rootlessness. (Jørgensen 1977: 264, my translation)

---

16 There is no room here to more than gesture towards the long-standing argument between liberalist developmentalists and its critics, which includes post-developmentalists, such as Arturo Escobar and James Ferguson.

These two quotations represent a rarity in Danish academic literature about modernisation and development aid discourse, simply by linking the two. Modernisation has been seen as an intrinsic part of 'Greenlandic studies', in Denmark associated primarily with Eskimology, Anthropology and to some extent Political Science, whereas development aid belongs to the realm of Development Studies, Political Science, Economics and Anthropology. However, given their coexistence over several decades one might have expected there would have been studies that sought to link, what is so obviously overlapping discourses, whose shared interests are readily identified at the time. The next and more important question is does it matter now? In order to answer this question, it is necessary to return to the initial issue raised in this chapter, that both discourses potentially challenge the idea of Denmark as a naturally enclosed nation space. Bringing them together shows that there is a layeredness of cultural differentiation that operates within the Danish perception of its national identity. To put it provocatively, if Denmark didn't have the ability to produce Greenland and its intervention in the Third World as a mirror image of its own infallibility as a modern welfare nation, the domesticity of the discourse would be obvious and render it obsolete, or it would problematise whether the infallibility might be an overstatement. It would reflect merely what was there for all Danes to observe as citizens of their own country, and they would be able to critically interrogate the claim. 'Migrants', Greenland and development aid in this way become important showcases to demonstrate the infallibility of the naturalised majority self. The self that is constructed as 'white', but at the same time rendered invisible, as a naturalised norm. Hence critical questions coming from people working in the field of studies related to the three 'categories', or for that matter from those who experience the social manifestation of the discourses on their bodies cannot destabilise the norm, because it is invisible, or rather it renders itself invisible. However, in the process of rendering itself invisible it also exposes itself in its moves to deflect the critique. This is very clear in political discourse because that is typically the clumsiest form it takes. In academic discourse it is more difficult to expose. This situation is not helped by the fact that there is a remarkable shortage of literature that even engages critically with the premise of modernisation and development aid in a Danish context.[17] The literature that exists tends instead to resign itself to descriptive accounts of what happened when and where, and some biographical material on the entrepreneurial spirits behind both processes. What can be garnered from the literature in both fields is the unquestioned assumption that with all its faults the processes were carried out with the best of intentions, indeed an attitude relentlessly repeated by various administrators and government representatives, including PMs, but more problematically a position sustained in the academic literature. The curious nature of the field of literature is then a constantly nagging anxiety that there is critique

---

17 Ironically this is a complaint raised by Bach (15), who bemoans the lack of attention given to the evolution of Danish development aid, yet nowhere in his book does any critical examination of Danish motives or interests emerge.

out there, which has to be met. However, the critique very seldom materialises. In the case of Greenland, Viemose, Dahl and Brøsted and Fægteborg represent the only thorough critique of the Danish administration of Greenland. In the case of development aid, Jørgensen's unpublished PhD represents the only thorough critique. All of these books were published in the 1970s and 1980s, since then the accounts have served more it seems to bolster the official rhetoric behind development aid/modernisation, rather than criticising them.[18]

Two large-scale research projects in recent years, in fact two of the biggest research projects in the two areas illustrate this problem. One account is the investigation of the Danish inclusion of Greenland into the Danish realm, which for that reason focuses on the period immediately after 1945. The other is the tome on the history of the evolution of Danish development aid from 1945–2005. In their capacity as relatively recent books that reflect back on a period that is commonly referred to as a period with a dated vision of modernisation and development aid, one would expect to see them address the problematic attitude represented by simplistic modernisation thought. Yet neither of them delivers. Bach et al.'s, *Idealer og realiteter* is a descriptive account uncritical in all its assumptions about what might have driven development aid internationally, and what drove Danish development aid more specifically. When the book occasionally ventures into the territory of addressing the question of development aid on a more general level, it quickly reveals its absence of critical distance:

> The main emphasis in the presentation will be on the 'developing nation aspect', or to be more precise the development aspect of Danish policy vis-à-vis the countries in the Third World ... The developing nations [are] in relation to the most developed industrialised nations in Europe and North America way behind in economic and social development – a condition which they and the rest of the international community from a range of different motivations have seen a common interest in changing by promoting their economic and social development ... It has been a relatively steady point of view in Danish development policy that free trade will benefit the developing countries and be an important precondition for their economic growth. (Bach et al. 2008: 16–17)

Given the long-standing critique of the early phase of development aid's craze for modernisation, and more generally the critique of a lack of genuine involvement of the recipient countries (parallel again to the Greenlandic situation), it is amazing that this book does not find it necessary to even address this critique, but instead mindlessly reproduces the image of the Rest as trailing the (it would seem disinterested) West. The contemporary investigation into the transition of Greenland from colony to integrated part of the Danish Commonwealth, *Afvikling*

---

18 Especially in relation to literature, Kirsten Thisted and Karen Langgård have pointed to the continuity of representational patterns of Danes and Greenlanders, and their interdependence.

af Grønlands kolonistatus 1945–54. En historisk udredning follows the same mode of storytelling:

> It was a dominant trait in the Danish attitudes to the possessions in Greenland that Greenland as economic, social (including health-wise) and politically backwards country was both unique and extremely vulnerable. Consequently, Denmark was obliged to protect the Greenlanders and their vulnerable society against economic influence from abroad and as widely as possible advance Greenland's development towards a modern society ... The modernists felt that after the war one should take the first steps towards an economic and political development corresponding to the one, Denmark had gone through over several centuries ... By contrast the traditionalists felt that Greenland was not ready for such a development. (DIIS 2007: 11, my translation)

Even if the report speaks of the patriarchal attitude betrayed in Denmark's administration of Greenland, the report does not even begin to address the *real* problem of the Danish presence in Greenland, that is, the defence of its national interests, nor does it take into account the long Greenlandic tradition of criticising Danish authoritarian attitudes to Greenlanders. Although the report distances itself historically ('*was* a dominant trait'), nowhere in the report does it begin to address the relationship between this attitude and the Danish rule in Greenland. Similar to *Idealer og realiteter*, where policies are simply described, not discussed, seldom analysed, which renders them as transparent accounts of a period in Danish history, which although 'of its time' needs no words to emphasise, through distancing, what reservations are required in order to read these histories, with the benefits of what we may, or may not have known then. As such they act as patrolling accounts that prevent the emergence of more critical assessments. Both accounts readily reproduce deeply stereotyped representations as Greenland/the Third World as lagging behind and insert Denmark as the benevolent helper.

References

Anderson, B. 1991. *Imagined Communities: Reflections on the Origin of Nationalism*. London: Verso.

Bach, C.F., T.B. Olesen, S. Kaur-Pedersen, J. Pedersen. 2008. *Idealer og realiteter: Dansk udviklingspolitiks historie 1945–2005*. Copenhagen: Gyldendal.

Bhabha, H. 1994. Dissemination: Time, narrative and the margins of the modern nation, in *The Location of Culture*. London: Routledge, 139–70.

Brun, E. 1985. *Mit Grønlandsliv*. København: Gyldendal.

Brøsted, J. og M. Fægteborg. 1985. *Thule – fangerfolk og militæranlæg*. Copenhagen: Jurist- og Økonomforbundets Forlag.

Butcher, J. 2007. *Ecotourism, NGOs and Development*. London: Routledge.

Dahl, J. 1986. *Arktisk selvstyre*. Copenhagen: Akademisk Forlag.

Debes, H.J. 2001. *Færingernes land*. Torshavn: Multivers.
DIIS. 2007. *Afvikling af Grønlands kolonistatus 1945-54. En historisk udredning*. København: DIIS http://www.stm.dk/publikationer/grludredning07/DIIS.pdf.
DUPI. 1997. *Grønland under den kolde krig: Dansk og amerikansk sikkerhedspolitik 1945-68*. Copenhagen: Dansk Udenrigspolitisk Institut.
Escobar, A. 1995. *Encountering Development: The Making and the Unmaking of the Third World*. Princeton: Princeton University Press.
Hall, S., D. Held, D. Hubert and K. Thompson (eds). 1996. *Modernity: An Introduction to Modern Societies*. London: Blackwell.
Jørgensen, K. 1977. *Hjælp fra Danmark: En studie i dansk u-landspolitik 1960-71*. Odense: Odense Universitetsforlag.
Koch, L. 1996. *Racehygiejne i Danmark 1920-56*. Copenhagen: Information.
Krogh, T. 1989. Humanitet og politik i det danske efterkrigshjælpearbejde 1945-51, in *Historie/Jyske Samlinger, Bind ny række*, 18(2), http://www.tidsskrift.dk/visning.jsp?markup=&print=no&id=73418.
Lidegaard, M. 1973. *Ligestilling uden lighed*. Copenhagen: Schultz Forlag.
Lynge, A. et al. 2000. *The Right to Return: Fifty Years of Struggle by Relocated Inughuit in Greenland*. Nuuk: Atuagkat.
Marquardt, O. 2009. H.J. Rink, in *Grønland – en refleksiv udfordring*, edited by O. Høiris. Aarhus: AAUF, 129-54.
Nauerby, T. 1995. *No Nation Is an Island*. Aarhus: Aarhus University Press.
Rünitz, L. 2000. *Danmark og de jødiske flygtninge 1933-40 En bog om flygtninge og menneskerettigheder*. Copenhagen: Museum Tusculanum.
Steenstrup, K.J.V. 1893-94. Dr Phil. Hinrich Johannes Rink, in *Geografisk Tidsskrift*, 12, 163-6.
Thorleifsen, Daniel. 2003. Kampen for etnisk identitet og krav om ekstern selvbestemmelsesret. Bevæggrunde for grønlandske ønsker om selvstyre 1950-2000, in *De vestnordiske landes fælleshistorie*, edited by Daniel Thorleifsen. Inussuk. Arktisk forskningsjournal 2.
Viemose, J. 1977. *Dansk kolonipolitik i Grønland*. København: Demos.

Chapter 8
Bodies and Boundaries

Kirsten Hvenegård-Lassen and Serena Maurer

On page 6 of the 2007 (English) edition of the booklet *Citizen in Denmark: Information to new citizens about Danish society*, the former Danish Ministry for Refugees, Immigration and Integration Affairs welcomes newcomers to Denmark:

> Dear New Citizen,
>
> Beginning a new life in a new country often involves considerable upheaval. You will encounter new people and new ways of doing things.
>
> This handbook is intended to help you get started in your new life in Denmark and make your daily life that little bit easier. It outlines Danish society and provides practical information which you may require as a new citizen in Denmark.
>
> ...
>
> It is a challenge for one and all – for both new and native Danes – to retain and develop an open society offering freedom, progress and opportunity. The diversity which you and others bring from the outside can lead to increased dynamism and renewed innovation.
>
> In the hope that you will become actively involved in the society of which you are now a part, we warmly welcome you to Denmark. Good luck with your new life in Denmark.

This welcome address intonates the ambivalent positioning of 'new' and 'native' Danes that characterizes the remainder of the Ministry 'handbook'. The booklet is criss-crossed with oscillating boundaries between bodies marked by nativity and newness. Initially, these boundaries enable coterminous proclamations of unity (all of us 'on the inside' are Danes) and division (diversity is 'new', or 'from the outside'). In what follows we map how these boundaries emerge and shift across the pages of the booklet. Our mapping zooms in on three thematic moments in the booklet: its profiles of 'model' immigrants, its discussion of 'the body and sex' in Denmark, and the photographic representation of a family mantelpiece opening the booklet's chapter on 'family'. We choose these moments as our foci for the ways in which they represent the slippery and contradictory boundaries between 'citizens' and 'new citizens' surfacing throughout the booklet.[1]

Our analysis draws on Homi Bhabha's (2004) notion of colonial authority to theorize the ways in which *Citizen in Denmark* (*CID*) reproduces and recomposes a co-constitutive boundary between 'native' and 'new' Danes. Colonial authority is, according to Bhabha, a power formation that works through an ambivalent and multilayered continual production of the colonized's difference from the colonizer as both absolute (menace) and almost, but not quite, like us (mimicry). Colonial mimicry is one modality of colonial authority, which Bhabha defines as 'the desire for a reformed, recognizable other, as a subject of difference that is almost the same, but not quite' (Bhabha 2004: 122). This desire for sameness is continually interrupted by the anxious reproduction of the colonial other as menacing difference. Bhabha develops this framework in order to grasp how mimicry opens a space of performativity and subversion for the colonized subject. However, in this chapter we are concentrating on the production of the Danish self, that is, the unstable production of (Danish) authority through an oscillation between the other as 'almost but not quite' like us and the other as absolute, menacing difference. In our interpretation, mimicry and menace are layered co-presences in *CID*'s positioning of the immigrant other as a subject of difference. The oscillation between the two has to do with what is foregrounded and backgrounded in specific representations. Our focus on the co-presence of mimicry and menace means that instead of analysing current Danish immigration policies and practices as representing one type of discourse or another (for example, universalist or particularist), we consider the discursive field and the subject positions on offer as constructed through ambivalent, multilayered representational practices.

We turn to a terminology of race in our analysis to make sense of the ways in which *Citizen in Denmark*'s constructions of Danishness and immigrant otherness work through representations of whiteness and non-whiteness. Race is a concept generally evaded in continental Europe (Gullestad 2004; Hervik 2004a; 2004b; Sawyer 2008; Hübinette and Lundström 2011). This erasure works through a discourse of race that articulates the concept with the colonial and racist practices of other powers out there – that is *outside* Europe. Goldberg (2006) argues that race – and indeed racism – is only seen as a European phenomenon in connection with anti-Semitism and the Holocaust. As a consequence, discourses of race and racism are in the European context either deemed irrelevant or associated with individual delusions. It is within this context that race has evaporated as a speakable term

---

[1] The boundaries appearing in the handbook are, of course, inserted in – written against, breaking away from and reproducing – the broader landscape of Danish discursive practices concerning immigration, integration, social cohesion, national 'values', and so on. This broader landscape is alluded to in the course of the chapter, but space does not permit a more thorough treatment here. For analyses of various pieces of this broader landscape, see: Andreassen 2005, 2011, 2012; Brun and Hersh 2008; Hervik 2004b, 2006; Koefoed and Simonsen 2007; Larsen 2009; Marselis 2008; Siim and Skjeie 2008; Yilmaz 2011.

while concepts like 'ethnicity' and 'majority and minority' have become the norm in European academic and popular analyses of immigration. While these terms have their merits, they also facilitate a non-engagement with the racial taxonomies at play in contemporary European – including Nordic – policies of immigration and the linkages between these taxonomies and historical moments of colonialism. This is what Stuart Hall calls colonial amnesia (Hall 2000), or the 'forgetting' of colonialism as something internal to and formative of Europe. The erasure of colonialism's role in Europe's internal past is in the Nordic countries coupled with another amnesiac move concerning our participation in the happenings of the elsewhere of colonialism. In this way, Nordic exceptionalism is a sort of opting out of colonialism all together. Which means there is no 'burden of guilt' (Marselis 2008) for the Nordic countries to carry–about the set of historical practices popularly understood as 'colonialism', or about other historical and contemporary discourses and practices of producing differentiation and inequalities we might also, in a postcolonial vein, name 'colonial'.

While racialization in Europe, as elsewhere, tends to centre on the production of difference, or otherness, it is never uni-directional. As a relational system of categorization, racialization also always involves the construction of an unmarked category against whom difference is constructed. As Ruth Frankenberg has argued about whiteness in an American context:

> ... continual processes of slippage, condensation, and displacement among the constructs 'race', 'nation', and 'culture' continue to 'unmark' white people while consistently marking and racializing others. (Frankenberg 1997: 6)

Frankenberg and other scholars within critical whiteness studies (cf. Dyer 1997; Razack 1998, Byrne 2006) direct our attention to discourses and practices that establish whiteness as an implicit and unmarked norm that is an essential component of racial taxonomies and the unequal power relations they produce. Whiteness maps a racialized reality shared and lived by everybody, but largely unrecognized by those who are interpreted as white. In line with Frankenberg, we do not see whiteness as an essential or fixed category (see also Blaagaard 2006). As Bridget Byrne argues:

> It should be clear that whiteness needs to be approached as a historicised and contextualized construction. It is produced in a series of instances where discursive and psychic processes lead to identifications with subject positions that are constructed as the norm, the neutral, the centre, which is defined by and through the construction of a racialised other. These moments of construction are at the same time gendered and classed. (Byrne 2006: 26)

What counts as 'white', then, shifts over time and between locations. This means that specific groups of people may pass from non-white to white – as, for instance, in the case of the subject position 'Irish' (Byrne 2006: 22–3). The distinction itself – and hence the modern idea of race – is, however, bound up with a specific historical moment: that of European 'enlightenment', colonialism and imperialism *and* modern naturalist science. Here the ground for the figuration of human beings as the family of man, distinguished by hierarchical gendered and racial relations (McClintock 1995) is laid. In that sense whiteness is the point of departure – the summit being the white patriarch – for the establishment of the social imaginings of race as such. Located within a regional context that, in Bolette Blaagaard's words, 'is in several ways the epitome of whiteness in the Western and Nordic European consciousness' (Blaagaard 2006: 1), Denmark itself emerges as the summit of these racialized constructions of the family of man. Even as Nordic whiteness is in this sense highly marked as such, it 'easily becomes simultaneously the 'norm' as well as something invisible – everything and nothing' (Blaagaard 2006: 1, see also Hübinette and Lundström 2011).

As pointed out by Byrne in the quotation above, the distinctions that are drawn between whites and non-whites are not only raced, but also gendered and classed. In our analysis of the handbook, we especially turn our attention to how gender emerges as a constituent in discourses and practices that establish (Danish) whiteness as the summit of civilization.[2] Here, we draw on postcolonial feminist research which in recent years has demonstrated how gender equality has been highlighted as a specific characteristic of different European countries as well as sometimes, more generally, as a pan-European value and condition (cf. Andreassen 2011, 2012; Lewis 2006; Tuori 2007, 2009). Gender equality (often in conjunction with 'tolerant attitudes towards homosexuals') hence becomes a national characteristic, something obtained by the Danes (as well as by the Finns, the Norwegians, the Swedes and so on) – *and* a discursive resource in the formation of distinctions between the national us and the immigrant other. In Denmark, the discourse of gender equality articulates Danishness and (universal) modernity. In doing so, it signifies a co-constitutive boundary between gender equal Danish women and men and non-Danish women victims of a gender hierarchy installed and reproduced by their non-Danish men that calls up and reworks colonial notions of saving brown women from brown men (Spivak 1988: 296).

New Citizens in Denmark

The English version of the (2007) second edition of *Citizen in Denmark* is a small booklet of 169 glossy pages richly illustrated with colour photos.[3] Also published

---

    2   Class also appears as an intersecting category in the handbook; albeit in a less direct way than gender. Hence the emphasis on gender reflects our interests, but also that gender seems to be stuck to race in more spectacular ways than class gets attached to race in contemporary Denmark.

    3   The handbook is also published in an online version accessible from the Ministry's webpage, available at: www.nyidanmark.dk/en-us/citizenship/citizen_in_

in 17 other languages, the handbook is co-authored by an editorial team consisting of members of the Ministry itself and a private communication and project management company entitled Commitment Kommunikation ApS.[4] Visually, the booklet combines the look of a tourism brochure advertising the Danish flag, the royal family and other national icons with more prosaic photos of people engaged in the daily activities of paid employment and everyday life. The booklet contains 10 thematic chapters offering general information about Denmark ('Geography and population,' 'How the country is governed') as well as 3 chapters specifically directed at immigrants ('Entry and residence in Denmark,' 'New citizen in Denmark' and 'Repatriation').

While the English booklet is a translation of the Danish version, the English title (*Citizen in Denmark: information to new citizens about Danish society*) speaks to a formal, rights-bearing kind of citizenship while the Danish one (*Medborger i Danmark. Information til nye borgere om det danske samfund*) refers to citizenship as practice, or performativity. *Medborgere* denotes the everyday practices of living together as a national community rather than legal citizenship, which in Danish is conveyed by the term *statsborgerskab*. Both versions of the title offer a promise of sameness or unity in the sense that 'new' and 'old' Danes are all *medborgere*, *borgere*, or citizens. But when we place the English and Danish versions alongside one another, the English title's use of 'citizen' highlights the Danish title's erasure of the barriers to 'new citizens'' access to the formal rights of citizenship, barriers that both versions of the booklet matter-of-factly detail in the chapters specifically directed at 'new citizens'.

According to the Ministry, the handbook is distributed to 'newcomers'. But the text and photos partly subvert this broad reach by spotlighting particular kinds of 'newcomers' as those best served by the information the booklet has to offer. Hence in Chapter 4, entitled *New citizen in Denmark*, the handbook is situated as 'a supplement to and clarifi[cation of] many of the topics listed in the Declaration [regarding integration and active citizenship]' (*CID*: 38).[5] As *CID* explains, this Declaration must be signed by refugees or other people without Nordic or EU citizenship who have joined their family in Denmark – 'third country citizens' in the official lingo – as part of their integration contract with the local authorities. The integration contract includes a specification of the contents of the three-year

---

denmark/Medborger.htm.

4 [Online]. Available at: www.commitment-aps.dk/. The company's homepage is – despite the partly English name – in Danish. As the Danish text explains, Commitment Kommunikation ApS is a consulting group that works with public, semi-public and private institutions, organizations and companies on a broad range of communicationprojects.

5 See the full wording of the Declaration here: www.nyidanmark.dk/NR/rdonlyres/7A32FAD0-E279-467C-91E3-3074249ED586/0/integrationserklaering_engelsk.pdf.

introductory programme offered to this group of immigrants.[6] The (objectified) informational purpose of the handbook hence is interrupted by its relation to this quasi-legal document, which limits the scope of the 'new citizens' targeted by *CID* as it 'informs you (that is, 'third country', 'new citizens') about a number of values and rules in Danish society' so that 'you will know what society expects of you as a new citizen' (*CID*: 38). When we look at the declaration itself, we can see that the 'third country' 'new citizen's' signature on the declaration binds her or him to the performative speech act it installs: 'I, the undersigned, hereby declare that I will actively endeavour to ensure that I and any of my children and spouse/cohabitant who reside in Denmark will be integrated and become active citizens in Danish society.'

This vague and far-reaching promise of active citizenship contained in the declaration takes shape through 16 commandments through which the 'third country' 'new citizen' pledges that s/he '[understands] and [accepts]' a detailed list of modes of performing Danishness. Many of these reproduce popular discourses about unacceptable (menacing) 'immigrant practices' in Denmark,[7] such as the following:

> I understand and accept that in Denmark all children shall be given equal respect and self-expression – be they boys or girls – in order for them to grow up and become active and responsible citizens who are capable of making their own decisions. I shall ensure that my children have the best possible childhood and adolescence, schooling and integration in Denmark. I shall amongst others ensure that my child learns Danish as soon as possible and does his/her homework throughout the school years, and I shall actively collaborate with my child's day care institution and school. I understand and accept that it is illegal in Denmark to hit one's children. I understand and accept that circumcision of girls and the use of force to contract marriage is illegal in Denmark. (http://www.nyidanmark.dk/en-us/coming_to_dk/permanent-residence-permit/permanent-residence-permit.htm)

---

6 The (municipal) integration programmes contain Danish language education, courses in Danish history and society and/or job-related training. Signing the Declaration is a condition for obtaining a permanent residence permit in Denmark. In 2007 other requirements included, in the wording of *CID* 'that you have had a job or worked for a time, that you pass a Danish language proficiency test, that you do not owe the state more than a certain sum or that you have not committed a serious crime' (30). These conditions have since been reformulated in terms of a point-system, where you will not be granted permanent residence until you score 100 points. The current point system can be seen here: www.nyidanmark.dk/en-us/coming_to_dk/permanent-residence-permit/permanent-residence-permit.htm.

7 For an analysis of the gendered dimensions of the declaration see Andreassen 2012: 148–9.

As the booklet situates itself as a handbook for the individual immigrant ('I') who must sign on to 'be integrated and become [an] active citizen ... in Danish society', it underlines *CID*'s focus on the performing individual immigrant vis-à-vis the established norms of Danish society indicated in the handbook's explanatory subtitle ('information to new citizens about Danish society'). It also reproduces (neo)liberal notions of individual responsibility for self-improvement (Valverde 1996; Rose 1999); the successful self here being the immigrant who can, through his or her own active performance of Danishness, achieve belonging in the national community, or 'citizenship,' despite the legal and economic barriers to this belonging.

Following Bhabha, we interpret the contradictions between *CID*'s calls for individual immigrant responsibility and unproblematically generalized (re)productions of immigrant menace as evidence of an ambivalent production of (immigrant) difference along lines of mimicry and menace. *CID* reproduces immigrant difference both as it teaches the targeted immigrant how to properly perform, or mimic, Danishness and as it evokes discourses and legal practices that reproduce the immigrant as menace. Thus the booklet figures the immigrant as, on the one hand, absolutely different and, on the other, almost, but never quite like, us. The two kinds of difference are relational in so far as representations of the immigrant as menace incite the calls for mimicry that themselves reproduce menace as the threat against which they must continuously be produced.

Model Immigrants

CID's call to mimicry is most clear in the booklet's presentation of a set of eight (textual and photographic) 'newcomer' profiles that teach the reader the ins and outs of the activated immigrant performance. We interpret these profiles as tools for the fulfilment of a desire for a reformed other. These profiles of what we're calling *model immigrants* teach the newcomer how s/he can move into a position of mimicry (and avoid menace) in order to pave his or her way into Danish society.

The origins of the eight model immigrants profiled in the handbook are representative of the populations of 'third country' immigrants that tend to emerge as the focus of contemporary Danish integration campaigns: Pakistan, Iraq, Turkey, Palestine, Somalia, Macedonia and Afghanistan, all of which are popularly associated with Islam.[8] In profiling these particular 'newcomers' as

---

8 According to Statistics Denmark, immigrants and their offspring regardless of (Danish) citizenship make up 9.1 per cent of the Danish population, only 6.2 per cent (again: of the total population) originated in the 'non-Western' countries highlighted in CID's immigrant profiles. Top-score origins among all immigrants are: Turkey and Iraq, followed by Germany. The entire population in Denmark is just below 5.5 million. The numbers are published in the 2008 population statistics from the Ministry for Refugees, Immigration and Integration Affairs.

the immigrants to model, *Citizen in Denmark* calls up contemporary popular and state discourses about immigration and integration in Denmark that write the immigrant as a Muslim other. We see the kinds of difference these discourses associate with the Muslim other echoed in the passages of the declaration of active citizenship cited above (patriarchal, violent, dispassionate about and inactive in their children's schooling).

Scattered throughout the handbook, each of the individual portraits of the five men and three women are accompanied by a short paragraph recounting the immigrant's country of origin, when they arrived in Denmark and what they are doing here. This paragraph serves as a sort of backdrop to each model immigrant's narrative about 'Danish society' and how to become an active 'new citizen'. The statement of middle-aged Nevzat Ibisi from Macedonia is, for instance, subsumed under the headline: 'I like the Danish system' (*CID*: 119), while Amna Amin, a woman from Iraq, reminds the reader that: 'Speaking the [Danish] language opens a lot of doors' (*CID*: 36).

While the origins and former residence of the eight model immigrants are highlighted alongside their photographs, the stories of and reasons for migration are not selected as relevant. Hence the individual histories of the eight model immigrants – and, by extension, of all 'new citizens'– are erased, along with the larger global histories and power relations shaping their migration to Denmark. What matters is what happens in 'the hereafter', here situated as a time and place in which the immigrant emerges as a clean slate on which we can start writing the codes of conduct associated with Danishness.

The first of *CID*'s model immigrants appears on page 16, in a section entitled 'How the country is governed.' Perwez Iqbal left his native Pakistan in 1970, the reader is informed by the box of text floating alongside his photograph. Superimposed on the photograph itself is the quotation 'I think it is our duty to become involved'– a statement that calls up the 'active citizenship' alluded to in the declaration as it emerges as a headline for all advice set forth by the model immigrants in the handbook. The spectacles and whitening hair suggest that Iqbal is the kind of older and wiser immigrant man other immigrants should listen to and model, a father figure whose commitment to and knowledge about Denmark and Danishness is proven by his decades of experience. With sand-coloured clothes that give off the air of a relaxed professionalism in keeping with what is worn by a large part of the Danish male population of Iqbal's age, Iqbal is also proof of active immigrant citizenship done well – or, in Bhabha's terms: mimicry. The handbook's visual and textual representations of Iqbal simultaneously erase his difference (his dress and stance familiar, commonplace, harmless, even) and point to its existence (his name, country of origin, skin and hair tones marking racial/national difference).

Bodies and Boundaries 127

Figure 8.1 *CID:* 16; photo: Michael Daugaard

Alongside the photograph, in quotation marks, we read:

> In my opinion, it is the duty of every immigrant to become actively involved to whatever extent they can and pass on the benefit of personal experience. There are great opportunities for gaining influence at local community level; it's simply a question of using them. I, myself, became active back in the 80s because I wanted to comment on what is being said about immigrants in the media. The experience taught me a lot; I met lots of very different people and today I have many Danish friends. By taking an active part in discussions, I have helped to alter the perception of many Danes towards immigrants and influenced integration initiatives in Albertslund Municipal Authority. (*CID*: 16)

What stands out here is the idea that influence is there, ready to be picked up by anyone who makes an active effort. Doing so is the duty or responsibility of the individual immigrant, but the duty also has a collective dimension: as an immigrant you have a duty to pass on your experiences to other immigrants and to alter some Danes' (erroneous) perceptions of immigrants. The statement is overtly about political influence, but in a broader sense it captures how the relation between old and new citizens is imagined in the handbook – and in the greater imaginings of integration in which the booklet is inserted. In the shadows against which the figure of the successful immigrant mimic comes to light, we also glimpse *menace*: the immigrant, who – through his/her passivity – becomes responsible for Danish perceptions of immigrants as unemployed subjects relying on welfare benefits, uninterested in their new society and its ways.

When we move from the profile of Iqbal to the set of model immigrants following in his footsteps in the handbook, it becomes apparent that the 'active citizenship' required by the declaration and embodied by the model immigrants follows a gendered pattern. As demonstrated by Iqbal (and confirmed in the rest of the profiles), immigrant men's activity takes place in relationship to 'public' matters – politics, the welfare system, jobs and education.

The activity of model immigrant women, on the other hand, focuses on Danish language proficiency and immigrant children's upbringing in Danish society. It also emerges in the context of model immigrant women's mimicry of Danish women's presence in the labour market (all three model immigrant women work outside the home). These are working women who challenge popular stereotypes of immigrant women as victims of repressive Muslim men – victims who speak no or very little Danish and are prevented by their husbands from entering the labour market or taking Danish language classes.[9] The booklet in this sense goes against the grain through its move away from these stereotypes.

Sabah Elawi is one of these model immigrant women. The text tells us that she is a schoolteacher, an identity the photograph of her sitting relaxed in a primary school classroom on one of the pupils' tables underscores (*CID:* 77). Her face – sweetly smiling – is framed by a sand-coloured *hijab* tucked into a high turtleneck, worn under a patterned red dress and a white cardigan. Her skin is covered, but her body is not obscured. While the visual representation of Perwez Iqbal only very vaguely hints at physical markers of racial difference between him and 'the old citizens', Elawi's difference is announced by an obvious and heavily loaded, or 'sticky', sign (Ahmed 2004): the *hijab*. The inclusion of Elawi amongst the model immigrants seems to point in another direction than the representation of Iqbal, where difference only emerges as diluted traces. The *hijab* overtly marks Elawi as different, but still she is presented as a source of valuable advice to other newcomers to Denmark, and, as such, she signals a Danish acceptance of difference.

---

9 These stereotypes are in circulation across social domains in Denmark. The media and political debates may be the most prominent sites of production and reproduction (cf. Andreassen 2005, 2011, 2012; Siim and Skjeie 2008), but they also seem to be employed in the administrative practices associated with integration and other social work (cf. Larsen 2009).

Figure 8.2 *CID:* 77; photo: **Michael Daugaard**

The representation of Elawi is, however, ambiguous and multilayered. Another layer emerges with the statement overlaid on Elawi's photo – 'It's all about securing our children's future' – and the body of text alongside. When we read this text in relationship to the picture, it becomes unclear whether Elawi is offered the speaking position of a professional teacher – or if she speaks as a mother:

> It's important to attend parent-teacher meetings and take part in school-parent collaboration in order to stay abreast of developments and build a bridge between Danish and Arab society. It's about securing our children's future. You get to know other parents and have the opportunity of influencing your children's education. You have to be open and prepared to tell people what you think and let them know what you are capable of. You mustn't become isolated. And most important of all, you have to learn the language so you can get to know Danes better, and vice versa. (*CID:* 77)

The text speaks directly to the commandments of the declaration of active citizenship quoted above and hence indirectly points towards established notions of what is wrong with the immigrants, including in terms of their lack of involvement in their children's schools. While Elawi is explicitly labelled 'schoolteacher' in the text, in this statement she appears to speak less as a representative of Danish educational institutions and more as a representative of 'Arab society', or, perhaps more specifically, as an *Arab mother* who tries to bridge the difference between that society and Danish society. The *hijab* hence becomes the visual marker of difference that correlates with the textual reference to 'Arab society' as it solidifies 'our' understanding of 'Arab society' as patriarchal, and thus as an arena within which Elawi's representation as family/care worker rather than school teacher makes sense.

As Meyda Yegenoglu observes, the European obsession with the 'Oriental veil' is rationalized in terms of: "civilizing', 'modernizing', and thereby 'liberating' the 'backward' Orient and its women, making them speaking subjects'. (Yegenoglu 2003: 548). But the representation of Elawi is neither 'backward' Oriental woman nor liberated European one. Although she seems to have succeeded in a partial 'liberation' through her successful mimicry of the working Danish woman, the sticky presence of the hijab continues to redress her body in the menace of immigrant difference=patriarchal oppression that confines the horizon of her active citizenship to matters of the family and social reproductive/care work.[10] As we illustrate in the next section, the menace Elawi's *hijab*-clad form embodies emerges in stark contrast to the 'proof' of gender equality located in the body of the unclothed Danish woman surfacing in *CID*'s textual and visual representations of Danish 'bodies and sex'.

Nudity and Modernity

Throughout *Citizen in Denmark*, the model immigrants' performances are situated in relationship to representations of the kinds of Danishness they should seek to mimic. One set of these representations emerges towards the end of the chapter on 'Family' in a photo and accompanying body of text entitled 'the body and sex'. The photo is of a wide lawn covered with towels and bathing suit-clad bodies. The text alongside reads:

> Whether or not you approve, you will often come across sex and nudity in Danish society. Newspapers write articles about sex and sex life, and adverts and commercials visually exploit the human body.

---

10   It should be noted here, that as we interpret Elawi as in some ways mimicking the 'liberated' figure of the working Danish woman, we are not asserting that Danish women themselves have been liberated from a gendered labour market. Although the overwhelming majority of Danish women are included in the labour market, this labour market is to a large degree gendered, and public sector care work in Denmark is predominantly occupied by women (cf. Siim 2000). While families (and welfare provisions) in Denmark are in many ways built on a dual breadwinner model, patriarchal family norms continue to lurk beneath the surface.

Bodies and Boundaries 131

This reflects a general social trend towards a more liberal view of sexual life. In the last decade, new ways of living together have come into being as well as greater freedom to decide over one's own body and improved conditions for homosexuals, for example. With this freedom, however, comes responsibility.

This means there are limits on what you can and can not (sic) do, and no one is allowed to force others to do things against their will. The assumption is that we respect each other's person and sexual boundaries.

Semi-naked sunbathers in the park and on the beach or scantily clad or naked bathers, for example, should not be seen as an open invitation to sex. In the same way, neither a person's body language nor provocative fashion should be interpreted as an open invitation to sex. Sexual assault must be reported to the police so that the offender(s) can be prosecuted.

Figure 8.3 *CID:* **65; photo: Jørgen Schytte**

While the text mentions 'new ways of living together' and 'improved conditions for homosexuals' as two examples of Danish modernity when it comes to matters of the body and sex, there is no visual or textual evidence of these in the remainder of the booklet. But the landscape of bare skin stretching across the photo does offer ample evidence of Danes exhibiting 'greater freedom to decide over one's own body.' The photo creates a visual link between public nudity and sexual/bodily freedom that is confirmed in the text (beginning with the opening line: 'you will often come across sex and nudity in Danish society'). The half-naked sunbathers are not explicitly gendered in the text, but when we look at the photograph, the majority of those Danes who are free to disrobe appear to be donned with breasts and bikinis. This photographic illustration of Danes' bodily and sexual freedom as a landscape of largely unclothed women brings a particular feminist notion of freedom into focus, one that links it with women's bodily autonomy.

As we discuss in the introduction to this chapter, representations of liberated views on women as part of what constitutes Danishness are not surprising within a contemporary Nordic context in which "being good at gender equality' is seen as an essential and inherent part of the social landscape' (Tuori 2009: 158). It is even less surprising that this representation of a belief in women's right to govern their bodies and sex *as* Danish emerges in the context of immigration, a terrain where, as Salla Tuori points out, gender equality has become 'one of the cornerstones in discourses on multiculturalism' (Tuori 2009: 158). But the emphasis on women's bodily and sexual autonomy as an essential component of gender equality does seem to be more pronounced in Denmark than in the other Nordic countries. And covering up – as in the case of Sabah Elawi – floats through debates about immigration as a sign of coercion, a restriction on women's free choice. Thus the contrast between undressed Danish female bodies and covered 'oriental' women lurking in the shadows of 'the body and sex' text and photo becomes a line of difference written between the national body and its others.

The whiteness of the (free) Danish woman's body and nation surfaces through a gathering together of bits of photographic evidence on display: light-skinned bellies, backs and limbs and blonde hair aren't the only body parts on display, but they do fill up enough of the landscape to effectively mark it as inhabited by a Danish corporeality that tends to circulate, along with other Nordic bodies, as a personification of True Whiteness. As Lena Sawyer has argued, 'blond hair, blue eyes, and pale skin' (Sawyer 2008: 90) function as signifiers of a Nordic/Scandinavian whiteness within and outside contemporary Nordic contexts. The sense that the unclothed Danish women's bodies in 'the body and sex' embody the Nordic 'epitome of whiteness' (Blaagaard 2006: 1) we reference above is enhanced by their location in a chapter on 'family'. Bloodlines are involved here as families, or, a national family, of white bodies reproduce liberated Danish women, and thus Danish modernity, over time. The free Danish woman's emergence in the context of the 'family' also connects her with contemporary constructions of a Scandinavian/Nordic ancestry surfacing across the Nordic region whose whiteness is produced through its differentiation from immigrant racial otherness (Sawyer 2008). As Tobias Hübinette and Catrin Lundström have illustrated in a Swedish context, this differentiation of Nordic whiteness and its immigrant others is emerging as 'a racialized juxtaposition' between white and non-white women that:

> ... reflects the ideological function that the family plays in the construction of the nation as naturalizing gendered and national boundaries, and indeed how the politics of family values nurtures nationalistic ideals and in the end the (re) production of Swedish whiteness. (Hübinette and Lundström 2011: 49)

Danish whiteness also surfaces in 'the body and sex' as a set of practices and beliefs. The claims of tolerance (for homosexuality) and displays of gender equality-as-sexual liberation speak to a modern, liberal Danish whiteness that, as framed in *CID*'s opening letter, '[offers] freedom, progress and opportunity' to all – different and familiar – within its territorial reach. This characterization of Denmark as a land of tolerance and women's freedom frames Danishness within hegemonic constructions of Europe–and its people–as 'a universal standard of humanity' (Lewis 2006: 89) 'distinguished by its core principles of freedom, of family and private life and respect for and promotion of tolerance' (Lewis 2006: 91). In this imaginary, Europe's 'sociopolitical advancement and superiority ... rests upon an image of women's freedom and a particular kind of gender order between women and men' (Lewis 2006: 92–3), one that eschews hierarchy and embraces equality.

In the opening line of 'the body and sex' text – 'Whether or not you approve, you will often come across sex and nudity in Danish society,' – the whiteness of the liberated Danish women's bodies in question also surfaces in direct relationship to the 'new citizen' reader of *Citizen in Denmark*. As it situates the 'you' = 'new citizen' as an observer of contemporary practices of 'sex and nudity in Danish society', the text places this reader outside the liberated space of Danish territory and its national families' free nude women. This is consistent with the didactic tone taken throughout the booklet that produces the 'new citizen' as someone who is unfamiliar with, and therefore must be taught about, Denmark's modern, liberated ways. But here, the 'new citizen' appears not only unfamiliar with, but likely to be *against* Danish ways.

The text's repetitive concluding claims that 'semi-naked sunbathers in the park and on the beach ... should not be seen as an open invitation to sex' and 'neither a person's body language nor provocative fashion should be interpreted as an open invitation to sex' evokes a 'new (male) citizen' who has moved into the heart of Denmark, and is now standing in its parks and on its beaches. This 'new citizen' retains a menacing (sexually predatory, patriarchal) difference that necessitates he be told more than once not to take advantage of Danish women's sexual liberation. The final statement in this set of warnings – 'sexual assault must be reported to the police so that the offender(s) can be prosecuted' – homes in on the urgency behind 'the body and sex' teachings about sex/gender liberated Denmark: the protection of the Danish woman's freed body and the liberated national landscape it represents from the unliberated gender and sexual beliefs and practices of the menacing migrant male. While this call for protection aims to secure the liberty of white women, it also reaffirms their vulnerability in the presence of the (shadowy) figure of the menacing non-white immigrant man.

As these pieces of the text work to safeguard the liberation of the Danish woman/landscape, they redraw the boundaries of Danish 'freedom' around the (white) bodies whose freedom must be protected in order to preserve the modernity of the nation.[11] In this way, they echo the ways in which the imaginary of the European as the modern standard of humanity 'closes down questions as to whose identity, autonomy, family and privacy are to be respected, at whose cost and with what consequences for Europe's potential for an economy of gender equality' (Lewis 2006: 93). They also reproduce gendered colonial constructions of European whiteness and racial otherness that constituted the foundation of the reproduction of colonial authority. As Ann Laura Stoler has argued:

> A defense of community, morality, and white male power was achieved [in colonial settings] by increasing control over and consensus among Europeans, by reaffirming the vulnerability of white women, the sexual threat posed by native men, and by creating new sanctions to limit the liberties of both. (Stoler 1991: 70)

Tradition and Modernity

As 'the body and sex' produces Danishness in the realm of 'family' as a modern sort of *medborger* embodied in the performance of the free-to-be-unclothed Danish woman, the full-page photograph opening the handbook's chapter on 'family' grounds the practices of the modern Danish family in and against a more tradition-bound familial past. The mostly black-and-white photo gallery of a family lineage resting on old-fashioned furniture and out-of-date, faded wallpaper evokes the truth and authority of a national historical archive. The gallery establishes tradition, ancestry, and the depth of historical origin as the secure points of departure for modern Danish society as well as its projection into the future (Bhabha 2004: 203). What is on display here is hence out of reach of the immigrants, or 'new citizens', addressed by the handbook. The picture demarcates the limits of the space of active (new) citizen performativity. This is *our* – that is the nation's – past; and the setting from which *our* modernity has taken off. It is a genealogy of the Danish nation narrated visually – showing us the (white) looks of Danishness – or, following Sara Ahmed, the bodies that ground *the ideal image of the nation:*

> ... the promise of the nation is not an empty or abstract one that can then simply be fulfilled and transformed by others. Rather, the nation is a concrete effect of how some bodies have moved towards and away from other bodies, a movement that works to create boundaries and borders, and the 'approximation' of what we can now call 'national character' (what the nation is *like*). Such a history of movement 'sticks', so that it remains possible to 'see' a breach in the ideal image of the nation in the concrete difference of others. (Ahmed 2004: 133)

---

11   This is our interpretation of dominant media and political discourses of immigrant difference as the opposition between the modern Danish self and the traditional immigrant others (see, for instance, Hervik 2004a; 2004b; Koefoed and Simonsen 2007).

Figure 8.4 *CID:* **54; photo: Anne-Li Engstrom**

While the photo marks the limits of new citizen performativity, it can also be read in other ways. The clothing and positioning of the brides and grooms in the array of wedding photos in the picture – her in front, below, dressed in layers of feminine lace, him behind, above, in black tails and tie – suggest a patriarchal national past captured in the safety of marital heteronormativity. This suggestion seems to fit well with the representations of the patriarchal gender relations of the 'new citizens' emerging in the shadows of the declaration of active citizenship and the profiles of model immigrants discussed above. In this way, the photo alludes to a universalized notion of the route from tradition to modernity, where the others' present corresponds to 'our' past.

Here the promise of integration or active citizenship might be seen as a full entry into modernity on 'our' level. And indeed the past evoked in the family pictures seems in contrast to the contemporary Danish trend towards 'new ways of living together' spoken to further on in the 'Family' chapter in 'the body and sex.' But it also appears to illustrate the first line of text in another section in the chapter, entitled 'family life and partnerships': 'most families in Denmark consist of a father, mother and children'. In this way it seems that the (national) family picture gallery photo illustrates the continuity of Danishness as the unbroken whiteness of the traditional family line that both secures the racial normativity of the 'modern' nude white bodies in the park and enables the modern break with the national family tradition. This sense of a break with the traditions of the nation's past is enhanced by the historical breaking point established by the picture: judging from the fashion (and not least the hair dressing), the latest wedding picture is from the late 1960s or the early 1970s. That is, co-terminus with both the rise of immigration to Denmark as part of post-WWII global migration flows and the feminist movement around 'sexual revolution' that equated freedom with women's liberation from sexual and gender norms.

There is, however, at least one more layer of meaning present in the family photo. A trace that – if we follow it – seems to suggest a completely different genealogy of the Danish nation from the one captured in the discourse of unproblematic and internal national continuity. In the centre of the photo – and, one might add, the centre of the national family shrine – is a small black statue of what appears to be a naked African woman with a vessel on her head sitting alongside what looks like an Asian porcelain Buddha. In the midst of this landscape containing an all-white (and heteronormative) national past, a patch of non-whiteness appears. Even if this non-whiteness appears in the form of objects designed for decoration that are there for *our* pleasure, we might still see their emergence as an interruption of the race-erasing discourse on the Danish nation, indicating that the non-white other is already here, internal to our past and defining the existence of Danishness in profound ways.

Conclusion

Our focus in this reading of *Citizen in Denmark* has been on the ways in which the booklet produces Danishness as a particular kind of modernity in relation to the 'new citizens' it addresses. *CID*'s production of Danish modernity is premised on two discourses: (1) the 'new citizens' should become like 'us' Danes to be modern, but also – and more subtly – (2) 'our' modernity is underwritten by the fact that they should mimic it (and shadowed by the danger of subversion if they don't). Hence the universality of the teleology from Danish tradition to Danish modernity is somehow 'proven' by their mimicking it. The universal is, however, tied to the particulars of the Danish nation, which is projected backwards and forwards into a seamless linking of past, present and future, employing what Homi Bhabha terms the pedagogic discourses of the nation (Bhabha 2004: 203). And while the 'new citizens' are invited to perform in relation to the modernity of the nation, they will never be part of the Danish past projected in this pedagogic discourse. This means that, no matter how well they perform the role of the mimicking immigrant laid out in the pages of the 'new citizen's' 'handbook', the nativity alluded to in the opening address of the handbook is out of reach.

In *CID* the family is the site where nation, race and gender slide into each other to produce Danish modernity and tradition. As Ann McClintock (1995) argues: '[the family] offers a "natural" trope for figuring historical time' (McClintock

1995: 357). Paradoxically, the family – in order to attain its status as a 'natural' unit – is separated from history and thus from change, and at the same time offers what McClintock calls a 'domestic genealogy', where the time of the nation unfolds as an organic evolution figured through the child's process of growing up. This domestic genealogy crucially hinges on the family as a gendered (and heteronormative) hierarchy, something Danishness relies on in establishing its organic historical roots. This is the backdrop against which the (modern, half-naked) bodies of white Danish women in a rather traditional way come to mark the boundaries of the nation. They are, like their imperial foremothers, vulnerable and in need of protection. Gender equality in this way becomes trapped in a racialized national narration; on the one hand it is something 'we' have and 'our' unliberated others don't, and, on the other, it is under threat from the outside by these others. Embodied in the liberated white body of the Danish woman, this nationally particular brand of gender equality is central to *CID*'s production of Danishness as a modern sort of performative whiteness grounded in both a heteronormative familial national lineage and the tenets of modern liberal northern European beliefs.

References

Ahmed, S. 2004. *The Cultural Politics of Emotion*. Edinburgh: Edinburgh University Press.
Andreassen, R. 2005. The Mass Media's Construction of Gender, Race, Sexuality and Nationality: An Analysis of the Danish News Media's Communication about Visible Minorities from 1971 to 2004. PhD thesis. Toronto: University of Toronto.
Andreassen, R. 2012. Gender as a Tool in Danish Debates about Muslims, in *Islam in Denmark*, edited by J.S. Nielsen. Plymouth: Lexington Books, 143–60.
Andreassen, R. and Dutje, L. 2011. Veiled Debates: Gender and Gender Equality in European National narratives, in *Politics, Religion and Gender: Regulating the Muslim Headscarf*, edited by S. Rosenberger and B. Sauer. London: Routledge, 17–36.
Bhabha, H. 2004. *The Location of Culture*. London: Routledge Classics.
Blaagaard, B.B. 2006. Relocating Whiteness in Nordic Media Discourse, in *Rethinking Nordic Colonialism: A Postcolonial Project in Five Acts*. Kuratorisk Aktion, Nordic Institute for Contemporary Art. [Online]. Available at: www.rethinking-nordic-colonialism.org [accessed: 21 October 2011].
Brun, E. and Hersh, J. 2008. The Danish Disease: A Political Culture of Islamophobia. *Monthly Review*, June, 11–22.
Byrne, B. 2006. *White Lives: The Interplay of 'Race', Class and Gender in Everyday Life*. London: Routledge.
Dyer, R. 1997. *White*. London: Routledge.

Frankenberg, R. (ed.) 1997. *Displacing Whiteness: Essays in Social and Cultural Criticism*. Durham: Duke University Press.

Goldberg, D.T. 2006. Racial Europeanization. *Ethnic and Racial Studies*, 29(2), 331–64.

Gullestad, M. 2004. Blind Slaves of Our Prejudices: Debating 'Culture' and 'Race' in Norway. *Ethnos*, 69(2), 177–203.

Hall, S. 2000. The Multicultural Question, in *Un/Settled Multiculturalisms: Diasporas, Entanglements, Transruptions*, edited by B. Hesse. London: Zed Press, 209–40.

Hervik, P. 2004a. Anthropological Perspectives on the New Racism in Europe. *Ethnos*, 69(2), 149–55.

Hervik, P. 2004b. The Danish Cultural World of Unbridgeable Differences. *Ethnos*, 69(2), 247–67.

Hervik, P. 2006. The Emergence of Neo-Nationalism in Denmark. 1992–2001, in *Neo-Nationalism in Europe and Beyond: Perspectives from Social Anthropology*, edited by A. Gingrich and M. Banks. Berghahn Books, 136–61.

Hübinette, T. and Lundström, C. 2011. Sweden after the Recent Election: The Double-Binding Power of Swedish Whiteness through the Mourning of the Loss of 'Old Sweden' and the Passing of 'Good Sweden'. *NORA – Nordic Journal of Feminist and Gender Research*, 19(1), 42–52.

Keskinen, S., Touri, S., Irni, S. and Mulinari, D. (eds) 2009. *Complying with Colonialism: Gender, Race and Ethnicity in the Nordic Region*. Farnham and Burlington: Ashgate.

Koefoed, L. and Simonsen, K. 2007. The Price of Goodness: Everyday Nationalist Narratives in Denmark. *Antipode*, 39(2), 310–30.

Larsen, N.B. 2009. Institutionalized Nationalism and Orientalised Others in Parental Education, in *Complying with Colonialism: Gender, Race and Ethnicity in the Nordic Region*, edited by S. Keskinen, S. Tuori, S. Irne and D. Mulinari. Farnham and Burlington: Ashgate, 225–40.

Lewis, G. 2006. Imaginaries of Europe: Technologies of Gender, Economies of Power. *European Journal of Women's Studies*, 13(2), 87–102.

McClintock, A. 1995. *Imperial Leather: Race, Gender and Sexuality in the Colonial Contest*. New York: Routledge.

Marselis, R. 2008. Descendants of Slaves: The Articulation of 'Mixed Racial Ancestry' in a Danish Television Documentary Series. *European Journal of Cultural Studies*, 11(4), 447–69.

Razack, S.H. 1998. *Looking White People in the Eye: Gender, Race, and Culture in Courtrooms and Classrooms*. Toronto: University of Toronto Press.

Rose, N. 1999. *Powers of Freedom: Reframing Political Thought*. Cambridge: Cambridge University Press.

Sawyer, L. 2008. Engendering 'Race' in Calls for Diasporic Community in Sweden. *Feminist Review*, 90, 87–105.

Siim, B. 2000. *Gender and Citizenship. Politics and Agency in France, Britain and Denmark*. Cambridge: Cambridge University Press.

Siim, B. and Skjeie, H. 2008. Tracks, Intersections and Dead Ends: Multicultural Challenges to State Feminism in Denmark and Norway. *Ethnicities*, 8(3), 322–44.

Spivak, G.C. 1988. Can the Subaltern Speak? in *Marxism and the Interpretation of Culture*, edited by C. Nelson and L. Grossberg. Basingstoke: Macmillan Education, 271–313.

Stoler, A.L. 1991. Carnal Knowledge and Imperial Power: Gender, Race and Morality in Colonial Asia, in *Gender at the Crossroads: Feminist Anthropology in the Post-Modern Era*, edited by Michaela Di Leonardo. Berkeley: University of California Press, Berkeley, 51–101.

Tuori, S. 2007. Cooking Nation: Gender Equality and Multiculturalism as Nation-Building Discourses. *European Journal of Women's Studies*, 14(1), 21–35.

Tuori, S. 2009. Post-Colonial and Queer Readings of 'Migrant Families' in the Context of Multicultural Work, in *Complying with Colonialism: Gender, Race and Ethnicity in the Nordic Region*, edited by S. Keskinen, S. Tuori, S. Irne and D. Mulinari. Farnham and Burlington: Ashgate, 155–70.

Valverde, M. 1996. Despotism and Ethical Liberal Governance. *Economy and Society*, 25(3), 357–72.

Yegenoglu, M. 2003. Veiled Fantasies: Cultural and Sexual Difference in the Discourse of Orientalism, in *Feminist Postcolonial Theory*, edited by R. Lewis and S. Mills. Edinburgh: Edinburgh University Press, 542–66.

Yilmaz, F. 2011. The Politics of the Danish Cartoon Affair: Hegemonic Intervention by the Extreme Right. *Communication Studies*, 62(1), 5–22.

Chapter 9
Intimacy with the Danish Nation State: My Partner, the Danish State and I – A Case Study of Family Reunification Policy in Denmark

Linda Lund Pedersen

Introduction

Family reunification policy is currently one of the most politically contested immigration issues in the EU. In many regards it has become the last legal pathway into fortress EU for so-called third country nationals to obtain their first residence permit. This is also mirrored in Danish politics and policy debates. Since Denmark and other EU/EEA countries introduced an official cessation of immigration in the early 1970s, spouses or partners have comprised one of the largest single category of non-EU/EEA immigrants through main entry clearance routes to take up residence.

I did not set out to study discrimination or multiculturalism in Denmark through detailed research as an outside observer of the implications of family reunification policy. I found myself inevitably in the eye of hectic, whirling political debates about my rights and deprived of the right to live with my partner as a Danish citizen living in Denmark. Family migration policy has constantly been an issue in electoral campaigns and it is so important that parties actually win or lose votes depending on the position they take on family reunification.

In this chapter I draw on my own experience as a Danish citizen who, between 2007 and 2009, applied for family reunification with my spouse, a Colombian national, in Denmark. The materials that will be the object of this study are the requirements and the application packet that we had to meet and fill in, applying for a residence permit in Denmark through the family reunification system.

Through a close reading of the application form published by the Danish Immigration Service, I intend to examine how Danishness can overlap with whiteness and how race privileges may present as unarticulated and qualifying norms in the application process. By analysing the intersections of race, gender, age and class, I will show what it is that *some* bodies 'can do' as Sara Ahmed has argued (Ahmed 2007).

Although this chapter draws on my own experience in applying for family reunification, it will likely resonate with that of the many other transnational couples who have had to fill in the same application forms and therefore my story cannot aspire to be any different than the application process other couples had to go through in the same time period. They too had to qualify and fulfil the requirements that would allow them to qualify as 'capable' of civic integration to the Danish society.

Theoretical Approach

My argument here has a broader purpose than displaying the discrimination of 'ethnic' groups in Denmark since the focus tends to stay on minoritized groups and particularly the 'ethnic minoritized woman' than whose interest does the policy serve. With this perspective the norms and standards that are embedded in the policy seem to stay unchallenged (Puwar 2004). The difficulties in being family reunified in Denmark is a matter for both Danish and foreign citizens residing in Denmark. I will therefore turn to theories that have challenged and sought to interpret differentiation within nation states.

What I intend to trace here can with a terminology from the political thinker Hannah Arendt be called a 'story of an opinion', which seems to display a certain kind of restlessness in family migration policies in the attempt to exclude the unwanted subject/other (Arendt 1968/1951: 183). I consider the need for frequently changing a policy towards a subject as an expression of *opinion* that can further be said to shape a structure of thinking about an object. The experience of such rapid changes in policies and politics seems to have revitalized a steady urge to discriminate between desired and undesired subjects. Additionally the process of shifting policies appears also to lead to a limitation of civic rights that seems to be situated in a tradition alien to democratic thinking. Iris Marion Young suggests that the legitimacy of a restless policy might lie in the idea that '[M]ost people believe that their rights of freedoms will not be threatened' (Young 2003: 12). Consequently, it does not meet a lot of resistance within the borders of the nation state, which it might have if it was the entire group of nationals who were being subjected to limited rights and citizenship. The division of people within the nation state through their different entitlements to family reunification becomes clearer when analysing it through the different devices/techniques of requirements.

Hannah Arendt argues that 'race' was discovered during the first period of imperialism together with 'bureaucracy' as new devices for political organization and the legitimacy to rule over foreign people. Race was the main principle for a 'body politic' and bureaucracy was the key principle of 'foreign domination' (Arendt 1968/1951: 185). Arendt locates the discovery of race inside the era of colonialization and in particular to the European vision of the 'Dark Continent' and race:

[W]as the emergency explanation of human beings whom no European or civilized man could understand and whose humanity so frightened and humiliated the immigrants that they no longer cared to belong to the same human species. (Arendt 1968/1951: 185)

Race was used as a device to 'explain' the difference between European civilized people and what Europeans saw as a savage people who scared them. With this conceptualization of race and bureaucracy as a part of modernity, it draws up the contours of potential harm of the European modernization project as Arendt is pointing out. Though it has to be emphasized that modernity is neither inherently positive nor destructive which is indeed reflected in the concept of bureaucracy entailment of securing rights and simultaneously excluding other from enjoying the same rights (Arendt 1968/1951). For Arendt, one of the harmful implications of bureaucracy thinking is the practice of racism (Taylor 2011). Race thinking (or racism) is harmful when groups/persons within a given society are treated as inferior by, in one way or another, delimited or denied from enjoying equally and full rights in the society. Generally, their condition within the sphere of social, political and economic mobility has been limited. In addition, if the inferiority is superimposed upon these groups, and they are trying to figure out ways of resisting this inferiority position, bureaucracy would, in this case, work to develop other modes of preserving and enacting its policy, as Hannah Arendt argues: '[I]t sharpened and exploited existing conflicting interests or existing political problems, but it never created new conflicts or produced new categories of political thinking' (Arendt 1968/1951: 183). Considering Arendt's definition of race and bureaucracy as potential devices to control people's affinities and framing their mobility, it can serve as an interpretative framework for analysing the restrictions on family migration. Paul Gilroy further supports this argument in *Against Race* (2000) where this way of thinking creates a different space between camp thinking. Gilroy argues further that modernity opened up for an understanding of a new role for its citizens which was strongly entangled with 'territory, individuality, property, war and society was dramatized in this historical phase' (Gilroy 2000: 55). The correlation between citizens, race thinking, individuality and property are all thematized in different ways in the Danish policy on family reunification as I will show in the following.

Danishness, Whiteness and Other Nationalities

To adopt whiteness as a theoretical inspiration is a way of questioning prevalent perspectives and interests within bureaucratic thinking as I explored through the lens of race in the previous section.

The state directs us to and withdraws us from certain people through its regulation of requirements for being able to share a residency within the nation state boundary. To desire some *bodies* is less troublesome than other *bodies*. The whiteness of my body seems to have transformed in its proximity or directedness to a non-white/non-EU body; it arrested me from enjoying the same rights prior to my meeting with the other body.

To critically examine this process of nation preservation through different parameters of stratification of citizenship I rely on Arendtian, feminist and postcolonial perspectives and theories. The enterprise of immigration regulation is to demarcate a line of who belongs here and who belongs elsewhere (Andersson 2012; Fiona 1995; Lewis 2000). The demarcation of nation boundaries assumes some commonalities within the boundaries, like the communal subscription to the idea of a shared past intensified through myths of origins. This is what Benedict Anderson calls imagined communities, which have concrete effects through their different levels of desirability for people to inhabit these places (Anderson 1991; Gilroy 2000; Yuval-Davis 1997). In *A Phenomenology of Whiteness* Sara Ahmed shows us how it 'helps us to show how whiteness is an effect of racialization, which in turn shapes what it is that bodies "can do"' through the assumption that 'how whiteness is "real", material and lived' (Ahmed 2007: 150). Migration policies embark on an inherited formation of the nation state to protect its borders and citizens (Arendt 1968/1951; Kaplan, Alarcón and Moallem 1999). Racism is not a publicly considered principle for the organization of the Danish immigration policy, for obvious reasons, and as such neither race nor ethnicity is used in the formal documents but an overt emphasis on nationalities that appear more compatible for the Danish society than others. Nationality then appears to be the marker in line with ethnicity and race which has been used to distinguish between people and groups (Gullestad 2006). Relatedness or likeness to Danishness occurs to be a norm for other nationalities to aspire to if access to Denmark is desired. Danishness becomes closely related to whiteness though it would be difficult to argue for a full overlap but that whiteness is strongly influential in forming ideas of Danishness. So, the context for my intervention, to contest whiteness as a norm, a set of privileges and capability, informed by devices to prevent certain nationalities entry clearance. Therefore, I have been searching for perspectives that would enable an understanding of the experiences and bodies that family migration policy allows through its different stratification of citizenship and obvious discrimination of couples.

A Restless Story – A Short History of Danish Immigration Policy

The Danish Immigration Service is a directorate under the Ministry of Refugee, Immigration and Integration Affairs.[1] It is the service organ that administrates the Danish Alien Act and is therefore the main body responsible for the processes and guidelines for applications concerning asylum, visas, residence and work

---

1 Previously, the Ministry of the Interior handled these issues, in the time of the Social Democrats and Social-Liberals coalition (1992–2001).

permits, family reunification, and so on. The Danish Immigration Service, under the Liberal-Conservative government, resided within a ministry solely created to handle so-called refugee, immigration and integration issues as the name of the ministry indicates.

The previous government, constituted by the right-wing, Liberals and Conservatives (*Venstre-Konservative*), with the support of the openly anti-Muslim and ultra right-wing Danish People's Party (*Dansk Folkeparti*), introduced in 2002 stricter rules for family reunification with a threefold purpose: to decrease immigration, to prevent arranged and forced marriage[2] of young people and sham marriages / marriages of convenience, and lastly to secure better integration of people already residing and new immigrants (Olsen, Liisberg and Kjærum 2004).

During the period of the centre-left government, Social Democrat-Social Liberal (*Socialdemokraterne and Radikale Venstre*), two amendments of the Alien Act had taken place with the official intended purposes of preventing arranged and forced marriages and sham marriages, and to further limit immigration in order to promote better integration. The first change in 1998 made it possible to refuse family reunion in cases where it seemed that a third party had set up the marriage/partnership. The second change came in 2000 and concerned the formal legal right to family reunification; it was repealed for persons between 18 and 25 years of age. Family reunification could only be granted if the marriage was considered to be made between two consenting persons and there was no suspicion or signs of a third party being involved in the arrangement of the marriage.

The former Conservative-led government (1982–93) was forced to resign over a case where it had illegally obstructed Tamil refugees residing in Denmark from having their family members brought to Denmark from Sri Lanka. The Minister of Justice received a six-month conditional suspended sentence for unconstitutional ministerial misconduct in the case (Brochmann and Hagelund 2010).

With 2002 as the hallmark for the stricter course on immigration and integration, as mentioned earlier, the legislation has changed for family reunion several times since it was passed in parliament with the proviso of continuous review in order to observe if it has had the intended effect over the years.

The prior evolution of the Alien Act through tightening of family immigration can be interpreted as sowing the seed to what in 2002 becomes the 24-year rule, with its full exclusion of family reunification for persons under 24. Denmark was one of the first countries to introduce an official minimum age higher than the national age of consent for the applicants of family reunifications. The Danish example has served as model for other countries, such as England (raised in 2004 from 16 to 18, and again in 2008 from 18 to 21 and lowered in 2011 from 21 to 18) and the Netherlands (which has introduced a similar higher minimum age)

---

2   In the Danish context forced and arranged marriages are typically not distinguished between, see Peter Hervik and Mikkel Rytter for a critical overview of the discussion on forced and arranged marriage in a Nordic context, though with an emphasis on the Danish case (Hervik and Rytter 2004).

(Phillips 2010). The minimum age in these countries was not raised as high as in Denmark (24) and Greenland (25)[3] (in most cases on 21 years of age) since it followed the minimum age that the EU commission suggested as a maximum in the directive from 2003 (Frattini 2003; Ruffer 2011).[4]

The EU directive from 2003 was initiated for the prevention of forced or sham/marriages of convenience. The proposal to prevent forced marriage was to introduce a higher age restriction for the involved couples and it would consequently lead to a better integration: "In order to ensure better integration and to prevent forced marriages Member States may require the sponsor and his/her spouse to be of a minimum age, and at *maximum 21 years*, before the spouse is able to join him/her' (EU Council Directive 2003/86/EC). This EU suggestion is not only about the age of the moving spouse but also a matter of the age of the partner (in the citation called sponsor) already living inside the EU jurisdiction.

I focus on the Danish Alien Act, which might be interpreted as an extreme version of current tendencies in EU member countries to decrease immigration from third countries, particularly in regard to the Danish family reunification policy. Denmark might not only be singled out as an extreme version of the assimilationist approach with a strong emphasis on national belonging but, together with UK and Sweden, also has a factual exception to the EU family migration legislation that in the case of Denmark facilitates stricter legislation (Antonsich 2012; Jørgensen 2012).[5]

---

3 The applicants can receive a dispensation for the Greenlandic minimum age if there are no doubts that the person already residing in Greenland entered the marriage/partnership/relationship voluntarily and/or under special circumstances from the age of 18, contrary to the Danish minimum age which cannot be overruled or dispensed from. I have not been able to trace any literature dealing with the different legislations within the Danish Commonwealth (*Rigsfællesskabet*) on family migration. Within the Danish Commonwealth the three nations have different rules for family reunification. The Greenlandic Alien Act relies partly on the Danish Alien Act. The Danish Immigration Service takes care of family reunification on behalf of Greenland though in accordance with the terms of Ordinance 150 of 23 February 2001 – 'Application of the Aliens Act in Greenland'. The third nation in the Danish Commonwealth, the Faeroe Islands, is likewise administrated by the Danish Immigration Service in accordance with the terms of Ordinance 182 of 22 March 2001 – 'Application of the Aliens Act in the Faeroe Islands' they have no age-requirement but is following more the common course of housing, subsistence and residing permanently in the Faeroe Islands, requirements can be suspended under special circumstances. Lastly it has to be noted that the Faeroe Islands and Greenland are not member states of the EU and therefore do not partake in the free movement of people, see for further information (Danmark 2012).

4 Here, I only implied applications between EU/Nordic nationals and third-country nationals since partnerships or marriages which qualify to be treated under the legislation of the EU right for family reunification and family life have different requirements for a successful application process than partnership/marriages qualifying for a bilateral process.

5 In this study I have excluded the changes of policy that came into effect in January and July 2011 where a fee and a point system were introduced.

The family legislation opens up for its member countries to adopt a minimum age higher than the normal national age of consent for national/EU partnerships/marriages. Countries who are exempted from this directive are Sweden, UK and Denmark. The EU suggested minimum age is 21 years though this has to be seen in the light of a recent UK Supreme Court case, where the Court ruled that it is a violation of the Article 8 in the European Convention on Human Rights and Fundamental Freedoms 1950 (ECHR). It is noteworthy that the effect or, more precisely, the lack of the desired effect, that is, to hinder forced marriages among immigrant youth, in the Danish practice was used as evidence against upholding the British minimum age. One of the weighty arguments was that the British act was disproportional in regard to how many couples were living in genuine marriages and who were hindered family life compared to the few it might have protected. The British judgment stated that:

> At the time when the ages were raised, it was argued not only that the change would promote better integration of foreign spouses into Danish society but also that it would contain forced marriage. But subsequent research in Denmark did not confirm that the reform had reduced forced marriage; and it highlighted negative – and socially alienating – effects on the reasonable aspirations of young spouses whose marriages were not forced. (The Supreme Court 2011)

In this case the British Supreme Court judged that there is no evidence or support to continue the policy of a higher minimum age for family reunification therefore the 21-year rule was dismissed. The British authority immediately ruled back the policy to the practice prior to 2008 and couples that have been rejected on the grounds of age restriction could reapply to have their case reconsidered.

Following the British judgment that the minimum age of 21 breached Article 8 in ECHR, it inevitably raises the question if the Danish Alien Act likewise is violating Article 8. A Danish lawyer and researcher, Louise Halleskov Storgaard, has pointed out that the British minimum age and the Danish minimum age are two different acts since their purposes are not identical, as a response to the British Court judgment. Storgaard suggests that the Danish act is not only invoked to obstruct arranged and forced marriages but as well to secure better integration of immigrants and their descendants already residing in Denmark (Fischer 2011), though I would think it cannot be *de jure* that this will be the outcome of an actual appeal case in Denmark and/or trial at the EU Court of Human Rights.

In this sense, I have explored whiteness as a complex expression of racism embedded in Danish legislation on family migration. Furthermore, it examined Denmark as a location where privileges are explicitly articulated through the requirement towards the applicants and the legitimacy of their relationship through financial capability. It is even publicly acknowledged that the strict requirements are needed in order to prevent 'forced marriages' and as well to limit the overall number of immigration of 'third country' nationals in order to promote better integration of the immigrants who are already residing in Denmark. The nation state fosters politics which conceives bodies as in need of protection (to be saved) through regulatory strategies. Anne Phillips argues that the argument of protection of some bodies can be the vehicle to introduce paternalistic policies '... force marriage as the main argument to introduce paternalistic protection of mainly minorities' youth' (Phillips 2010). This argument is also established in other EU member countries which have introduced similar policies with the intention to prevent force marriage. Phillips is critical of the effect to protect young people through legislation from becoming victims of forced (or arranged marriages in the case of Denmark) as there are already international convention and national legislation in place to prevent force marriages as proven in the UK judgment.

Sweden and the UK sought different approaches to immigration and integration despite their exception to the Council Directive 2003/86/EC. Sweden adopted, already in 1974, an official concept of multiculturalism in their approach to immigration and integration policies; though from the 90s it was marked by racist outbreaks and tightening of immigration and integration legislation. However, with the changes in Sweden, multiculturalism is still considered as official state policies (Hübinette and Lundström 2011; Scuzzarello 2008). The UK has been toughening the line and as mentioned earlier had to bring the minimum age down following a Supreme Court judgment in 2011. In these cases an exception from the EU's directive does not necessarily follow a restrictive national legislation or that national legislation can accommodate strict immigration's laws on family migration, following the cases of the UK, Sweden and Denmark (Hedetoft 2006, 2010).

A Life through Documents – The Application Form and the Process of Applying

The experience of filling in the application form for family reunification can be interpreted as what Mónica Moreno Figueroa calls *racist moments* (Figueroa 2010: 390). She defines racist moments as, 'the moments when racism is expressed, noticed, talked about or sensed in a different level of intensity that makes it somehow recognizable. Racist moments are both an exception and a pointer to racism's distributed intensity' (Figueroa 2010: 395). You are called in, noticed and sense your mode of belonging as a citizen who is transgressing the nation state's border. Your race, accommodation, family history, age, financial situation and proximity are all structuring your experience of yourself and how your body is (not) allowed in a specific location (Arendt 2006/1961). Translated into my own experience and situatedness as a 'white' Danish citizen living in Denmark/EU with no family history of immigration these features did not have any conscious significance to the way I could live my life in Denmark as a Danish citizen. Though unarticulated, they mattered to the extent that I was able to live in privileged situation qua being (in-)visibly a part of the norm as whiteness in the location. The application process is 'experiencing racializing practices' triggered by my meeting with a non-Danish person (Hübinette and Lundström 2011: 44). It was first in this meeting with my partner from a 'third country' that I became aware of my national membership and the significance of its entailments.

So what does proximity do in the case of my meeting or contact with, to stay within Ahmed's terminology, a Colombian national? My Danishness and inherited proximity of/in whiteness can be said to have delimited and constrained my life/intimate-world in regard to the possibility to cohabitate a shared space with my Colombian partner. Ahmed suggests that likeness is a matter of proximity in space 'This saying suggests for me that likeness is as an effect of the proximity of *shared residence*' (Ahmed 2007: 155 emphasized in original). In my contact with the other body, my whiteness became noticeable and it mattered in the way that the other's body was associated with my whiteness and unhindered accessibility:

> White bodies are habitual insofar as they 'trail behind' actions: they do not get 'stressed' in their encounters with objects or others, as their whiteness 'goes unnoticed'. Whiteness would be what lags behind; white bodies do not have to face their whiteness; they are not orientated 'towards' it, and this 'not' is what allows whiteness to cohere, as that which bodies are orientated around. When bodies 'lag behind', then they extend their reach. (Ahmed 2007: 156)

The *reach* of bodies/persons is what I am going to explore in the next paragraphs to establish who can do or who has access.

When a couple are looking for information on the application process and the requirements it will be directed to the website www.nyidanmark.dk which translates literally into 'new' in Denmark. The website contains information for citizens about migration and integration and the entire content of the website can be read in Danish and English, whereas guidelines in other languages are mainly describing the life as a new citizen in Denmark, serving as guidelines for civic integration into the Danish society.

The application packet is 29 pages long and consists of two identical parts, one part for the sponsor and another part for the applicant.[6] In the application packet you have to answer a series of questions about your relationship and your status, such as how you stay in contact, who decided upon your marriage, who arranged it, did you meet before the marriage, were you present at the marriage, do you share close ancestry, and so on. Beside these intimate questions, you have to attach evidence of adequate accommodation, subsistence/income, the marriage certificate, rental contracts, and so on. The application could be handed in in Denmark and any other country with a Danish representation. In order to have your application considered you have to qualify through some different requirements.

---

6 I am following the guidelines and application forms applicable for the procedure in 2007/9, which has changed several times since we applied. See www.nyidanmark.dk for an updated version.

One of the ways I had to prove my qualification to be eligible to live with my spouse was that I had not received any welfare support as for example unemployment benefits within the year prior to the day of handing in the application form[7] and if afterwards I wanted to make a claim for welfare support, we would no longer be qualified to renew my partner's residence visa.

Following the precedence set by the Eind and Metock court judgments, Denmark was obliged to follow the EU regulations on the right of free movement. In the Eind case, the right to *continue* living together with your partner/spouse was emphasized. In the case of EU nationals who have been residing in another EU member state, they may claim the right to continue living together with their third national spouse in their country of origin. In the Metock case, which seems to be the most well known of the two ruling appeal cases, it was emphasized that the requirements in the Danish Alien Act of the 24-year rule and combined attachment can be bypassed if the applicants qualify within the EU right of free movement.[8] The Metock judgment caused much headache for the Danish government since it seemed to undermine much of the ruling national regulation in regard to requirement for family reunification in Denmark. The furore was followed up by several attempts from the government and its supporting party, to find legal ways to opt out of the EU ruling (Hornbech 2008).

The application process is divided into three types: one entails a 'self-service' fast track application process for cases which are assumed to be straightforward as long the applicants have provided sufficient documentation and their 'bodies' and partnership are not violating or falling outside the regulation and norms of the requirements. The other process type is labelled complex cases where the authority has to evaluate and assess more closely whether the partnership is eligible and qualifies for a family reunion clearance. Lastly, the third possibility to obtain entry clearance is through the EU granted right of free movement and the right to a family reunification where the Danish citizen prior to the application moment has resided in another member state before the EU directive can be pleaded as the base for granting family reunification.[9]

Here I am only considering the application processes for bilateral family reunion, which means cases between Danish citizen/residence holders and third country nationals. But before I return to the successful application procedure I find it useful to map out the two rejections we received prior to the family reunification

---

7 This was extended to a three-year period with the amendments of the requirements from January 2011.

8 See for further details the Eind and Metock the Judgments, (C-291/05, 2007) and (C-127/08, 2008).

9 Here it has to be noted that any third country national has the right to enter EU as long as they are traveling with their spouse or partner who is residing within the borders of EU and can prove their relationship through official documents such as a marriage certificate. According to Article 5 of EU Directive 38/2004, you do not need a visa for travel to for example Denmark, but you must be accompanied by your EU/EEA spouse/partner.

was awarded. When we were applying for family reunification in 2007 we were denied the residence permit for my partner on the grounds that we were subletting our flat, which was incorrect since we had a permanent rental contract with the landlord. But, what is of interest here is that we had previously lived and studied together in Finland, another member state of the EU and the Nordic Union. When the judgment of the Metock case was announced, we filed a complaint about the rejection and claimed that we had the right to *continue living* together in another member country. Furthermore, we applied again for family reunion through the 'normal' procedure. Our complaint was rejected with the stated reason that there was no connection between my date of return to Denmark and us applying for continuation of family life. This rejection was followed up with a granted residence permit a few weeks later through the normal procedure. It was later announced on the website for the Danish Immigration Service that only a few couples had been entitled to the EU granted right of a family life, and who had previously been unlawfully rejected.[10] It makes me question how many other couples have been in a similar situation since a EU granted right permit would be preferable because it grants you a permit immediately for five years, whereas a Danish permit has to be reissued every second year until a permanent residence or citizenship can be granted. Furthermore, the sponsor does not have to provide collateral for the residence permit. In conclusion, the EU granted right is a more convenient solution for transnational couples if it is available as an option.

The rejection on the grounds that I was subletting my flat suggests discrimination based on a hierarchy between subtenants, tenants and owners (Olsen et al. 2004: ch. 1). It is not only in the case of possessing an appropriate accommodation that owners are privileged, but also in the requirement of collateral where a property can serve as the guarantee, which was approximately €6,700 in 2007. If the sponsor does not have the option of making a bank guarantee in the form of a property, they must deposit the full amount in a barred bank account. People's financial capability and ownership of property become significant qualifier for their possibility to choose family life in Denmark. Or people simply are forced to give up a transnational partnership. This suggests that the person's property relations become the vehicle for having rights. Celia Lury and Beverley Skeggs show through the concept possessive individual how individual is defined through the 'capacity to own property in his person' (Skeggs 2004: 4–5). The 'possessive individual' becomes the norm whose interest is legitimized through the policies (Lury 1998; Skeggs 2004). The possessive individual has historically been equivalent to the protective white man who had the right to own property. In relation to family reunification requirements about subsistence, collateral and sufficient accommodation the privileges that the possessive individual enjoys becomes substantial compared to other groups.

The financial capability of the applicants becomes the determining factor in deciding whom you can live with and at the structural level a device for organizing

---

10 See www.nyidanmark.dk press lease from 0809–2009, *Et år efter Metock dommen.*

society. The organization of people through what they can afford suggests that 'economic politics are also racial politics' (Hübinette and Lundström 2011: 48). Through this analysis of the relation between qualifying for family reunification and the requirement of accommodation the policy appears as being working in the interest for particular couples. In the following section I will continue the analysis of privileging certain groups interest over others and attempts there has been to consolidate these 'rights'.

Racialized Privileges as Policy Generator

It may be the current case that it is more likely to be granted family reunification as a 'white' Dane, as many of the requirements give native 'white' Danish citizens privileges they are only in possession of because of their birthright and membership of the whiteness/majority group (Rytter 2010). A further example of privileged entitlement is the combined attachment requirement,[11] which is enforced if the applicants have had Danish citizenship or a coherent period of legal residence in Denmark for less than 28 years.[12] The attachment requirement hints at what normative aspiration we seem to be driven towards. Even if the sponsor already is a Danish national it would appear insufficient to merely have a formal membership of the state, some cultural bonds also need to be in place. Prior to the introduction of the 28-year limit amendment of the combined attachment requirement, a discussion had emerged on the rightfulness in rejecting Danish citizens' application to return to Denmark with partners they have met when they have been abroad for some years. The Social-Liberals have on two occasions, in 2003 and 2008, suggested a 'Love card'[13] arrangement to mitigate the strict rules and requirement for family reunification (Jelved, Vestager, Østergaard and Ammitzbøll 2008).[14] The Love card was meant as a one-year entry visa for foreigners who had a relationship with a Danish citizen without the possibility of prolonging the period of their love visa. An example of couples that this visa will prove relevant for are students who cannot return to Denmark with their partners or are 'forced' to marry in order to fulfil the requirements of genuine relationship.

---

11   Was introduced already in 2000 and further tightened in the 2002 revision of the Alien Act. Prior to 2002 it was only the newcomer's attachment to Denmark that was assessed and not the sponsor. From 2002 both partners' attachment to Denmark were evaluated (Olsen et al. 2004).

12   This amendment was added in 2003 because several couples had been denied family reunification on the basis of an evaluation stating that they did not meet the requirement of having a stronger attachment to Denmark than any other country. This act was changed due to an intervention from the Danish Human Rights Institute. The current act is known as the 28 year rule.

13   With an allusion to the Green card arrangement known from countries such as US and Canada.

14   The proposal was rejected by parliament on both occasions.

These attempts can be read as a counter strategy to the Danish immigration politics hardliners. The Social-Liberals promoted the suggested bill as a trial period for young people who live in a transnational relationship with a third country national where they can test the stability of their relationship. In 2003, the Refugee Minister Bertel Haarder (Liberals) supported the bill in the beginning though with some proposed alterations. He suggested instead to create more 'working holidays' visa agreements with western oriented countries. Furthermore, Haarder stated that there are no plans to establish working holiday agreements with such countries as Pakistan, Turkey, Somalia or Thailand (Emborg and Thomsen 2003). A working holiday visa would allow people in the age group 18–32 to stay in Denmark for up to one year depending on the bilateral agreement their country of citizenship has negotiated with Denmark. Seven countries have presently such an arrangement, all highly industrialised: Argentina, Australia, Canada, Chile, Japan, New Zealand and South Korea. It is noteworthy that people qualifying for a working holiday visa are not eligible to bring family members including children.[15] Furthermore, as Peter Hervik also points out, the notions of immigrant and foreign cultures are not referring to all foreigners who are moving to Denmark, as it is explicitly shown in this case (Hervik 2001). With the possibility to apply for a holiday visa it grants applicants from these countries a privileged position compared to other countries and especially Muslim majority countries that do not have any such arrangements with the Danish state. Thereby spurring a view that it is not all cultural differences that are taken up as a threat but merely non-Western cultures (Hervik 1999). The privileged position becomes more significant when we are looking at the assessment of the attachment requirement, which is an assessment of the applicants' combined ties to Denmark. The ties to Denmark have to be considered greater than to any other country. For transnational couples, whiteness is called into question and losing its capability to 'freely' move even into previous spaces of comfort and ease such as the nation state of citizenship (Puwar 2004). Some bodies stay in distress for a longer period of time than others (Ahmed 2007: 161), dependent on the merits of the applicants in the beginning of the application process. The strong wish from the Danish state to direct its citizens *in spe* and citizens towards it as the singular point of reference can be seen through its demand to denounce former citizenships, if possible, in the process of naturalization. As a Danish citizen residing in Denmark you are meant to only hold one national citizenship, unless it cannot be avoided.

Concluding Remarks

To write a conclusion on a restless story seems rather contradicting since the Danish family immigration policy is still in transformation. What I have portrayed

---

15   In 2003 Denmark only has working holiday visa agreements with Australia and New Zealand.

here has only been a small sequence of the story of opinions and I have attempted to understand and reveal what might be the 'thinking' behind the ever-changing policies. My concerns are those that have fuelled whiteness as a social and political norm and its entanglement with invisibilized and naturalized privileges that some groups enjoy in a given society and others do not have equivalent access to, due to their marked (and/or problematized) identities/bodies. The intimacy I had felt with the Danish state through the application process has been a stressful period. One could never be sure that you had fulfilled the right criteria and for the period of the process my partner was stripped of rights to participate in the Danish society which left him in limbo. This has been the case for the many couples who have tried to seek family reunification in Denmark some more successful than others. This chapter has shown that when nation states becomes insecure about their identities the personal decision to cross borders becomes a threat to the nation state played out as a disguised moral fear about protecting minoritized group against unwanted marriage or against 'their own'.

It is yet to be proved if the strict admission requirements into Denmark and other countries do 'save' anyone from unwanted/forced marriage/partnership and if therefore they support better integration (Phillips 2010). More troubling, however, is that the question, which is still unanswered, is whether this is actually what is the intention of the legislation. It seems rather transparently to work primarily as a device to control to whom people should direct their desires and in which locations their bodies are allowed proximity.

References

Ahmed, S. 2007. A Phenomenology of Whiteness. *Feminist Theory*, 8(2), 149–68.
Anderson, B.R.O.G. 1991. *Imagined Communities: Reflections on the Origin and Spread of Nationalism*. London: Verso.
Andersson, M. 2012. Seeing through the White Gaze: Racialised Markings of (un) Familiar Bodies in Swedish Transnational Adoption Policy. *GJSS: Graduate Journal of Social Science*, 9(1).
Antonsich, M. 2012. Exploring the Demands of Assimilation among White Ethnic Majorities in Western Europe. *Journal of Ethnic and Migration Studies*, 38(1), 59–76.
Arendt, H. 1968/1951. *The Origins of Totalitarianism*. New edition with added prefaces. San Diego: Harcourt.
Arendt, H. 2006/1961. *Between Past and Future*. London: Penguin Books.
Brochmann, G. and Hagelund, A. (eds). 2010. *Velferdens grenser*. Oslo: Universitetsforlaget.
Danmark, Ny i. 2012. *Family reunification in Greenland*. [Online]. Available at: http://www.nyidanmark.dk/en-us/coming_to_dk/greenland/family-reunification.htm [accessed: 14 February 2012].

Emborg, R. and Thomsen, C.B. 2003. Kærlighedsvisum på vej. *Politiken*, 21 February.
EU Council Directive 2003/86/EC of 22 September 2003: On the Right of Family Reunification 2003.
Figueroa, M.G.M. 2010. Distributed Intensities: Whiteness, Mestizaje and Logics of Mexican Racism. *Ethnicities*, 10(3), 387–401.
Fiona, W. 1995. Race/Ethnicity, Gender and Class in Welfare States: A Framework for Comparative Analysis. *Social Politics – International Studies in Gender State and Society*, 2(2), 127–59.
Fischer, A. 2011. Britisk højesteret underkender 21 års regel [Radio]. At http://www.dr.dk/Nyheder/Udland/2011/12/19/154811.htm [accessed: 8 June 2012].
Gilroy, P. 2000. *Against Race: Imagining Political Culture beyond the Color Line*. Cambridge, MA: Belknap Press of Harvard University.
Gullestad, M. 2006. *Plausible Prejudice: Everyday Experiences and Social Images of Nation, Culture and Race*. Oslo: Universitetsforlaget.
Hedetoft, U. 2006. *Multiculturalism in Denmark and Sweden*. Copenhagen: http://www.diis.dk/graphics/publications/Briefs2006/hedetoft_multiculturalism_dk_sweden.pdf [accessed: 08 June 2012].
Hedetoft, U. 2010. Denmark versus Multiculturalism, in S.V. a. S. Wessendorf (ed.), *The Multiculturalism Backlash*. Oxford: Routledge.
Hervik, P. (ed.). 1999. *Den generende forskellighed danske svar på den stigende multikulturalisme*. Copenhagen: Hans Reitzel.
Hervik, P. 2001. Lighedens diskrimination: Den danske farveblindhed i det flerkulturelle samfund. *Nordic Journal of Human Rights*, 2, 41–53.
Hervik, P. and Rytter, M. 2004. Med ægteskab i focus, in B.K. Olsen, M.V. Liisberg and M. Kjærum, 2004. *Ægtefællesammenføring i Danmark: Udredning* (vol. 1). Copenhagen: Institut for Menneskerettigheder.
Hornbech, B.R. 2008. *Integrationsministeren offentliggør juridisk notat om Metock-dommen*. [Online]. Available at: http://www.nyidanmark.dk/da-dk/nyheder/nyheder/integrationsministeriet/2008/september/integrationsministeren_offentliggor_juridisk_notat_om_metock_dommen.htm [accessed: 3 September 2008].
Hübinette, T. and Lundström, C. 2011. Sweden after the Recent Election: The Double-Binding Power of Swedish Whiteness through the Mourning of the Loss of 'Old Sweden' and the Passing of 'Good Sweden'. *NORA – Nordic Journal of Feminist and Gender Research*, 19(1), 42–52.
Jelved, M., Vestager, M., Østergaard, M. and Ammitzbøll, S.E. 2008. *B108 Forslag til folketingsbeslutning om et 'love card'*. www.folketinget.dk
Jørgensen, M.B. 2012. Danish Regulations on Marriage Migration: Policy Understandings of Transnational Marriages, in K. Charsley (ed.), *Transnational Marriage: New Perspectives from Europe and Beyond*. London and New York: Routledge, 101–34.

Kaplan, C., Alarcón, N. and Moallem, M. (eds.). 1999. *Between Woman and Nation: Nationalisms, Transnational Feminisms, and the State*. Durham and London: Duke University Press.

Lewis, G. 2000. *'Race', Gender, Social Welfare: Encounters in a Postcolonial Society*. Cambridge: Polity Press.

Lury, C. 1998. *Prosthetic Culture: Photography, Memory and Identity*. London and New York: Routledge.

Olsen, B.K., Liisberg, M.V., Kjærum, M. 2004. *Ægtefællesammenføring i Danmark: Udredning* (vol. 1). Copenhagen: Institut for Menneskerettigheder.

Phillips, A. 2010. *Gender and Culture*. Cambridge: Polity Press.

Puwar, N. 2004. *Space Invaders: Race, Gender and Bodies out of Place*. New York: Berg.

Ruffer, G.B. 2011. Pushed beyond Recognition? The Liberality of Family Reunification Policies in the EU. *Journal of Ethnic and Migration Studies*, 37(6).

Rytter, M. 2010. The Family of Denmark and the Aliens: Kinship Images in Danish Integration Politics. *Ethnos*, 75(3), 301–22.

Scuzzarello, S. 2008. National Security versus Moral Responsibility: An Analysis of Integration Programs in Malmö, Sweden. *Social Politics – International Studies in Gender State and Society*, 15(1), 5–32.

Skeggs, B. 2004. *Class, Self, Culture – Transformations: Thinking Through Feminism*. London and New York: Routledge.

Taylor, D. 2011. Countering Modernity: Foucault and Arendt on Race and Racism. *Telos*, 154(Spring), 119–40.

Young, I.M. 2003. The Logic of Masculinist Protection: Reflections on the Current Security State. *Signs*, 29(1), 1–25.

Yuval-Davis, N. 1997. *Nation and Gender*. London and New York: Sage.

Legal Judgments

Judgment of the Court (Grand Chamber) of 11 December 2007.
Minister voor Vreemdelingenzaken en Integratie v R. N. G. Eind.
Reference for a preliminary ruling: Raad van State – Netherlands.
Freedom of movement for persons – Workers – Right of residence for a family member who is a third-country national – Return of the worker to the Member State of which he is a national – Obligation for the worker's Member State of origin to grant a right of residence to the family member – Whether there is such an obligation where the worker does not carry on any effective and genuine activities.
Case **C-291/05**.
European Court reports 2007 Page I-10719.

European Union: European Court of Justice, *Reform*, Case **C-127/08**.

Metock and Others *v* Minister for Justice, Equality and Law Reform , 25 July 2008, available at: http://www.unhcr.org/refworld/docid/48a574262.html [accessed 8 June 2012].

The Supreme Court of The United Kingdom. Judgment for the case:
R (on the application of Quila and another) (FC) (Respondents) *v* Secretary of State for the Home Department (Appellant).
R (on the application of Bibi and another) (FC) (Respondents) *v* Secretary of State for the Home Department (Appellant) (12 October 2011).

Chapter 10
Aesthetics and Ethnicity: The Role of Boundaries in Sámi and Tornedalian Art

Anne Heith

Aesthetics, from the Greek *aesthesis* (perception, sensation, experience), is a concept of great significance for the arts. Ever since the beginnings of Western philosophy the arts have been an important object of investigation. 'What is art?' and 'What is the purpose of art?' are recurrent questions which have been answered in various ways. One answer to the first is that 'art is a vehicle for the expression or communication of feeling' (Hanfling 1995: viii). The second question, 'What are the arts for?', is extremely complex as people's experiences of art may vary considerably. In classical aesthetics experiences such as 'pleasure' and 'delight' are often highlighted, and the ideal of 'disinterested contemplation' promoted. When examined with perspectives from Critical Race and Whiteness Studies this attitude becomes problematic as the normative role of whiteness is being ignored. The circumstance that the implied producers and recipients of works of art are privileged whites is a fact never acknowledged.

When discussing interconnections between whiteness, race and art from an American vantage point Maurice Berger concludes that whiteness has functioned as 'a norm that had been so pervasive in society that white people never needed to acknowledge or name it'. (Berger 2004: 26). The aim of this article is to examine interconnections between aesthetics and ethnicity in Sámi and Tornedalian art. Both the Sámi and the Tornedalians have been constructed as the racialized others of the Aryan standard proposed as the superior race by twentieth-century race biologists (Lundborg and Linders 1926, Kemiläinen 1998). While Swedish race biologists did not hesitate to use the concept of 'race' when examining the racial character of the Swedish population in the early twentieth century (Lundborg and Linders 1926), the concept has practically disappeared from the academic debate in the later part of the century. Rarely has the normative and unself-critical whiteness of the majority population been a theme for critical investigation, although whiteness as a source of power has influenced all sectors of society and culture, including aesthetics. White aesthetics has perpetuated understandings of art which have marginalized minorities, while at the same time creating myths of purity and disinterestedness. This kind of aesthetics invariably fails to acknowledge its own 'racial character'. It also fails to provide tools for analysing works of art expressing experiences of minorities by drawing attention to abuse and marginalization. Sámi and Tornedalian specimens of such works of art will be discussed in this chapter.

The Sámi are the only indigenous people of north-western Europe and the Tornedalians are a national historical ethnic and linguistic minority in Sweden. During the 1960s and 1970s the cultural mobilization of both groups intensified. In this context art played a central role for creating ethnic identities which distinguishes the Sámi and Tornedalians, respectively, from the majority populations of the nation states they inhabit. Art became part of cultural production which challenges the othering of minorities and the cultural homogenization of the modern Nordic nation states which marginalized the Sámi and the Tornedalians.

Sweden and the other Nordic countries are frequently thought of as modern welfare states whose cultural homogeneity has been disrupted by fairly recent immigration. However, prevailing images of historical purity are not true (Schoug 2008). The Nordic countries have always been multi-ethnic and multilingual, and the borders which demarcate the Nordic nation states have changed through history. The ancestral homeland of the indigenous Sámi, Sapmi, covers parts of northern Norway, Sweden, Finland and north-western Russia. Meänmaa (literally 'Our land'), the homeland of the Tornedalians, is situated on both sides of the Swedish–Finnish border. The status of the Swedish Tornedalians changed dramatically with the establishment of the Swedish–Finnish border at the conclusion of the 1808–1809 war between Sweden and Russia when Sweden lost Finland. The Tornedalian Finns on what became the Swedish side of the border were now Swedish citizens and consequently a minority with an ambiguous status. Part of the ambiguity is related to Swedish security politics and a fear of Russian expansionism (Åselius 1994, Rodell 2009). One idea at the time was that Finland, which had become a Russian Grand Duchy, was a space from where the Russian enemy might attack and pose a threat to Swedish sovereignty (Åselius 1994). This particular historical context provided a soil for constructing the Finno-Ugric Tornedalians as domestic others, whose loyalty one could not be sure of. The marginalization of the Sámi is related to the colonization of the north. The land in the north was considered empty and uninhabited, and consequently free for exploitation. As settlers arrived the areas which could be used by the reindeer-herding Sámi were diminished, and Sámi people were driven away from areas they had traditionally used.

Another context for the marginalization of the Sámi and the Tornedalians is provided by the discourse of race biology which flourished in the nineteenth and early twentieth century. Prominent race biologists in the 1920s and 1930s were of the opinion that the Sámi were a remnant from ancient times doomed in the modern world (Mebius 1999), while the Finno-Ugric Tornedalians were seen as racially inferior to the Nordic racial character (Kemiläinen 1998, Laskar 2008). Through history, constructions of domestic others and racial hierarchies have intersected with constructions of the majority population as the norm which provides a standard for normality which other groups may be measured against. Connections between ethnic majority status and notions of normality explain why processes which have othered minorities have continued long after theories of race biology have been dismissed. Richard Dyer describes the transformation from a focus on superiority to an emphasis on normality in social constructions of whiteness which privileges one group of people, while constructing other groups as deviant, in the following way: 'Power in contemporary society habitually passes itself off as embodied in the normal as opposed to the superior' (Dyer 1997: 458).

In a Swedish national context the building of the modern welfare state exemplifies how modernization intersected with cultural homogenization:

> Sweden, which never has been a monocultural society, has during the latter part of the nineteenth century and during the entire twentieth century gone through a sociopolitical process of homogenization, whose main aim was to create a strong nation state. A major step in this process was the state's welfare programme implemented with the intent to create a national 'folkhem' [people's home]. (Ehn and Klein 2007: 11, my translation)

One effect of this process was that people who were seen as deviant from the ideal of the modern, progressive, ethnic Swede were put under pressure to assimilate or else they would be excluded from the imagined community of the modern welfare state (Heith 2009a, Heith 2009b). The success of the model of the modern welfare state is one reason why notions of Swedish and Nordic exceptionalism came to prevail (Hettne, Sörlin and Østergård 2006: 211–23). Recently this kind of construction has been challenged, for example in a study which proposes that the concept of 'colonial complicity' may be useful for describing the establishment of structures which have marginalized groups of people who have not fitted the model of the ideal nation: 'The analyses of the Nordic welfare states have ... been predominantly conducted from a majority perspective ... [C]entral welfare state policies and discourses ... are deeply embedded in notions of 'race', gender and heterosexuality' (Keskinen et al. 2009: 11).

Tacit Majority Ethnicities

'Ethnicity' is a controversial concept. While it has been proclaimed irrelevant by some (Sollors 1986, Sollors 1989), ethnicity studies have also flourished (Singh and Schmidt 2000). Ethnicity researchers Fenton and May propose that the notion of 'majority ethnicities' has been suppressed in the context of modern nation-building and state formation, as 'ethnicity' has been associated with 'minority' and 'outsider' status:

> We can begin by acknowledging that all groups – both minority and majority ones – incorporate an ethnic dimension and the failure of the latter to recognize or acknowledge this has more to do with differential power relations between groups than with anything else. Ethnic majority status is an unaccustomed thought simply because the majority tends to assume, without much reflection, the normalized and normative status of their identity, and its (unquestioned) place of preeminence. In other words, majority group members, being neither 'ethnic'

nor a 'minority', simply represent modernity, or the modern (civilized) way of life. By extension, this tacit ethnic status almost certainly includes the equating of an ethnic majority with a (or even, the) nation. (Fenton and May 2002: 10–11)

Connections between, and even the conflation of, majority ethnicity and the modern nation state presents a normative framework for the othering of ethnic minorities in nation-building discourses. This relationship is discussed in a study of the modernization of Sweden, which highlights modernity's enhancement of the marginalization of minorities through repressive measures manifested in the cultural homogenization of Swedish society (Arvastson 1999, Mebius 1999, Vallström 1999). Although there are variations with regard to the implementation of assimilation politics in the different Nordic countries over time (Elenius 2006), the themes of assimilation and marginalization prevails in present-day Sámi and Tornedalian cultural production inspired by anti-colonial and postcolonial theory. However, it ought to be kept in mind that there is not a homogeneous history of assimilationist policies, nor a culturally homogeneous Sámi, or Tornedalian, population. There are several Sámi languages and groups of Sámi people with different traditional livelihoods spread over Sapmi (Solbakk 2006). When discussing the theme of policies of assimilation Solbakk points out that: 'From the early 19th century onwards, use of the terms "norwegianization" and "swedification" was justified when speaking of the official policies of these states, as their exact objective was the assimilation of the "alien" populations in their midst' (Solbakk 2006: 68–9). Solbakk also discusses the implications of the motto 'Lapps will be Lapps' adopted in Sweden towards the turn of the century. The motto refers to protective segregation aiming at the preservation of the lifestyle of the reindeer-herding Sámi:

> Behind this policy was a long-established paternalistic tradition, according to which the affairs of the Sámi were to be decided over their heads 'for their own good', especially in regards to reindeer herding and land use. The Sámi were now expected to find peace busying themselves with their reindeer, and their schools were to prepare them for this 'natural' pastoral nomadic way of life – certainly not for life in Swedish society. (Solbakk 2006: 72)

As the quotation indicates the reindeer-herding Sámi in Sweden were marginalized and excluded from the imagined community of modern Swedes through active measures which aimed at preserving their 'traditional' life style. In this context the reindeer-herding Sámi came to represent the exotic others on the fringes of the modern world (Mebius 1999). The life styles of other Sámi groups, the forest Sámi for example, not considered exotic and different enough to fascinate modern man, were not 'protected'. Rather these groups were expected to conform to the lifestyles of the majority.

The tacit role of majority ethnicity in constructions of national self-images during the building of the Social Democratic driven idea of People's Home, 'folkhemmet', is a theme which has not been much discussed. On the contrary the vision of the Social Democratic People's Home has come to represent Swedish exceptionalism. This in spite of the fact that Per Albin Hansson who launched the concept of 'folkhemmet' envisioned the people as a nation of ethnic Swedes (Hettne, Sörlin and Østergård 2006: 400). In the narrative of 'exceptional Sweden', progress, democracy and modernity are key concepts which function as markers of difference which distinguish Sweden from less 'advanced' nations.

Minorities in Advanced Industrial Societies

Yet there are counter trends to visions of cultural homogenization. For example in 2000 Sweden ratified the European Charter for Regional or Minority Languages and the Council of Europe Framework Conventions for the Protection of National Minorities. As a result Sámi and Meänkieli have become officially recognized minority languages in Sweden. A similar development has occurred in Norway where Sámi and the language of the Finno-Ugric Kven minority in northern Norway have been officially recognized. In 1999 Norway ratified the Council of Europe's Framework Convention for the Protection of National Minorities, and in 2005 the Kven language was granted the status of a minority language within the same framework. This manifestation of a shift away from the implementation of assimilationist policies and the vision of a culturally and linguistically homogeneous population may be related to a wider concern with minorities in advanced industrial societies (Hill Collins and Solomos 2010: 5).

Another important aspect of identity politics is that identities are not simply imposed, but also actively chosen and used. The Norwegian anthropologist Fredrik Barth emphasizes the role of boundary-marking for the construction of ethnic identities. Barth is primarily interested in how groups define themselves and how they distinguish themselves from other groups. In this context he highlights the role of ethnic markers. He emphasizes that 'we can assume no simple one-to-one relationship between ethnic units and cultural similarities and differences. The features that are taken into account are not the sum of 'objective' differences, but only those which the actors themselves regard as significant' (Barth 1998: 14). This analysis of the role of boundaries is quite different from for example Dyer's discussion of how constructions of norms and normality are used in order to exclude certain groups of people (Dyer 1997). Barth's discussion of how groups of people use ethnification in processes of self-definition introduces a qualitative difference in so far as ethnification is seen as a positive strategy. In the contexts of Sámi and Tornedalian cultural mobilization this strategy implies that alternatives to discourses which have excluded and marginalized the Sámi and the Tornedalians, respectively, may be expressed.

The Swedish Tornedalian writer Bengt Pohjanen's poem 'Jag är född utan språk', 'I was born without language', has been of great importance in Tornedalian cultural mobilization. The title reflects a feeling of loss and deprivation typical for the anti-colonial currents of the 1970s when the poem was published for the first time. Another work of art which will be discussed is Norwegian Sámi artist Geir Tore Holm's sculpture Tripod, which was part of the exhibition 'Same, same but different' at Umeå University's BildMuseet in 2004. For a Swede the name of the exhibition is quite ambiguous as 'same' is the Swedish word for 'Sámi'. The exhibition presented the artwork of three artists. All of them consciously addressed the issue of what Sámi art is, and what a Sámi cultural identity might be like in the modern world. In this context Geir Tore Holm was being framed as a contemporary Sámi artist who produces contemporary Sámi art. Pohjanen's poem and Holm's sculpture may both be related to discourses which have othered the Sámi and the Tornedalians. The backdrop of this history is the establishment of the nation state's ethnic majority as a norm which has contributed to the exclusion and marginalization of the Sámi and Tornedalians, respectively. Today, both Sámi and Tornedalian artists use ethnification consciously as a strategy for self-identification. This involves that ethnic markers are used to distinguish a specific Sámi and Tornedalian culture which differs from national mainstream culture. Both Pohjanen's poem and Holm's sculpture exemplify performances of ethnification through the emphasis of elements which distinguish 'Sáminess', and 'Swedish Tornedalian Finnishness', from national majority cultures. The term 'performance' is used here as these works introduce alternative perspectives on history, politics and identity. The concept of 'performativity' has been used in various ways in a number of disciplines. One central aspect of theories of performativity is that they focus on what utterances may achieve. According to J.L. Austin who introduced the idea of the performativity of speech acts in *How To Do Things With Words*, linguistic utterances may not only affect emotions and shape notions of identities, but also bring about something entirely new (Austin 1962). The idea of the performativity of speech acts and linguistic utterances has had a major influence on subsequent constructivist theories on how various categories are shaped (Butler 1990, Hall 2000, Schechner 2002). In this article the concept is used in order to analyse interconnections between performativity in art and literature on the one hand, and the shaping of ethnic identities on the other.

History

History constitutes one form of cultural material which is deployed extensively in Sámi and Swedish Tornedalian constructions of diacritical borders. These borders distinguish the Sámi and the Tornedalians from the ethnic majority groups of the nation states which they inhabit. Such a conceptualization requires the histories of the ethnic minorities to be presented as qualitatively different from those of the majority population, for example in the shape of colonized versus colonizers, oppressed versus oppressors. The present-day creation of positive self-images among indigenous peoples has gained strength from theoretical perspectives from ecocriticism's critique of modernity's devastating effects on the environment

(Garrard 2009, Huggan and Tiffin 2010). Geir Tore Holm's sculpture Tripod ('Stativ' in Norwegian) from 2003 to 2004 may be seen as an example of a bordering performance which projects dichotomies between the indigenous Sámi and processes which threaten traditional Sámi life.

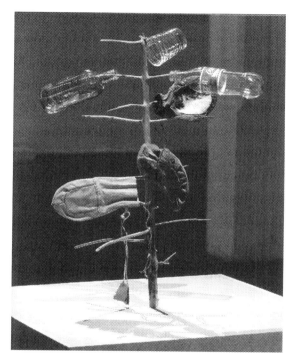

Figure 10.1   Tripod, 'Stativ', by Geir Tore Holm

Tripod displays an arrangement of items which draw attention to contrasts, and even conflicts, between Sámi traditions and ways of life, versus cultures which threaten traditions and indigenous value systems. The leafless branch of a tree which constitutes the tripod obviously does not represent a tree of life. A tree has roots, it grows vertically from the ground and up into the air. But this is not the case with Holm's Tripod, which is a dead branch disconnected from its roots. A chronology is indicated by the arrangement of the items hung on the twigs. The three objects on the bottom are all versions of Sámi coffee pouches handcrafted from reindeer skin and other traditional organic materials. As a contrast to these, the three objects on top all exemplify mass produced items which have been brought to the land of the Sámi by outsiders. While coffee is a drink which was brought to Sapmi by trading Sámi, vodka and Coca-Cola both function as metonyms connoting colonialism, consumerism and pollution. The materials, glass and plastic, pose as contrasts to the organic materials of the traditional Sámi pouches. If the vertical dimension of the tripod is considered, the drinking glass on its top may be interpreted as a representation of the pinnacle of diachronic 'evolution'. The fact that the glass is (or at least very much resembles) a glass from one of Ikea's collections further emphasizes the theme of modernity and cultural homogenization.

Another theme related to the interpretation of what the Sámi objects, on the one hand, and the bottles and the glass, on the other, may stand for is that of ethnically organized market relationships. While the coffee pouches connote trading with Sámi people as active agents making choices about what to import, the other objects represent forms of trading which have been imposed on the Sámi people by outsiders. In the case of coffee import the Sámi people may be described as agents choosing to make coffee a part of everyday life, as opposed to the introduction of alcohol by colonizing tradesmen during the era when settlers, missionaries and tradesmen came north. The persistence of the negative impact of trading with liquor is indicated by the Absolut Vodka bottle which, together with the Coca-Cola bottle, provides a reference to contemporary marketing of consumer goods by geographically distant multinational enterprises. Trading patterns constitute one form of ethnic boundary-marking when related to questions like: Does ethnicity matter in the construction of consumers? What is the relationship between ethnicity and profit-making?

As these observations suggest the tripod may be interpreted as a representation of diachronic transformations of Sámi culture and everyday life under the pressure of colonialism, modernity and globalization. One social significance of this kind of arrangement is that the sculpture functions as a form of protest and taking up a stand. This type of social significance is closely related to the context of cultural mobilization influenced by the mobilization of indigenous peoples, as well as anti-colonial and postcolonial theory which have inspired a number of Sámi artists from the 1970s and onwards. From the vantage point of indigenous or minority aesthetics the social significance of this kind of works of art is related to the issue of the role of ethnicity for cultural production and consumption, and not least for negotiating boundaries and values which affect the social organization of cultural differences.

Language

One central theme in both Sámi and Tornedalian artistic deployments of history is the problem of how to preserve the Sámi and Tornedalian languages. Language loss is intimately connected to the assimilationist policies implemented through discriminatory measures taken against minority languages in mandatory education and other institutions supervised by state authorities. Use of language may function as an overt sign of ethnicity, that is, the use of a minority language like Sámi or Meänkieli, the Tornedalian language. The reason why the use of a majority language frequently does not function as an ethnic marker is related to the equation drawn between majority status and modernity. This involves that majority group members are seen as unproblematically representing modernity and the modern civilized way of life. As Fenton and May point out this 'tacit ethnic status almost certainly includes the equating of an ethnic majority with a (or even, the) nation' (Fenton and May 2002: 11). This tacit ethnic status may be manifested in debates through the supposition that modern people, the majority, are somehow free from ethnic allegiances.

One implicit critique of a number of Sámi and Tornedalian literary works of art is directed towards the value system which has stigmatized and marginalized the Sámi and Tornedalian minority languages. The Swedish Tornedalian author Bengt Pohjanen, for example, has repeatedly highlighted the theme of language in his writing. One example is the poem 'I was born without language', first published in Swedish in 1973.

> Bengt Pohjanen, 'I was born without language' printed in *Meänkieli Rätt och lätt*.
>
> I was born without language
> umbilical cord speechlessly bandaged
> by a mute midwife
>
> I grew up at the border
> under the cross-fire from two languages
> which have whipped my tongue
> to dumbness
>
> I was raised
> with demands of clarity
> language and nationality
>
> I was whipped at school
> into language, clarity
> nationality
> I was whipped to contempt
> for that which was mine
> the want of a language
> and the border
>
> I was built by exterior
> violence
> as well as interior constraint
> on abbreviations
> and misunderstandings
>
> I was deprived of my identity card
>
> (translation from Swedish by Anne Heith)

The poem has been reprinted a number of times, for example in a Meänkieli grammar book published in Swedish in 2005 (Pohjanen and Muli 2005: 5). The fourth stanza reads: 'I was whipped at school/into language, clarity/nationality/ I was whipped to contempt/ for that which was mine/the want of language/ and the border' (my translation). A couple of decades later the same theme was highlighted by another Swedish Tornedalian author, Mikael Niemi, in his novel *Popular Music From Vittula*. In the fourth chapter the narrator enumerates what the children learned at school in the Swedish Torne Valley when he was a child. The enumeration ends as follows: 'We spoke broken Finnish without being Finns, we spoke broken Swedish without being Swedes. We were nothing' (Niemi 2000: 50, my translation). Pohjanen's poem and Niemi's novel both depict responses to bordering processes which have excluded the Tornedalian minority from a Swedish and Finnish national linguistic community. Both authors highlight the role of the educational system for socializing the Tornedalian minority into a culture of poverty. When this theme is explored by authors in the context of Tornedalian cultural mobilization coloured by anti-colonial and postcolonial critique, the marginalization of the Tornedalian language by institutions supervised by the state is presented as an abuse which has resulted in shame, identity loss and disempowerment (Heith 2008). The emphasis on this theme in works by present-day authors represents both resistance to a history of homogenizing modernity and a reversal of the basic value orientation guiding assimilationist policies and state-supervised strategies aimed at effacing the languages of minority groups.

Barth mentions language as an overt sign of ethnicity (Barth 1998: 14). However, the fact that language signals ethnicity has also been problematic in contexts where ethnic minority status has been stigmatizing. When discussing this theme from the vantage point of the Finno-Ugric Kven population in northern Norway Anna-Riitta Lindgren emphasizes that the recognition of the language of a minority is vital for the creation of a positive cultural identity (Lindgren 2003: 111). She argues that if the language of the Kvens in Norway was not recognized as an autonomous language, it would always be compared with the norm for Finnish in Finland, and as a result be found inferior. She makes the point that the language of the Kvens, as well as that of Swedish Tornedalians, has developed along other trajectories than that of Finnish in Finland. She highlights the fact that both the Kvens and the Swedish Tornedalians have experienced roughly a hundred years of assimilation politics and that as a result of this there is a need for a transformation of negative views on Kven and Tornedalian language and culture:

> It is fairly common that minorities internalize disparaging opinions about their own group and culture, and this has happened among the Kvens and the Tornedalians in the context of language shift from the minority language to the majority language. This is one reason why there is disagreement within minority groups concerning ethnie and linguistic identity. (Lindgren 2003: 111, my translation)

Lindgren's analysis points to the fact that stigmatization and shame contributed to a language shift which as time went by resulted in language loss. The process may be described as one of internal colonialism, which parallels the development on the Celtic fringes of Britain (Hechter 1975). Michael Hechter particularly highlights the role of education which has contributed to socializing the Celtic minorities into cultures of poverty. His study testifies to the fact that colonization may appear in various guises, for example in disempowerment through the colonization of people's minds and thoughts (Fanon 1968, Fanon 2000, Thiong'o 1986, Said 1978, Smith 2008). This theme is highlighted by Vuokko Hirvonen in the first academic thesis published in Northern Sámi (Hirvonen 1998). In 2008 an English Translation, entitled *Voices from Sápmi: Sámi Women's Path to Authorship*, was published (Hirvonen 2008). Hirvonen's book is pioneering both in the sense that it contributes to the revitalization of the Northern Sámi language, and in the sense that she presents an alternative literary history in which the achievements of Sámi women authors are analysed within the framework of anti-colonial, postcolonial and feminist theory.

The examples from the works of Pohjanen and Niemi highlight practices of exclusion and naming which have othered the Tornedalians. The ideological point of departure for these practices is the notion of 'one people – one language – one culture – one nation'. Within this brand of nationalism the cultures of the Sámi and Tornedalians are conceived of as problematic as they do not fit into the paradigm of a linguistically and culturally homogeneous nation state. When Pohjanen writes about abusive enforcements of assimilationist policies in the poem 'I was born without language' and the subsequent generation of feelings of shame and contempt directed towards Tornedalian language and culture, he invokes the situation of a person living on a border, that is in a zone which may be conceived of as a third space when seen in relation to the two nation states separated by the concrete border. The mental mapping of this space in the work of Pohjanen is influenced both by anti-colonial strategies of resistance to an oppressive majority culture implemented by state politics and institutions, as well as by postcolonial theories celebrating cultural hybridity and syncretism. One way of interpreting performances of critique of the ideal of assimilation and processes of homogenizing modernity is to relate these to postmodern and postcolonial challenges of notions of exceptionalism and purity (Ashcroft, Griffiths and Tiffin 2009a, Ashcroft, Griffiths and Tiffin 2009b, Bhabha 2008). This involves the scrutiny of complacent self-images entertained at times in the Nordic countries: 'The Nordic countries have always seen themselves as liberal and tolerant to strangers, refugees as well as immigrants. This they have obviously never been in real life …' (Hettne, Sörlin and Østergård 2006: 211). One space of critical scrutiny discussed in this article is that of cultural production in which alternative voices express hitherto suppressed elements of the histories of the Nordic countries. The alternative histories suggested by the examples of Geir Tore Holm's Tripod and the poem 'I was born without language' by Bengt Pohjanen, draw attention to the fact that Norway and Sweden have been multi-ethnic, multilingual, and multicultural since way back in time.

Aesthetics and Ethnic Boundaries

Ascription of ethnic boundaries in production and interpretation of works of art is related to a field within aesthetics which is concerned with the social significance of cultural differences. This article discusses a couple of examples of how constructions of ethnic differences related to history and language may function as performances of anti-colonial and postcolonial critique of histories of homogenizing modernity and nationalism in the geographical context of northern Scandinavia. This critique has been inspired by the international indigenous movements in the 1970s and the emergence of indigenous and ethnic studies (Singh and Schmidt 2000, Smith 2008, Heith 2010). As a consequence of this development ethnicity has evolved as a major category in interpretations of the social significance of Sámi and Tornedalian art. One important theme in this brand of aesthetics stems from the construction of cultural similarities and differences which are regarded as significant by the actors, that is, producers and interpreters of works of art. However, it is important to recognize that ethnic boundaries are constantly being negotiated, multiplied and diversified. This implies that instances of boundary confusion occur, when actors cannot be sure, whether boundaries exist and, if they do, what they delimit. Instances of boundary transgression are also found in deconstructions of boundaries which result in new cultural combinations. This is manifested in a kind of poetics which may be called a poetics of hybridization, or syncretization (Ashcroft, Griffiths and Tiffin 2009a, Ashcroft, Griffiths and Tiffin 2009b, Bhabha 2008). Elements from various cultural traditions have always been combined in artistic performances, and borders have never been stable. However, there is a new sensibility when interferences, crossings and adaptions are seen as the rule in cultural production, and not as exceptions. It is obvious that this kind of aesthetic sensibility either is unfamiliar to, or suppressed by, the populist parties in Denmark, Finland, Norway and Sweden, which all are at war with 'multiculturalism', which is seen as a threat to 'original purity'. In this context new myths are created, recirculating old ideas of Nordic exceptionalism. However, as the discussion of Sámi and Tornedalian art above suggests, both historical and present-day notions of exceptionalism are also being challenged, when whiteness and race are used as analytical concepts in interpretation, and when ethnicity and boundary-marking are recognized as significant for the interpretation and production of art.

References

Anderson, B. 2006. *Imagined Communities: Reflections on the Origin and Spread of Nationalism*. London: Verso.

Arvastson, G. 1999. Inledning, in *Järnbur eller frigörelse? Studier i moderniseringen av Sverige*, edited by G. Arvastson. Lund: Studentlitteratur.

Åselius, G. 1994. *The 'Russian Menace' to Sweden: The Belief System of a Small Power Security Élite in the Age of Imperialism*. Stockholm: Akademitryck AB.
Ashcroft, B., Griffiths, G. and Tiffin, H. 2009a. *The Empire Writes Back*. 2nd edition. London and New York: Routledge.
Ashcroft, B., Griffiths, G. and Tiffin, H. 2009b. *Post-Colonial Studies: The Key Concepts*. London and New York: Routledge.
Austin, J.L. 1962. *How To Do Things With Words*. Cambridge, MA: Harvard University Press.
Barth, F. 1998. Introduction, in *Ethnic Groups and Boundaries: The Social Organization of Culture Difference*, edited by F. Barth. Long Grove: Waveland Press.
Berger, M. 2004. *White: Whiteness and Race in Contemporary Art*. Issues in Cultural Theory 7. Baltimore County: Center for Art and Visual Culture, University of Maryland.
Bhabha, H.K. 2008. *The Location of Culture*. London and New York: Routledge.
Butler, J. 1990. *Gender Trouble: Feminism and the Subversion of Identity*. New York: Routledge.
Dyer, R. 1997. *White*. London: Routledge.
Ehn, B. and Klein, B. 2007. *Från erfarenhet till text: Om kulturvetenskaplig reflexivitet*. Stockholm: Carlsson Bokförlag.
Elenius, L. 2006. *Nationalstat och minoritetspolitik: Samer och finskspråkiga minoriteter i ett jämförande nordiskt perspektiv*. Lund: Studentlitteratur.
Fanon, F. 1968. *The Wretched of the Earth*. New York: Grove Press.
Fanon, F. 2000. *Black Skin, White Masks*. New York: Grove Press.
Fenton, S. and May, S. 2002. Ethnicity, Nation and 'Race': Connections and Disjunctures, in *Ethnonational Identities*, edited by S. Fenton and S. May. Houndmills, Basingstoke, and New York: Palgrave Macmillan.
Garrard, G. 2009. *Ecocriticism*. London and New York: Routledge.
Hall, K. 2000. Performativity. *Journal of Linguistic Anthropology*, 9(1–2), 184–7.
Hanfling, O. 1995. Introduction, in *Philosophical Aesthetics: An Introduction*, edited by O. Hanfling. Oxford, UK and Cambridge, USA: Blackwell.
Hechter, M. 1975. *The Celtic Fringe in British National Development, 1636–1966*. Berkeley: University of California Press.
Heith, A. 2008. Förhandlingar och förvandlingar av det nationella i den tornedalsfinska Litteraturen. *Horisont*, 3, 17–19.
Heith, A. 2009a. Millenarianism and the Narration of the Nation: Narratives about the Korpela Movement. *Journal of Northern Studies*, 1, 13–29.
Heith, A. 2009b. 'Nils Holgersson Never Saw Us': A Tornedalian Literary History, in *Cold Matters: Cultural Perspectives of Snow, Ice and Cold*, edited by H. Hansson and C. Norberg. Umeå: Northern Studies Monographs, 1, Umeå University, 209–21.
Heith, A. 2010. Särskiljandets logik i en kolonial och en antikolonial diskurs. Nils-Aslak Valkeapääs *Beaivi áhčážan, Edda. Nordisk tidskrift för litteraturvetenskap*. 4, 335–50.

Hettne, B., Sörlin, S. and Østergård, U. 2006. *Den globala nationalismen: Nationalstatens historia och framtid*. 2nd revised edition. Stockholm: SNS Förlag.
Hill Collins, P. and Solomos, J. 2010. Introduction: Situating Race and Ethnic Studies, in *The Sage Handbook of Race and Ethnic Studies*, edited by P. Hill Collins and J. Solomos. Los Angeles, London, New Delhi, Singapore and Washington: Sage.
Hirvonen, V. 1998. *Sámeeatnama jienat: sápmelaš nissona bálggis girječállin*. Guovdageaidnu: DAT.
Hirvonen, V. 2008. *Voices from Sápmi: Sámi Women's Path to Authorship*. Kautokeino: DAT.
Huggan, G. and Tiffin, H. 2010. *Postcolonial Ecocriticism: Literature, Animals, Environment*. London and New York: Routledge.
Huss, L. 1999. *Reversing Language Shift in the Far North: Linguistic Revitalization in Northern Scandinavia and Finland*. Uppsala: Uppsala University.
Kemiläinen, A. 1998. *Finns in the Shadow of the 'Aryans': Race Theories and Racism*. Studia Historica 59, Helsinki: Finnish Historical Society.
Keskinen, S., Tuori, S., Irni, S. and Mulinari, D. 2009. *Complying with Colonialism: Gender, Race and Ethnicity in the Nordic Region*. Farnham and Burlington: Ashgate.
Laskar, P. 2008. Den finska rasen: Finska kranier i 1800-talets vetenskap. *Ord and Bild*, 2, 142–9.
Lindgren, A.R. 2003. Språklig emansipasjon eller språkdöd blant kvener og tornedalinger?, in *Innsyn i Kvensk språk og kultur: Seminarrapport, Tromsö, mars 2002*, edited by R. Mellem. Tromsö: Norske kveners forbund.
Lundborg, H. and Linders, F.J. 1926. *The Racial Characters of the Swedish Nation*. Anthropologica Suecica MCMXXVI, Stockholm.
Mebius, A. 1999. Föreställningen om samerna som de Andra: Rasbiologi, genetik och självidentifikation, in *Järnbur eller frigörelse? Studier i modernizeringen av Sverige*, edited by G. Arvastson. Lund: Studentlitteratur.
Niemi, M. 2000. *Populärmusik från Vittula*. Stockholm: Norstedts.
Pohjanen, B. 2005. Jag är född utan språk, in *Meänkieli rätt och lätt: Grammatik i meänkieli*, edited by B. Pohjanen and E. Muli. Överkalix: Barents Publisher.
Rodell, M. 2009. Fortifications in the Wilderness: The Making of Swedish–Russian Borderlands around 1900. *Journal of Northern Studies*, 1, 69–89.
Said, E. 1978. *Orientalism*. New York: Vintage Books, Random House.
Schechner, R. 2002. *Performance Studies: An Introduction*. London: Routledge.
Schough, K. 2008. *Hyperboré: Föreställningen om Sveriges plats i världen*. Stockholm: Carlsson.
Singh, A. and Schmidt, P. 2000. On the Borders between U.S. Studies and Postcolonial Theory, in *Postcolonial Theory and the United States: Race, Ethnicity and Literature*, edited by A. Singh and P. Schmidt. Jackson: University of Mississippi Press.

Smith, L.T. 2008. *Decolonizing Methodologies: Research and Indigenous Peoples*. London and New York: Zed Books.
Solbakk, J.T. 2006. *The Sámi People: A Handbook*. Karasjok: Davvi Girji OS.
Sollors, W. 1986. *Beyond Ethnicity: Consent and Descent in American Culture*, New York: Oxford University Press.
Sollors. W. (ed.). 1989. *The Invention of Ethnicity*. New York: Oxford University Press.
Thiong'o, N.W. 1986. *Decolonizing the Mind: The Politics of Language in African Literature*. London: James Currey.
Vallström, M. 1999. Att möta andra: Etnologins praktik och reflexivitetens Konsekvenser, in *Järnbur eller frigörelse? Studier i modernizeringen av Sverige*, edited by G. Arvastson. Lund: Studentlitteratur.

Index

Bold page numbers indicate figures, *italic* numbers indicate tables.

aesthetics
    and the arts 159
    and ethnic boundaries 170
Africa
    Norwegian colonial encounters in 19
    Norwegian migration to 18–19, 20–25
Afrikka-kirja (The Africa Book) Gallen-Kallela) 97–9
Afvikling af Grønlands kolonistatus 1945–54 (DIIS) 115–16
Against Race (Gilroy) 143
Ahluwalia, P. 4
Ahmed, Sara 134, 149
Akseli Afrikassa (Akseli in Africa) (radio play) 97, 98
ambivalence 23–4, 24–5
    concept of in colonial discourse 13
amnesia, colonial 120–21
Anderson, Benedict 105, 144
Arendt, Hannah 142–3
arts and aesthetics 159
Ashcroft, B. 4
Austin, J.L. 164
authority, colonial 120

Bach, C.F. 115
Balcony Gods (Parvekejumalat) (Snellman) 74, 76–8, 81–3, 83–4
Bang, A.K. 19
Barth, Fredrik 163, 168
belonging, sense of 57–8, 67
Berger, Maurice 159
Bhabha, H.K. 24, 25, 105, 106, 120, 125
Blaagaard, Bolette 122
boundaries
    ethnic, and aesthetics 170

    geographical for Sámi and Tournedalians 160
    marking 163
Browning, Christopher 2
Brydon, Ann 58
Bryne, Bridget 121, 122
bureaucratic thinking 143

Cheng, Ann Anlin 46
Citizen in Denmark: Information to new citizens...
    appearance and content 122–3
    colonial mimicry 125–30, **127, 129**
    Danish/English titles compared 123
    evasion of race as subject in Europe 120–21
    model immigrants portrayed in 125–30, **127, 129**
    nativity and newness boundaries 119–20
    on nudity and modernity 130–34, **131**
    patriarchal family past 135
    photo gallery of family lineage 134–6, **135**
    representation of women 128–30, **129**
    sexual autonomy of Danish women **131**, 132–4
    as supplement to Declaration signed by migrants 123–5
    tradition and modernity 134–6, **135**
    welcome address 119
    whiteness of traditional Danish families 135–6
colonial amnesia 120–21
colonial authority 120
colonial complicity 15, 91n3, 94, 161

colonial mimicry 120, 125–30, **127, 129**
colonialism
    different views of 15–16
    erasure of in Europe's internal past 120–21
'coloured' as contested term 20
contact zone, concept of 16
Cooper, F. 15
Crenshaw, K.W. 6
Critical Race and Whiteness Studies 46–7, 121
cultural racism 7

Danish colonial exhibition, Copenhagen 1905 57, 61
'Dansk raceantropolgi i Grønland' (Duedahl) 29
Denmark
    colonization of Greenland by
        anthropological research 37–9
        as benevolent and caring 29–31
        Gundel, Peter, case of 33–5
        Instruction of the 19th April 1782 32–3, 35
        'Law regarding the government of the colonies in Greenland' 33, 33n7
        as racialized 31–6
        reluctance to address race 31–2
        subjective/objective violence 30, 35
        whiteness as an ideal 35–6
    gender equality as national characteristic 122
    gendered labour market 130n10
    national identity
        critiques of administration of Greenland 115–16
        domestic process, formation of as 105
        immigrants, presence of 106
        influences beyond geographic space 105–6
        modernisation/development aid to Greenland 106–16, 108n3
    sexual autonomy of Danish women 132–4
    see also Citizen in Denmark: Information to new citizens...; family reunification policy in Denmark
Department of Oriental languages 48–9
development aid to Greenland 106–16, 108n3
Dirks, Nicholas 5
discourse, colonial
    ambivalence 13, 23–4, 24–5
    colonial complicity 15
    colonialism, different views of 15–16
    contact zone, concept of 16
    hybridity 15, 25
    liminality 13, 21, 24–5
    metropole/periphery (colony) concepts 16–17
    Norwegian colonial encounters in Africa 19
    provincializing of Scandinavia 15
    studies of 14–15
    Thesen family in South Africa 21–3, 24
    see also Thesen family in South Africa
Duedahl, Poul 29, 31–2, 36–7, 38–9
Dyer, Richard 160–61, 163

Egede, Niels 35
Egede, Poul 29–30, 35
Einarsson, Oddur 59
Eind court judgement 150
Engh, S. 19
ethnicities, majority 161–3
exceptionalism
    defined 89
    Finland
        involvement in European colonial regime 96
        and national icons 97–100
        national self-image 100–101
        Nordic/European identity 96–7
        racism in 96
        school books 95–7
    Iceland 59–63, 66–7
    Nordic, meaning of 2
    Norwegian, challenging myth of 15
    Sweden 52–3
expressions, racist. *see* words and expressions, racist

Faeroe Islands 110, 111n12, 146n3
family reunification policy in Denmark
 application form and process
  148–52
 attachment requirement 152
 Danishness and whiteness 143–4
 financial capability of applicants
  151–2
 immigration policy, history of 144–8
 'Love card' arrangement 152–3
 minimum age 145–7
 property ownership 151
 racialized privileges as policy
  generator 152–3
 racist moments 148
 theoretical approach 142–3
 working holiday visas 153
Fenton, S. 161–2, 167
fiction and reality 83–5
Figueroa, Mónica Moreno 148
Finland
 exceptionalism
  compared to Nordic 90–91
  involvement in European colonial
   regime 96
  and national icons 97–100
  national self-image 91, 100–101
  Nordic/European identity 96–7
  racism in 96
  school books 95–7
 gains from colonialism 90
 immigration debates 74–5
 N-word, use of in 92–5
 racism in 83, 90
 racist representations of Africans 93
 see also minority families, gendered
  violence in
folkhemmet (People's Home) 162–3
forced marriages, prevention of 146–7
forestry management by Thesen family in
 South Africa 21–2
Frankenberg, Ruth 65, 121
Frello, B. 15

Gad, F. 32n5
Gallen-Kallela, Akseli 97–100
Gåseborg rock climbing tracks, names of
 44, 51–2

gender
 bodily and sexual autonomy of Danish
  women **131**, 132–4
 Danish handbook for new immigrants
  128–30, **129**
 Danish labour market 130n10
 equality as national characteristic
  122
 and Icelandic nationalistic discourses
  62–3
 racism as gendered 6
 violence in minority families
  debates about 73
  fiction and reality 83–5
  methodology for research 75–6
  *Minne tytöt kadonneet? (Where
   have all the young girls gone?)*
   (Lehtolainen) 74, 78
  Muslim/Western dichotomy 81–3
  Parvekejumalat (Balcony Gods)
   Snellman 74, 76–8
  Sweden 81
  transnational influences 85–6
  veil, symbolism of 78–80, **79, 80**
  whiteness, identification with
   normative 85–6
 and whiteness 122
Gilman, S. 6
Gilroy, Paul 143
Glick Schiller, Nina 100
Goldberg, David Theo 91, 120
Greenland
 colonization of by Denmark
  anthropological research 37–9
  as benevolent and caring 29–31
  Gundel, Peter, case of 33–5
  Instruction of the 19th April 1782
   32–3, 35
  'Law regarding the government of
   the colonies in Greenland' 33
  as racialized 31–6
  subjective/objective violence 30,
   35
  whiteness as an ideal 35–6
 critiques of Danish administration of
  115–16
 minimum age for family reunification
  146n3

modernisation/development aid from Denmark 106–16, 108n3
Grundlingh, A. 21
Gullestad, Marianne 91n4
Gundel, Peter 33–5

Haarder, Bertel 153
Hall, Stuart 106
Hansen, Søren 38
Hechter, Michael 169
hegemonic whiteness 52, 83
Hervik, Peter 153
hijab as mark of difference 128, **129**, 130
Hirvonen, Vuokko 169
history as cultural material 164–6, **165**
Hjulström, Carin 50
Høiris, Ole 31
Holm, Geir Tore 164, 165–6, **166**
honour-related violence. *see* minority families, gendered violence in
Huber, Sasha 98–100
Hübinette, Tobias 132
Huyssen, Andreas 100
hybridity 15, 25

'I was born without language' ('Jar är född utan språk') (Pohjanen) 163–4, 166–8
Iceland
    application for UN Security Council seat 66–7
    belonging, sense of 57–8, 67
    Danish colonial exhibition, Copenhagen 1905 57, 61
    exceptionalism 59–63, 66–7
    as existing outside colonialism and imperialism 66–7
    gender and nationalistic discourses 62–3
    Icelanders seen as different 61
    images produced of colonized people 60–61
    immigration to 63
    independence demands 60–61
    language and literature 60–61
    misconceptions about 59–60
    multiculturalism in 63–7
    Skírnir journal 60–61

'Ten little negroes,' republication of 64–6
transnational influences 86
Idealer og realiteter (Bach) 115
identity, choice in 163
illocutionary speech acts 47
Imagined Communities (Anderson) 105
immigration
    Finland 74–5
    Iceland 63
    see also family reunification policy in Denmark
Instruction of the 19th April 1782 32–3, 35
Ireland 86, 91

Jacobson, M.F. 6
'Jar är född utan språk' ('I was born without language') (Pohjanen) 163–4, 166–8
Jensen, L. 15
Jónsson, Arngrímur 59
Jónsson, Jón 60
Judd, D. 24

Kahle, Sigrid 48
Kariuki, Peter 94
Keskinen, S. 161
Kvens, language of 168

language
    Icelandic, and literature 60–61
    Kvens 168
    minority, official recognition of 163
    as overt sign of ethnicity 168
    Sámi and Tournedalian art 166–9
Lehtolainen, Leena 74
liminality 13, 21, 24–5
Lindgren, Anna-Ritta 168–9
Linné, Carl von 5
'Love card' arrangement 152–3
Löyttyjärvi, Kaisla 94
Lundström, Catrin 132
Lury, Celia 151

majority ethnicities 161–3
Marcus, George 92n6
marriages, forced, prevention of 146–7
Massey, D. 16

Maurer, S.K. 15
May, S. 161–2, 167
Metock court judgement 150
metropole/periphery (colony) concepts 16–17
migration, Norwegian, to Africa 18–19, 20–25
mimicry, colonial 120, 125–30, **127**, **129**
minimum age for family reunification 145–7, 146n3
Minne tytöt kadonneet? (Where have all the young girls gone?) (Lehtolainen) 74, 78, 81–3, 84–5
minority families, gendered violence in
   debates about 73
   fiction and reality 83–5
   methodology for research 75–6
   Minne tytöt kadonneet? (Where have all the young girls gone?) (Lehtolainen) 74, 78
   Muslim/Western dichotomy 81–3
   Parvekejumalat (Balcony Gods) Snellman 74, 76–8
   Sweden 81
   transnational influences 85–6
   veil, symbolism of 78–80, **79**, **80**
   whiteness, identification with normative 85–6
missionaries, Norwegian, in Africa 19
modernisation/development aid to Greenland 106–16, 108n3
Motzfeldt, Peter Hanning 32n5
multiculturalism
   Iceland 63–7
   use of term 8
Muslim families, gendered violence in
   debates about 73
   fiction and reality 83–5
   methodology for research 75–6
   Minne tytöt kadonneet? (Where have all the young girls gone?) (Lehtolainen) 73, 78
   Muslim/Western dichotomy 81–3
   Parvekejumalat (Balcony Gods) Snellman 73, 76–8
   Sweden 81
   transnational influences 85–6
   veil, symbolism of 78–80, **79**, **80**

   whiteness, identification with normative 85–6

N-word, continued use of term
   Sweden 44
   use of in Finland 92–5
national icons and Finnish exceptionalism 97–100
national identity
   domestic process, formation of as 105
   immigrants, presence of 106
   less formalised forms 106
   modernisation/development aid to Greenland 106–16, 108n3
national self-image 91, 91n4, 162–3
'negro,' continued use of term
   Finland 92–5
   Sweden 44, 49–51
Niemi, Mikael 168
Norðdal, Sigurður 59
Nordic countries
   defining region 14n1
   history of relationships between 3–4
Nordic exceptionalism
   compared to Finnish 90–91
   as opting out of colonialism 121
North America, Norwegian migration to 18, 18n7
Norway
   colonial encounters in Africa 19
   as colonial nation 17–18
   migration to Africa 18–19, 20–25
   missionaries in Africa 19
   as neutral entity, self-positioning of as 14
   shipping in 19th century 18
   Thesen family in South Africa 20–25
nudity, Danish handbook for new immigrants 130–34, **131**

'oriental,' continued use of term 44, 48–9
Orientalism (Said) 4, 48
Oslund, Karen 60
Oxfeldt, Elisabeth 58

Palmberg, Mai 90
Parvekejumalat (Balcony Gods) Snellman 74, 76–8, 81–3, 83–4

People's Home (folkhemmet) 162–3
performativity 164
periphery (colony)/metropole concepts 16–17
Perko, Jukka 97
Phillips, Anne 148
Pohjanen, Bengt 163–4, 166–8
Popular Music from Vittula (Niemi) 168
possessive individual, concept of 151
postcolonialism 4–5
provincializing of Scandinavia 15

race
   biology 160–61
   discovery of 142–3
   evasion of as subject in Europe 120–21
   whiteness and art 159
racial melancholia 46
racialization as relational system of categorization 121
racism
   biological approach to race 36–7
   categorisation of human diversity 5–6
   as consequence of bureaucratic thinking 143
   cultural 7
   Finnish society 83
   as gendered 6
   genealogical approach to race 36
   global and European perspective 5–9
   reluctance to address race in Denmark 31–2
   'Ten little negroes,' republication of in Iceland 64–6
   use of the N-word in Finland 92–5
   see also whiteness; words and expressions, racist
racist moments 148
Rastas, Anna 65
reality and fiction 83–5
relationships between Nordic countries 3–4, 17n4, 17n5
religion, Norwegian missionaries in Africa 19
Ripatti, Matti 98
Riste, O. 17n6
rock climbing tracks, names of 44

Said, Edward 1, 4, 48
Sámi art
   aesthetics and ethnic boundaries 170
   boundaries, geographical 160
   boundary-marking 163
   history as cultural material 164–6, **165**
   identity, choice in 163
   language 163, 166–9
   majority ethnicities 161–3
   modern welfare state 161
   People's Home (folkhemmet) 162–3
   performativity 164
   protective segregation 162–3
   race biology 160–61
   'Tripod' (Holm) 164, **165**, 165–6
Sawyer, Lena 132
Scandinavia
   defining region 14n1
   provincializing of 15
Schiebinger, L. 6
school books, Finnish exceptionalism in 95–7
self-image, national 91, 91n4, 162–3
sexual autonomy of Danish women **131**, 132–4
sham marriages, prevention of 146–7
shipping
   Norway in 19th century 18
   Thesen family in South Africa 20–21
Skeggs, Beverley 151
Skeie, K.H. 19
Skírnir journal 60–61
Smith, Andrea 58
Snellman, Anja 74
Solbakk, J.T. 162
Sørensen, Axel Kjær 33
South Africa
   hybridity 23–4
   social dislocation, periods of 23–4
   see also Thesen family in South Africa
Stoler, Ann Laura 15, 58, 134
Storgaard, Louise Halleskov 147
Sträth, Bo 96
Stuart Hall 121
Surridge, K. 24
Sveinsson, G. 57, 62

Sweden
  continued use of racist words and
    expressions 43–4
  Department of Oriental languages 44,
    48–9
  exceptionalism 52–3
  hegemonic whiteness 52
  honour-related violence in 81
  immigration and integration
    approaches 148
  'negro,' continued use of term in 44,
    49–51
  'oriental,' continued use of term 44,
    48–9
  rock climbing tracks, names of 44,
    51–2
  'The Name is Negro ball' Facebook
    group 44, 50–51
  white melancholia 45, 46, 53
  whiteness and Swedishness 45

'Ten little negroes,' republication of 64–6
textbooks, Finnish exceptionalism in 95–7
'The Name is Negro ball' Facebook group
    44, 50–51
Thesen family in South Africa
  monopoly, allegations of towards 22
  as occupying a third space 24–5
  reburial of A.L. Thesen 23
  shipping and forestry activities 20–22
Thisted, K. 34
Thomsen, Hanne 30–31
Thoroddsen, Þorvald 59
Tournedalian art
  aesthetics and ethnic boundaries 170
  boundaries, geographical 160
  boundary-marking 163
  history as cultural material 164–6, **165**
  identity, choice in 163
  'Jar är född utan språk' ('I was born
    without language') (Pohjanen)
    163–4, 166–8
  language 163, 166–9
  majority ethnicities 161–3
  modern welfare state 161
  People's Home (folkhemmet) 162–3
  performativity 164
  protective segregation 162–3

race biology 160–61
transnational influences 85–6
'Tripod' (Holm) 164, **165**, 165–6
Trophy I (Huber) 99–100

United Kingdom, immigration and
    integration approaches 148

veil
  as mark of difference 128, **129**, 130
  symbolism of 78–80, **79**, **80**
violence
  in minority families
    debates about 73
    fiction and reality 83–5
    methodology for research 75–6
    *Minne tytöt kadonneet? (Where
      have all the young girls gone?)*
      (Lehtolainen) 74, 78
    Muslim/Western dichotomy 81–3
    Parvekejumalat (Balcony Gods)
      Snellman 74, 76–8
    Sweden 81
    transnational influences 85–6
    veil, symbolism of 78–80, **79**, **80**
    whiteness, identification with
      normative 85–6
  subjective/objective 30
Violence: Six Sideways Reflections (Žižek)
    30
*Voices from Sápmi: Sámi Women's Path to
    Authorship* (Hirvonen) 169
Vuorela, U. 15, 16, 91n3, 94

Wallerstein, I. 17n3
welfare state, modern 161
*Where have all the young girls gone?
    (Minne tytöt kadonneet?)*
    (Lehtolainen) 74, 78, 81–3, 84–5
white melancholia, Swedish 45, 46, 53
whiteness
  as an ideal in Greenland as colony of
    Denmark 35–6
  as changeable category 121–2
  of Danish women's bodies **131**, 132–3
  and Danishness 143–4
  and gender 122
  hegemonic in Sweden 52

hegemony of 83
identification with normative 85–6
Nordic context 7–8
race and art 159
and Swedishness 45
'Ten little negroes,' republication of 65–6
traditional Danish families 135–6
see also racism
Wimmer, Andreas 100
woodcutters, impoverishment of 21–2
words and expressions, racist
    continued use of in Sweden 43–4
    decline in use of 43
    Department of Oriental languages 44, 48–9
    illocutionary speech acts 47
'negro,' continued use of term in Sweden 44, 49–51
'oriental,' continued use of term 44, 48–9
rock climbing tracks, names of 44, 51–2
'The Name is Negro ball' Facebook group 44, 50–51
as wounding 46–7
working holiday visas 153
World System Theory 17n3

Yegenoglu, Meyda 130
Young, Iris Marion 142
Yuval-Davis, Nira 58, 67

Žižek, Slavoj 30, 35

Printed in the United States
by Baker & Taylor Publisher Services